DYNAMICS

of

WORSHIP

DYNAMICS
of
WORSHIP

Foundations and uses of liturgy

RICHARD
PAQUIER

Translated by
Donald Macleod

Fortress Press   *Philadelphia*

This book is a translation of *Traité de Liturgique*, (Manuels et Précis de Théologie, XXV), published in 1954 by Delachaux & Niestlé S.A., Neuchâtel (Switzerland)

Library of Congress Catalog Card Number 67-19040

4069D67   Printed in U. S. A.   1-227

Translator's Preface

This volume represents not only the product of long years of thought and labor in the general area of Christian worship, it is an invaluable contribution to that growing list of definitive writings in the Reformed tradition that delineate our heritage of liturgical concepts and forms from historical and theological perspectives. Reformed worship is based ultimately upon the Christian doctrine of God and is centered in the person and work of Jesus Christ who is "the image of the invisible God." With such an orientation, the contemporary resurgence of interest in the nature and meaning of Reformed worship can not be merely a fad, but is bound to find permanent expression in books of lasting value and significance.

Undoubtedly two of the most authentic voices in Europe in the area of Protestant liturgiology today are Richard Paquier and Jean-Jacques Von Allmen. The latter, professor of practical theology at the University of Neuchâtel, published his *Cours de Liturgique* in 1965 and it is now available in English: *Worship—Its Theology and Practice* (New York: Oxford University Press, 1965). Paquier's *Traité de Liturgique*, however, is more distinctively in the Genevan tradition, while Von Allmen's work may be said to be more broadly Protestant, although both writers manifest a thorough comprehension of those sources from which our differing streams have taken their common origin.

In the series of *Manuels et Précis de Theologie*, Richard Paquier's volume appeared early (Neuchâtel & Paris: Delachaux & Niestlé, 1954). As the founder and faithful sponsor of the movement "Church and Liturgy," Pastor Paquier pursued one of his major concerns: the publication of liturgies for the enrichment of our resources of worship in the Reformed churches. However, he was anxious to record his conviction that liturgical renewal is not a matter of forms and texts only. Hence this essay was written as a discussion of the necessary relationship between the structure of worship and its theological foundation. Of the twenty-one chapters, eighteen are translated here; the other three are obviously oriented more toward the European situation and would not be in their concrete details of even general relevance to the situation in America.

Part One, entitled "The Initiative of God," consists of five chapters which deal with the bases and character of Christian worship, with its origin in and its focus upon a God who acts, and with the reality of the divine presence in Christ as he calls a people to himself in the community of fellowship, namely the church.

Since God's appeal is to the whole man and his aim is the transformation of the latter through the power of his grace, Paquier goes on to discuss what man says and does in the divine presence in the formal act of worship. Part Two, "The Response of Man," presents in much detail and with unusual thoroughness every aspect and item of liturgical responsibility, including prayers, music, Christian Year, vestments, interior arrangements of the sanctuary, and so forth.

In Part Three, "Ecclesiastical Order," Paquier turns to the actual service of the word and the sacrament of the Lord's Supper and shows how the theological presuppositions and liturgical traditions explored in Parts One and Two combine to influence and shape what the community of God's people do in the sanctuary on Sunday morning.

Liturgical scholars and teachers will find in this book much of what is generally known, but they will become aware of what is essentially a unique blending of theological, biblical, and historical strains that informs us with an authentic ring not only of what to do and how to do these things, but principally of why we do them at all. The translator is grateful to Dr. Paquier for allowing his work to be given to the wider English public and for his courtesy in reading carefully the final draft of the manuscript. The translator wishes to thank especially the Reverend Peter de Haas, D.Th., of Belgium and Professor Georges A. Barrois, Th.D., of Princeton, for their expert assistance in unraveling many complicated French idioms; without their willing assistance the final production of this work would have been slowed very considerably. A word of appreciation is fitting also to Mrs. Jean Bour and Miss Valerie J. Gillen for their competence and accuracy in typing the manuscript.

Donald Macleod

Princeton Theological Seminary
Princeton, New Jersey

Preface to the American Edition

In the life of the universal church, the first half of this century has been marked by the appearance and development of three new currents whose vitality and breadth are such that they have made a distinctive impression upon the style and spirituality of all denominations. I refer to the ecumenical movement, the return to biblical sources, and the liturgical renaissance. There is an obvious connection between these three manifestations of the Holy Spirit unceasingly at work in Christianity. Any turning back to scripture for a deeper understanding of it can but sharpen our awareness of the divine plan of salvation, namely: "To gather together in one all things in Christ" (Eph. 1:10 KJV). We are reminded how urgent it is, therefore, that the visible unity of the church be restored. From another point of view, however, the true nature of the biblical narratives, and particularly their cultic overtones and context, having been brought to light by the exegetical method of the *Formgeschichte*, were bound to call our attention to the problem of worship; a problem otherwise emphasized only by ecumenical encounters or by the reciprocal discovery of the various liturgical, or even non-liturgical forms, used in sundry confessions and denominations. Thus, the interdependence between Bible, worship, and ecumenism, became obvious.

Indeed, the liturgical movement, which alone need concern us here, dates in its "prehistoric" stage from the past century. The studies of the Benedictine monk Dom Guéranger in the Roman church; the Oxford or Tractarian movement in the Anglican Communion; the activity of Wilhelm Löhe in German Lutheranism and of Eugéne Bersier in French Protestant circles, were in a sense a prologue to the wide liturgical renaissance of the twentieth century. In such a movement which affects all the churches, we may be witnessing a kind of defensive reflex of a Christianity that has discovered its precarious situation in the midst of today's secularized world. Instinctively we have begun to feel how necessary it is for us to fall back on the living and life-giving center of our faith, even Christ, the Divine Gatherer of the community of brethren.

Now worship is the proper moment and place for this gathering around the Lord of the church. To be sure, it has not always and everywhere been what it ought to be. The spiritual backsliding which Christianity has shown in too many examples in the course of its history, has often prevented worship from actualizing its essence and from realizing its purpose. Some churches, endowed with a rich liturgical legacy, permitted a sort of sclerosis to set in, and allowed their worship to degenerate into merely an intricate performance of rituals. At the opposite extreme, however, other churches were dramatically impoverished, and their liturgy weakened by anemia. The Reformed churches strictly speaking—that is, the Calvinist Presbyterian or Zwinglian churches, especially in Switzerland, France, Holland, and Scotland—had no liturgy worthy of the name. They were content with a worship filled with the preacher's all too subjective monologue. We must take some satisfaction from the fact this was not the predicament of Anglo-Saxon Christianity. With the exception of Anglicanism, which is usually impartial ground for liturgics, it remains clear that the Methodists and Presbyterians of England and America were able to preserve, or eventually to restore, some elements of active participation of the congregation in the religious service, such as the so-called responsive readings, the Amen, the doxologies, and the Lord's Prayer recited in unison. As for the Lutherans, they had only to conserve a liturgical tradition which goes back to Luther himself; this legacy was kept more or less faithfully in the various sections and regions of Germany, or of Scandinavia, or among the groups of immigrants to America. At any rate much remains to be done, especially in Alemannic Switzerland and in the Netherlands, before the people of the church become clearly conscious of the true nature of worship, and of the active part—their part—in the divine service, which is the proper place for the exercise of the community's royal priesthood. For the time being, it is mostly in the monastic communities recently instituted in Reformed and Lutheran regions that liturgical life has regained fully its place and borne its fruit, such as at Taizé (France), Grandchamp (Switzerland), Iona (Scotland), and finally in Darmstadt and several other German localities.

The ecumenical movement, through its commission "On Ways of Worship," is equally concerned with the liturgical problem. Substantial agreement among the churches was reached on this subject, both at the conference in Lund in 1952 and Montreal in 1963. The Reformed World Alliance, in its assembly at Frankfurt in 1964, was able to face with even greater frankness the situation created by a defective Presbyterian Reformed worship, from which the celebration of the Holy Supper is still too often absent.

The greatest surprise of the past two years is by far the radical liturgical reform which began and is still going on in the Roman Catholic church as a consequence of decisions made by Vatican Council II. In the space of a few months the traditional features of the Roman Mass have changed considerably. Latin has been replaced by the vernacular in a sizable part of the service, and is expected to disappear altogether. The "canon," that is, the prayer of consecration of the host and of the chalice, which thus far was recited in a low voice by the officiating priest alone, is now to be spoken loudly and distinctly, or even to be chanted by all the priests assembled for the concelebration of the Mass. The officiants face the people—a repudiation of the so-called "eastward position" which, in the days of the Oxford Movement, was regarded as the touchstone of genuine Catholic liturgical spirit. Moreover, we are seeing also the miracle of a prompt and joyful readiness to accept these reforms on the part of a large majority of the faithful, whereas Reformed Protestants too often show their reluctance to accept the few liturgical reforms or improvements suggested to them. Yet a re-formation of Reformed worship cannot possibly be delayed much longer if a general breakdown of the life of these churches is to be avoided.

The plan of any treatise on liturgics can never be such as to demand immediate or general acceptance. One might easily devise several workable strategies. For instance, it would be quite feasible to build the entire treatise on Hebrews 8:1-2 as a foundation; that is, by beginning with Christ, our sovereign Sacrificer, who offers to God his Father, for us and with us, the one perfect worship, the true "liturgy." Thus everything could be organized clearly and easily with the advantage of being christologically centered. By so doing, however, one would run the risk of being suspect by all who are afraid lest our worship disclose even a slight semblance to meritorious service rendered by man to God. We thought, therefore, that it would be more preferable theologically, on Reformed or Lutheran grounds, to affirm from the outset the sovereignty of God and his prevenient grace, and then to stress the real presence of the Lord in worship. Too frequently Reformed Christians are less conscious of that presence than they ought to be, and indeed than Christians from other confessions actually are.

Liturgy is not a luxury item; rather it is the breath of this living body: the church of Christ. One is not free either to foster or neglect it since liturgy, no less than preaching of God's word, constitutes the encounter of the community and its Lord. Thus liturgy, as well as preaching, is also *event*, and consequently, "liturgical ineptitude shows not only a lack of good taste, but also quite often a lack of dedication" (Robert Will). We would add: even a lack of humility on the part of the minister who presumes to have the entire worship rest on the subjective foundation of his own personal ability and of his talent for improvisation. May God send again to the churches of the Reformation, which have received the particular charism of preaching, the no less important charism of the liturgy; and may these churches turn away from their one-sided posture from which the "sacred deposit" has suffered mutilation. May they be able, then, better to serve the one Lord of the one universal church.

July, 1966   R. Paquier

Table of Contents

Introduction:
The Threefold Office of the Church

The church of Jesus Christ reveals its proper characteristics and functions from the first moment of its existence. The well-known picture in the second chapter of the Acts of the Apostles presents clearly the main features of the life of the apostolic community: "And they devoted themselves to the apostles' teaching and fellowship, to the breaking of the bread and the prayers. And they sold their possessions and goods and distributed to all, as any had need."

The new people of God, gathered around the glorified Messiah, adheres to the *kerygma* of the gospel, through which it distinguishes itself from the old unfaithful Israel. It is constituted, therefore, upon the foundation of the faith of the apostles. It is the evangelical word taught by the apostles that forms the new community and creates and maintains its unity, its κοινωνία, or fraternal union.

This κοινωνία received from God as grace by means of the apostolic word, is confirmed in the breaking of bread and in common prayer. The young church responds to its Lord by celebrating its praises in unanimous collective worship, of which the token of the broken bread is the center.

Finally, the κοινωνία unfolds its useful and practical effects in daily life through mutual brotherly help. Material goods, seen as a gift from the Lord, are used equitably and charitably for the services of the brethren.

Therefore, the three constitutive elements of the life of the church are developed: witness, worship, service (or comfort), which are designated sometimes by the trilogy *martyria, leitourgia, diakonia.* [1]

a. The church explains its faith; it teaches it to the faithful; it bears witness to it before those on the outside. "And with great power the apostles gave their testimony to the resurrection of the Lord Jesus" (Acts 4:33).

b. The church offers to God the adoration and thanksgiving that are his due, and addresses its requests and intercessions to him. "And day by day, attending the temple together and breaking bread in their homes, they partook of food with glad and generous hearts, praising God . . . " (Acts 2:46). [2]

c. The church is a brotherhood that practices the sharing of goods for the joy and well-being of every member. God's love for his elect and his benevolence toward men calls in return for the love of the redeemed one for others (I John 3:16; 4:11, 19-21). "They had everything in common . . . every day some service of assistance was done" (Acts 4:32).

These three aspects of the common life of the first believers, even if clearly distinguished from each other, are nevertheless very intimately connected. The breaking of bread and the prayers, therefore, include necessarily the teaching of the faith and the declaration of the word; worship is done in a brotherly *agapé* and includes perhaps already an offering for the poor (cf. I Cor. 16:1-2). It is in prayer and in the fraternal and sacramental communion that the congregation nourishes its life in Christ and draws its strength in order to witness to the outside: it is there as well that the impetus is given to those charged with the dedication of themselves to their less fortunate brethren. When worship is neglected or degenerates, witness to the faith and charitable works dry up; and in-

---

[1] Cf. Wilhelm Stählin, *Bruderschaft*, Band 11 of the Series *Kirche im Aufbau*, 1940, p. 91; and K. B. Ritter, *Die Liturgie als Lebensform der Kirche*, 1947, pp. 5-6.

[2] The expression κατ'οἶκο · likely means a private house where the community is gathered for worship specifically Christian. Cf. Oscar Cullmann, "Early Christian Worship," *Studies in Biblical Theology*, No. 10. (Chicago: Henry Regnery, 1953), pp. 9-10.

versely, a church that is no longer missionary within its environment and gives only parsimoniously to help the poor, proves that the worship it celebrates is merely an empty formality.

The early church seems to have retained rather long the organic link and balance between the teaching of the word and the celebration of worship, and brotherly assistance. The Middle Ages experienced an eclipse of preaching and teaching; worship, according to the original design, had then degenerated, whereas assistance and relief survived through the monasteries and parochial fraternities. Through the Reformation the Holy Spirit revived the teaching of the word of truth; but the priority then urgently given to this doctrinal and prophetic element relegated the cultic element to the background, at least in the Zwinglian and Calvinistic churches. Benevolence has not been forgotten; but on account of its not being rooted in the cultic life, frequently it has become autonomous and even secularized.

It belongs to our century to receive from the Holy Spirit a renewed conception of the value of the church as the body of Christ and of the multiform richness of the life it receives from him who is its living head, its ever present chief, even Christ. Particularly, the authentic nature of Christian worship and its axial role in the church have been rediscovered during the last quarter of the century in almost all Christian confessions. The liturgical movement has taken on such dimensions everywhere that no one can ignore it or discount it as a fad or transient matter. As in every spiritual movement, it is easy to condemn the extremes or unskillfulness within it; but the "discerning of the spirits," which is a χάρισμα of the church of God, constrains us to recognize in the essential *élan* of this movement a gift of the Spirit to the church for the re-edification of the body of Christ that has been torn and fragmented by a long period of individualism, moralism, and pietism.

Part One
The Initiative of God

1

The Lord Calls His People Together

The whole Bible testifies that in the work of our salvation the initiative belongs entirely to God. It is he who calls; it is he who justifies and glorifies his elect (Rom. 8:30). Natural sinful man cannot rise from or by himself to God in order to know him or to honor and serve him as he ought. Man cannot offer him something which belongs properly to God himself, for "The earth is the Lord's, and the fullness thereof; the world and they that dwell therein" (Ps. 24:1 KJV). Man knows about God only what God really wants to reveal to him through his Word; and in his acts of honor and sacrifice, man can give to God only what God has given him already. "For all things come of thee, and of thine own have we given thee" (I Chron. 29:14 KJV).

Furthermore, man could not render God valid worship if already God himself had not consented and taught him. If man takes upon himself the authority to develop a body of cultic acts, conceived as an objective achievement, through which he can assure himself of the divine favor, he is flattering himself: indeed, this encounter that he seeks with God does not really take place. The appointment fails because it is up to God alone to initiate the encounter and to grant his grace

3

when and as he desires.[1] God can be the object of our worship only if he is first the subject, that is, the one who gives us the worship.[2] We can only offer him our service if he himself inspires and orders it first of all. To take up again the terminology of the Swedish theologian Nygren, the "eros" of human aspiration results only in a non-operating theurgy; only God's free and condescending "agape" to us can prescribe for us a worship that is agreeable to him.[3]

At the beginning Abel's sacrifice is accepted, whereas Cain's is rejected. God is free to decide in this way between them. The first act of worship of Abraham, the father of believers, is only a response to a call from God who makes himself known to his servant and causes him to hear his word. "And the Lord appeared unto Abraham and said, Unto thy seed will I give this land: and there builded he an altar unto the Lord . . . and called upon the name of the Lord" (Gen. 12:7-8 KJV). Again, having received the divine promises with regard to his posterity, Abraham built an altar to God at the oaks of Mamre (Gen. 13:14-18). His first sacrifice mentioned in the scriptures is offered by God's own command as a sign of covenant (Gen. 15). The same is true of the sacrifice which the patriarch wanted to make of his son Isaac (Gen. 22).

Abraham is only the first fruits of this election and call directed to a whole people. The promises God made to him are verified in the history of his descendants; the "house of Israel" is the society of men whom God has called to know him and to serve him as he wants to be served. The cultic ordinances of Exodus are presented to us as a command from God. It is by divine mandate that the assembly of Israel is called together for the religious ceremony of the consecration

---

[1] *Ubi et quando Deo visum est.*

[2] Cf. Robert Will, *Le Culte* (Strasbourg: Librairie Istra, 1925) "God alone is the subject of worship for he alone acts in it, he alone, the Absolute whose action is not submerged in the determinism of our experimental laws. Even there where man, in his mystical desire, believes he is lifting himself up on his own into the transcendent sphere, it is the mystery of God which draws him, without his being aware of the divine initiative: it is God who lets man find himself. Man can only imagine himself seeking God and consider God the subject of worship because he is not aware of the fact that the first impetus of his religious life and of his worship comes from God" (I, pp. 329-330).

[3] Anders Nygren, *Agapé and Eros*, Trans. Philip Watson, (Philadelphia: Westminster Press, 1953).

of Aaron and his sons (Lev. 8:3) and for the consecration of the Levites (Num. 8:9). Likewise it is God who commands the people to assemble for the various religious feasts. For this reason Chapter 23 of Leviticus is significant; the expression "holy convocation" comes back like a refrain, and it is God himself who orders the cultic gatherings of the sabbaths and of the feasts. "And the Lord spake unto Moses, saying, Speak unto the children of Israel, and say unto them, Concerning the feasts of the Lord, which ye shall proclaim to be holy convocations, even these are my feasts (verses 1-2) . . . These are the feasts of the Lord, even holy convocations, which ye shall proclaim in their seasons" (verse 4).[4]

The institution of the Levitical priesthood in its entirety and of the sacrificial rites is God's gift. In this respect biblical thought is clear. Nothing may be invented by pious human fantasy; everything is fixed by divine decision even to the smallest detail. So the ascending movement of the ceremonies and sacrifices is only the second beat of the rhythm of which the first is the condescending grace of God himself who indicates and gives to man the means of serving him. Only then may man, without fear and uncertainty, without conscientious scruples and false security, offer his worship to the Lord. "And Moses went up unto God, and the Lord called unto him out of the mountain, saying . . . Ye have seen . . . how I bore you on eagles' wings, and brought you unto myself . . . And ye shall be unto me a kingdom of priests, and an holy nation" (Exod. 19:3-6). "I have given your priest's office unto you as a service of gift" (Num. 18:7). So God's free grace has granted to poor people a royal priesthood, a holiness or "sacrality," with the right for this whole chosen people to come near their God in order to speak and pray to him. God himself bears them up "on eagles' wings" (Exod. 19:4) and brings them to himself. The worship of this people can now rise to God like a sweet smelling sacrifice, although "God is in heaven, and you upon earth" (Eccles. 5:2).

When the time had fully come God widened his call and extended his summons to embrace all men without any distinction of race. He sent his Christ, the living incarnation of the

---

[4] Cf. verses 7, 8, 21, 23-27, and 33-37.

divine Word, who calls and gathers men together. Christ is the shepherd who came to make his voice heard among the multitudes of men scattered and left to themselves, "being aliens from the commonwealth of Israel, and strangers from the covenants of promise, having no hope, and without God in the world" (Eph. 2:12). Through Christ, the children of God, scattered throughout the world, are gathered into one single body (John 11:52). Hence the *church* appears, a word which means etymologically "an assembly formed upon call."

Since there is only one Christ, there is only one church. When the New Testament speaks of churches, it is in a geographic sense. The church which is at Antioch, the church which is at Corinth, or the church which is at Rome, are only local segments of the unique and single Church of God. The dogmatic and liturgical Pauline passages speak of the church in the singular: "God hath put all things under his feet, and gave him to be the head over all things to the church, which is his body" (Eph. 1:22). "Unto him be glory in the church by Christ Jesus" (Eph. 3:21). And when Ignatius of Antioch at the beginning of the second century described the church as "universal" ($\dot{\eta}$ $\kappa\alpha\theta o\lambda\iota\kappa\dot{\eta}$ $\dot{\epsilon}\kappa\kappa\lambda\eta\sigma\iota\alpha$), he was only making explicit the biblical notion of the uniqueness and unity of the church. By this he was expressing the unanimous, not the individualistic, character of faith in Christ; to be a Christian is to be in the church. It is impossible to be saved by Him who is the head, without being integrated into His body. It is Christ-in-his-body who saves, justifies and reconciles sinners.[5] Paralleling the divine declaration of the old covenant about the people as priests is that of the new covenant in the words of the apostle Peter: "Ye also, as lively stones, are built up a spiritual house, an holy priesthood, to offer up spiritual sacrifices, acceptable to God by Jesus Christ" (I Pet. 2:5). The new people of God, which is the church,— more so and better than the old—can present themselves before their Lord with confidence and with the assurance of being received, heard, and accepted. A Christian "liturgy" is possible and legitimate as a transposition of the Judaic

[5] Cf. E. S. Abbott, H. J. Carpenter, *et al*, *Catholicity: A Study in the Conflict of Christian Traditions in the West*, (Westminster: Dacre Press, 1947), p. 13.

"liturgy" on the ground of the Holy Spirit and in full truth. The eucharistic liturgy of the ancient church shows full awareness of the fact that worship is a privilege one owes to the grace of God and not a human achievement valid on its own. The oldest complete eucharistic formula we possess, and which reflects the situation in the third century, says, "We offer to thee the bread and the cup, thanking thee that thou hast judged us worthy of presenting ourselves before thee to serve thee."[6] The same idea is expressed in most of the ancient liturgies in a still more concrete manner with regard to the sacramental elements: "We offer to thee that which is thine and which comes to us from thee."[7]

In worship then everything comes from God, entirely from his first "prevenient grace," which draws man out of his darkness, raises him from the dust of a very small and sinful creature, and tears away the veil which hides from him the knowledge of his Creator and Savior.[8] It is the Lord who calls together his people, it is he who holds assembly with them, and it is he who leads the divine service of his church.[9] Without this primacy of God, who gives grace to whomsoever he wishes and who determines himself the manner of encounter with his children, and without the sovereign liberty of the

[6] Hippolytus of Rome, *The Apostolic Tradition* Trans. B. S. Easton, (New York: Macmillan Co., 1934), p. 34. "Offerimus tibi panem et calicem, gratias tibi agentes qui nos dignos habuisti adstare coram te et tibi ministrare." The same idea is found expressed in similar terms in the liturgy called Clementine, of the "Apostolic Constitutions," which dates from the last quarter of the fourth century (see F. E. Brightman, *Liturgies Eastern and Western, I*. Oxford: The Clarendon Press, 1896, p. 21).

[7] Cf. Brightman, *op. cit.*, p. 329. To compare with the *de tuis ac datis* of the canon of the Roman Mass, 25.

[8] Cf. Robert Will, in *L'Esprit du Culte Protestant*. (Clermont-Ferrand: Imprimeries réunies, 1942), p. 20: "The initiative for coming together is due to God. It is God, who by his immanent action, urges souls to seek him. It is God, and God alone, who disposes them to hear his word. In a word, worship is a grace: all here is grace . . . God is thus the unique author of the cultic event. By affirming the sovereignty of his grace we confirm a fundamental principle of the Reformation." (See also pp. 36-37).

[9] Cf. Karl Barth, *The Knowledge of God and the Service of God*, Trans. J.L.M. Haire and Ian Henderson, (London: Hodder and Stoughton, 1938). "The church service is in the first instance primarily, in origin and substance, divine action, and is only then human action secondarily, by derivation, and as an accident of the former. What man should and can do here is to serve. And that this service is *divine* service is something which is brought about not by man but by God and God alone. It is *God* who wills that divine service be held. It is *God* who provides the media suitable for it. It is *God* who bears witness through them to his grace. It is *God* who by this means awakens, purifies and advances faith. All along the line it is God not man, and man at every point appears only as the one who serves and who carries out the will of God" (p. 192).

7

Holy Spirit, worship would be merely a human "work," a fiction deprived of value and efficacy.[10] Worship is a dialogue, but the initial call comes from God who begins the conversation.[11]

[10] Cf. Barth, *ibid.*, "The church service is an *opus Dei*, a work of God, which takes place for its own sake." (p. 194).

[11] Cf. *Ways of Worship* (The Report of a Theological Commission of Faith and Order), ed. P. Edwall, E. Hayman, and W. D. Maxwell. (New York: Harper & Brothers, 1951), p. 197: "The essence of worship is a double movement of the Holy Spirit. The initiative is, as always, on the side of God. His gracious approach to us through Christ is mediated to the believers by the Spirit . . . In their response of faith there is a movement of the Spirit back, as it were, from the human side to the Father." The author of this report, an Anglican, underlines very fortunately the value of the Trinitarian dogma as an expression of the worship cycle: the *lex orandi* has determined the *lex credendi*.

2

The Lord Present
Among His People

God invites his people to serve him. The people of God
respond by approaching their God and offering their service
to him. In worship an encounter takes place between God
and the community which belongs to him. The Lord is present
in his church, and the church is under the eye and attention
of its Lord. Only in God's presence is there truly divine
worship. Worship is possible only when the divine presence,
given by grace and received in faith, is recognized and grasped
in its reality and power.

In the Bible the divine presence is associated very frequently
with the mentioning of the divine name. The name of the
Lord is identified with the Lord himself in his person and
action. When God says his own name, "I am Jehovah thy
God," and when the people in turn call upon this name, he
causes himself to be present personally. "Unto thee, O God,
do we give thanks . . . for that thy name is near thy wondrous
works declare (or: "Thy name is present among us")."
Ps. 75:1.

Under the old covenant God is *with* his servants; he is
with his people by virtue of the past covenant with Abraham,
and received at Sinai through Moses as mediator. God is
present therefore in the life of his servants, not as a static,

impersonal, and unconditional presence, but in a personal and active way, conditioned by the destiny and mission assigned to his servants and his people. The same idea or notion of the divine presence colors the texts in which God is said to be *in the midst* of his people: "You shall not be in dread of them; for the Lord your God is in the midst of you, a great and terrible God. The Lord your God will clear away these nations before you little by little" (Deut. 7:21-22). "If you walk in my statutes and observe my commandments and do them . . . I will have regard for you . . . and will confirm my covenant with you. And I will make my abode among you, and will be your God and you shall be my people" (Lev. 26: 3, 9, 11, and 12). In case of disobedience and violation of the covenant, the divine presence does not become absence, but judgment (cf. Lev. 26:14 f). The *favorable* presence of God among his people is related always therefore with the faithfulness of this people to their vocation.

This presence, of which the divine name is the sign, God reveals through word and appearances; he makes himself heard and he makes himself seen. God *appeared* to Abraham in order *to speak to him* (Gen. 12:7). It was in a vision of a ladder reaching from the earth to heaven that he addressed his word to Jacob, and Jacob cried out when he wakened: "Surely the Lord is in this place . . . How awesome is this place! This is none other than the house of God, and this the gate of heaven" (Gen. 28:10-17). It was in the vision of a burning bush that God called Moses (Exod. 3:1-6), and later it was in the theophany on Sinai that he dictated the word of his commandments (Exod. 19:24, 33). It was in a sudden vision that he spoke to Elijah on this same mountain (I Kings 19:8-15). God appeared to Isaiah in the temple at Jerusalem (Isa. 6:1-8) and to Ezekiel on the banks of the Euphrates (Ezek. 1 and 2) to summon them to their mission.

So God reaches the man of his choice through the inner senses of hearing and seeing; he permits him to perceive words inwardly and he stirs up images within him. Word and vision are complementary means of communication between God and man; they are concomitant factors in the primary act of God making himself present to his servants. God uses these two human senses which are the most cognitive in making man aware of his immediate nearness. In Reformed circles sufficient attention has not been given to the considerable role that visible signs play in the Bible. Because of a one-sided insistence upon the heard word, we have closed our minds to the biblical emphasis upon sight and visions. God can reveal himself to us just as well through the interpretation given by our eyes as by our ears. Indeed one can say that in the old covenant, with its imperfections, the word of God was simply *heard*, while through the work of the new covenant, it has become *visible* in addition. "That which was from the beginning, which we have heard, which we have seen with our eyes, which we looked upon and touched with our hands, concerning the word of life . . . *that which we have seen and heard we proclaim*" (I John 1:1-3). At first John says: we have heard, we have seen; then, correcting himself, he says: we have seen, we have heard; thus he made clear the equality of the two means of knowledge and contact. It is a sign of mere prejudice always to give principal and systematic priority to one over the other, like the Reformers on the one side and Catholicism on the other.[1] It may be said, no doubt, that the word has the advantage over vision, for it is the word that gives the divine presence its intelligible content and the character or nature of a personal call. The vision is there to sustain the word and to provide for our spirit the indispensable support of the imagination; it is an auxiliary sign of the authenticity of the presence. Without the word, which is essential, the vision can be merely a hollow and empty dream; but without the vision which is a necessary help, the word might become only abstract theory.

With man the word is a detachable factor, and in fact is detached from the speaker. Far from expressing adequately

---

[1] Robert Will, *Le Culte*, II, p. 342: "The predominance either of the visual impressions, or of the auditive impressions, depends on the nature of the individual man, on the momentary state of his soul, on time, on place, on atmosphere, on gregarious suggestion . . . both spheres borrow reciprocally . . . Thought is not nourished exclusively by word and scripture, and the spirit does not live solely by visions. The word therefore is not *the* worship symbol above all others, but *a* symbol beside others." Also p. 109: "There is in Protestant circles an eternal nostalgia for worship in the spirit. It is only with a bad conscience they will allow ceremonial to enter. They prefer auditory symbols which are considered to be more spiritual than visual or pliable ones."

11

and fully the person who spoke it, the word conveys only a momentary aspect of him. Indeed the word may conceal the identity and nature of the speaker and disguise his real thought. It is often "the word of deceit" (Ps. 36:4; Isa. 59:13). But God is himself entirely and truly in his word. "By myself I have sworn, from my mouth has gone forth in righteousness a word that shall not return" (Isa. 45:23). The divine word in the Bible is identified with God himself. It is God himself in action; God himself turned toward his servants and interpreters in order to establish contact with them, and through them to his people. The word is the presence and power of God. Wherever this word is spoken, the Lord God is there who says it and fulfills it (Ps. 33:4; 6:8-9).

It is necessary, however, to underline here the biblical realism of the divine name and of the divine word. Modern idealistic presumption, and the disincarnate spiritualism that comes from it, have frequently reduced the one and the other to abstract concepts. They are little more than auditory symbols that conjure up in our minds *something* unreal and from far away, instead of indicating to us the immediate presence of *Somebody*.

The word and the vision are transitory for us, and the divine presence to which they testify would be sadly disjointed were it not that God, in the old covenant, remedied it by means of an object, a sensible permanent sign and concrete witness: the temple at Jerusalem and, more particularly, the ark of the covenant. The ark, visible and tangible, witnesses to the fact that God was continually with his people to guide and deliver them. But the ark was not an unconditional guarantee of the presence of God among his people. It was not an idol being substituted for God; it was the receptacle for the tables of the Law on which the religious and moral demands of the divine will were written. When the people were unfaithful to this Law, the ark did not protect them from misfortune or calamity (I Sam. 4:5); rather it restricted them, for the law which was contained in the ark judged the disobedient people. The ark confirms the presence of a holy God who judges and chastens a rebellious people.

After the word of grace came then the word of judgment; after the presence of God the Savior, then God the Judge. But it was the same unique and sovereign presence of which the ark was the sign and witness. The ark assured the people that God was wandering with them in this world. "I have not dwelt in a house since the day I brought up the people of Israel from Egypt to this day, but I have been moving about in a tent for my dwelling" (II Sam. 7:6). God becomes like a "stranger and traveler on the earth" in order to be present in a better way to his chosen people. Finally when the people have settled down in the Promised Land, the ark in the center of the temple in Jerusalem continues to testify that God is present in Zion and that he rules over his people.

What has been thus outlined in the old economy has found its fulfillment in Christ. Isaiah calls the Messiah *Immanuel*, that is to say, *God with us* (7:14). After hearing the words of Jesus of Nazareth and having seen his miracles, the people cried out, "We have seen strange things today" (Luke 5:26). "No man ever spoke like this man" (John 7:46). "God has visited his people" (Luke 7:16). Jesus Christ is the coming of God upon earth. In him is realized the living synthesis of word and vision, and also of the sign or witness that consolidates the one and the other.

Jesus of Nazareth is the very Word of God made flesh among men. He is the word which "has dwelt among us," more precisely which "has set up his tent or planted his tabernacle among us" (John 1:14). He is also a permanent *theophany;* in him we have the clear and enduring *vision* of God who is holiness and love. "He who has seen me, has seen the Father" (John 14:9). "Everyone who *sees* the Son *and believes* in him should have eternal life" (John 6:40). In this way Jesus is the living *sign* on earth, the faithful witness (Rev. 1:5; 3:14) of the divine presence and of the powers of the world to come. "This generation is an evil generation; it seeks a sign, but no sign shall be given it except the sign of Jonah. For as Jonah became a sign to the men of Nineveh, so will the Son of Man be to this generation" (Luke 11:29-30; cf. Matt. 12:38-40). Truly, one has complete "fullness of life in him" (Col. 2:10).

This presence endures. It has been promised "until the end of the world" (Matt. 28:20) to the community of disciples. It has been assured to all who together call upon the name of Jesus Christ, the divine name of the *Kyrios*, a name which is presence. It is in the fraternal group of believers, in the body which they form to call upon this name, that the Lord makes himself present. "For where two or three are gathered together in my name, there am I in the midst of them" (Matt. 18:20). This word is found in a clearly ecclesiastic context where the word *church* occurs in connection with the rules of discipline for the community (Matt. 18:15-20). Even if this passage had to be interpreted to a certain extent as a retrospective projection of the early community under the historical ministry of Jesus, it would not reveal any less the feeling of the first generation of believers towards the subject of the presence of the Lord in his church.

Paul teaches that the church is the body of Christ. What our physical body is for our personality, that is, a means of communication and action, the church is for the glorified Lord. It is through the church that Christ is present and active in the world. It is through the church that the incarnate presence of God in Christ is extended or prolonged in time and space. It is striking that each promise of the presence of Christ is made not to individuals as such, but always to the community (except for Acts 18:9-10). In the Old Testament we read that God said to a man: I am with *you* (singular); I shall be with *you* (singular). In the New Testament Christ says to the community of his disciples: I am with *you* (plural); I am among *you* (plural).

But the church cannot regulate like a master this presence of its Lord, as of a "thing" that was its own unconditional and inalienable property, just as Israel did not order God and his power through the mere fact that they had the ark. Christ lives in his church *through the Holy Spirit*. "And I will pray the Father, and he will give you another Counselor to be with you for ever" (John 14:16). The divine presence through the Holy Spirit is none other than the presence of Christ, for he has declared: "For he (i.e. the Holy Spirit) will glorify me, for he will take what is mine and declare it to you" (John 16:14). But the Holy Spirit is not only the Lord, who is with his church, in the midst of his own; it is God within their hearts; it is the divine life of Christ which has become internal and as immanent in his church and in the members of the church.

Now the conception we have been able to fashion for ourselves regarding the presence becomes clear and complete. Word, vision, and sign, united essentially in Christ, become real and effectual for us only through the action of the Holy Spirit. Ignatius of Antioch has written, "Where Christ Jesus is, there is the church universal."[2] In its anti-docetic context, this famous formula means: Where the Christ of the incarnation is, the Son of God who came in the flesh, there is the true church. But this saying has to be completed by the one which Irenaeus formulated in an anti-gnostic context half a century later: "For where the church is, there is the Spirit of God; and there where the Spirit of God is, there is the church, and every grace; but the Spirit is truth."[3] These two theses are complementary truths: Christ lives in his church as far as the church is open to the Holy Spirit.

The presence of the Lord in his church therefore is of another kind, of another degree, of another power than his universal presence in the world of which he, as the divine word, is the creator. In the church his presence is given as a function of the new eschatological creation through the Holy Spirit. This presence is a privilege peculiar to those who are able to confess through the Holy Spirit: *Jesus is Lord* (I Cor. 12:3), and who, having received the first fruits of the Spirit, groan inwardly as they wait for adoption as sons, the redemption of their bodies (Rom. 8:23). This presence is therefore *real* to the degree that it is *spiritual*, that is to say, declared and revealed by the Holy Spirit. From the warped perspective of the sixteenth century controversies, it has become customary to set *spiritual* presence in opposition to *real* presence, though these two determinations of the presence actually complement and correct each other. The formula *real presence*

---

[2] *Letter to the Smyrnists*, 8, 2. The Ante-Nicene Fathers, I Trans. A. Roberts and J. Donaldson. (New York: Chas. Scribner's Sons, 1899), p. 90.

[3] *Against Heresies*, III, 24, 1. The Ante-Nicene Fathers, *Ibid.*, p. 458.

seems to have risen out of the controversies of the eleventh century on the matter of the eucharist. This has been set over against virtual presence in order to underline the personal and concrete presence of the Lord, in contrast to a presence which would reveal itself only through its effects or faculties. By *real presence* we mean the discarding of everything that resembles abstractions in order to assure a personal encounter between the Lord and his own.[4] Real presence means also objective presence, given from outside and from above the subject, before it becomes internal for him. But in order to avoid having the term *real* entail in this connection a materialization or reification of the divine presence, we must add *spiritual presence*, a presence which becomes internal to us through the action of the Holy Spirit in us. On the other hand, in order to avoid having that spiritual presence decay in a purely subjective presence or confined to the limitations of our human spirit or conditioned by our capacity to understand men, we have to add: *real presence*. So the two formulas correct each other in order to define a transcendent presence, dominating the community and the individuals who comprise it, but penetrating them vitally by the influx of the Holy Spirit.[5]

The Lord lives in his church. The church, the body of Christ, shows *hic et nunc* the presence and action of its Lord. It extends in a certain sense the mystery of the incarnation in the unfolding of history. It is not, however, a literal extension of the incarnation of the Lord among us; for history is the place or arena of sinful men, and therefore the church and its

[4] Reformed piety itself demands this "existential" confrontation; for example, in the words of hymns.

> It is Thee—supreme God
> Thee whom I ask from Thee.
> Thy presence—Thy absence
> Is life or is death for me. (*Psalter*, No. 119). The Psalter of the French-speaking Swiss Church.

> I don't want the shadow which passes,
> The image which pales,
> But the substance of Thy grace
> Thee—self, Thy Spirit. (*Ibid.*, No. 331).

[5] It is in this sense and in order to avoid all sacramental reification that G. W. H. Lampe, the Anglican theologian, has indicated that he prefers to speak in terms of action rather than in terms of presence. Not, he says, that there might be in the last analysis a distinction between these terms, for the Lord cannot act while being absent, and he could not be present while remaining inactive (*Ways of Worship*, p. 200). Cf. also Robert Will, *op. cit.*, II, pp. 200-201.

institutions are heavily burdened and encumbered with human sin. The church is the consequence of the incarnation; it is the witness of it, the sign, the reflection. The church is the instrument, notoriously deficient, which the Lord uses to reveal his presence today in this transient and convicted world, while awaiting his clear and perfect revelation in the world to come.

The Lord Present In Worship

Worship is the propitious moment of encounter between God and his people. Worship is the peculiar or special occasion of the presence of the Lord in his church. It is through its worship that the church becomes aware of itself as the people of God and the body of Christ, and presents itself as such before the world. It is in worship that it reflects plainly and visibly the incarnation of its Lord, in demonstrating clearly his presence, word, and action. Matthew's Gospel associates the presence of Christ with common prayer, preaching, and the celebration of the sacrament. "Again I say to you, if two of you agree on earth about anything they ask, it will be done for them by my Father in heaven. *For* where two or three are gathered *in my name*, there am I in the midst of them . . . All authority in heaven *and on earth* has been given to me. Go *therefore* and make disciples of all nations, baptizing them in the name of the Father and of the Son and of the Holy Spirit . . . *And lo, I am with you* always, to the close of the age" (Matt. 18:19-20 and 28:18-20).

The fourth Gospel, moreover, associates common prayer with the promise of "being seen again." "So you have sorrow now, but I will see you again and your hearts will rejoice . . . In that day you will ask me no questions . . . If you ask anything of the Father, he will give it to you in my name" (John 16:22-23). Through both his divinity and humanity, which are closely united in the mystery of the incarnation, Jesus Christ becomes the unique and proper place for the encounter between God and men. He is their living bond and link, and therefore the center of worship; and his real presence establishes and makes the worship possible. As Son of God who came down to us, he establishes contact between God and us which we could never create by ourselves. As the risen and glorified Son of Man he carries and lifts us with him in his humanity to the throne of God. It is the incarnation and ascension that give to the worship of the church both existence and justification.

Worship would be emptied of its substance and spiritual dynamism if it were reduced merely to recollecting past events. The vast expanse of history would stand then between the divine acts of the past and the community of believers today. Indeed, worship becomes ineffective also when the divine transcendence is emphasized to the point of digging a chasm between the risen Lord and his church; or, to put it another way, to the point of splitting "the whole Christ," dissociating the Head from the body. There is then no longer any guarantee or certainty that the promises of Christ will spread their beneficent effects among his people. If worship is only a human act, purely symbolical, a simple calling to mind of things past and a platonic invocation of future realities, then it holds nothing vital for believers and they abandon it with a good conscience. They are not helped and healed by a history lesson or a course in morals.[1]

Actually the church believes and shows that its Lord is effectively present when it comes together around the word and the sacraments which he has entrusted to it. In worship the church really shares things from above as it participates

---

[1] Cf. Herbert Goltzen, in the Lutheran report, *Ways of Worship*, pp. 97-98. Also *Leiturgia, Handbuch des Evangelischen Gottesdienstes*, (Kassel: J. Stauda-Verlag, 1953), I, p. 215: "The idea that the preached word is simply recalling the saving work of Christ, which the hearer would have only to heed in order to be joined beyond this word and in the vague sphere of the Spirit to that work from which both time and space separate us, is one that is totally foreign to the witness of the New Testament and the biblical message."

in Christ and his kingdom.[2] Mysteriously it is in him and he is in it.

Jesus as a man was born in a stable. He was poor. He had "nowhere to lay his head" (Luke 9:58) and "he had no form or comeliness that we should look to him" (Isa. 53:2). He died on the cross as a criminal and an outcast. This is the scandal of the humiliation of the Son of God. But Jesus as God climbed the mountain of transfiguration where his face glistened as the sun and his clothes became white as snow. He entered Jerusalem as a king eight days before the Passover and he accepted the acclamation of the crowd. He walked on the water and his disciples, struck by religious fear, bowed down before him. He appeared to Paul in blinding light on the way to Damascus, and to the seer of Patmos as the glorified One who walks in the midst of golden candlesticks. The worship of the church must make real and visible these two aspects of the person of the Lord.

Moreover, traditionally the theology of the church fathers and of the reformers has recognized in Christ the threefold quality of *prophet*, *priest* (or sacrificer), and *king*. This is why the beginning of the Book of Revelation describes him in symbolic images. Worship has to declare and reflect this threefold office of Christ the Savior.

When Jesus preached the gospel of the kingdom and confirmed it by his miracles, the crowd said, " 'A great *prophet* has arisen among us!' and 'God has visited his people!' " (Luke 7:16). "This is indeed the *prophet* who is to come into the world" (John 6:14 and 7:40). The prophet is the spokesman of God to man, the Mediator in descending line. Who is able to be himself better than Christ, the divine Word, the living and personal Word of God? Sometimes his message assumed a solemn form and had a rhythm and euphony reflecting a divine origin and grandeur as in the Beatitudes, or certain themes in the fourth Gospel, or particular groups of *logia* whose poetical character is clearly recognizable. But

---

[2] Heb. 3:14. The term μέτοχος which is very broad in scope and significance, is found in Heb. 3:1 and 6:4, and I Cor. 10:17, 21, in a similar sense; likewise in Eph. 3:6 with the prefix συν it is still more expressive. Inversely, and as a counterproof of the real value of the word, Heb. 2:14 shows Christ *participating* in our flesh and blood condition.

Jesus spoke also in the freedom and spontaneity of the diverse circumstances of his own ministry.

Like its Head, the church is prophetic, and in its worship the Lord continues to make his word heard in these two ways. The gospel, preceded by the law or the prophets and commented upon by the apostolic letters, is read with a seriousness and solemnity which is appropriate in echoing faithfully the voice of the Master. The divine Prophet is there in the midst of his own and his voice resounds, not from the pulpit but from the choir of the church, close to the holy table, which is the sign of his divine and sovereign presence. Then comes the actualized message, transferred into the situation and the needs of the moment by the interpretation of the preacher. This is the sermon, declared from the pulpit, the appropriate place for religious discourse.

Christ is also *priest* or *sacrificer* (Heb. 8:1, 2). He is mediator in an ascending line between God and us. He offered the prayer of intercession, rightly called *priestly*, in which he offered himself to God (John 17). He yielded all his time, strength, and anxieties to the service of the Father as a living and holy sacrifice. He gave his life as a sacrifice on the cross, and in the very holy place of the heavenly tabernacle, he offers through eternity his own blood, once shed for all on Calvary (Heb. 9:12, 24). For he remains forever our sovereign sacrificer: "We have a great high priest who passed through the heavens, Jesus, the Son of God . . . he holds his priesthood permanently because he continues for ever" (Heb. 4:14 and 7:17, 24).

Now the church witnesses to the priesthood of its Lord. It expresses and reflects it. It is "a royal priesthood, a holy nation, a spiritual house to offer spiritual sacrifices acceptable to God through Jesus Christ" (I Pet. 2:9, 5). If there is a prophetic ministry of the church, there is also a priestly. Worship is as much sacrificial as prophetic. Christ, present in his community, as the head united with the body, continues to present to the Father, for the church and with it, the offering of the prayer, the offering of the whole life and being of his people, and the offering of his own redemptive death. The church in prayer, *Ecclesia orans*, prolongs in space and time the priestly prayer. When the church prays, it is Christ who prays in it. Christ extends his prayer in the church.[3] Thus all the petitions and praises that the body of Christ presents to God through its members are valuable only when passing through him who is the Head of the body, the Son of God. All the prayers of the church are offered to God "through Jesus Christ our Lord" or "in the name and for the sake of Jesus Christ." This is why the church must be careful how it expresses its prayers; they ought to be worthy, grounded and shaped in him who is truly "the hearer." The church must give to its prayers rigorous thought, right intention, spiritual fullness, and a propriety of tone and beauty of form that are in harmony with the divine person of Christ and his holy prayer, both in John 17 and Matt. 11:25-27 and in the Lord's Prayer, Matt. 6:9-13.

Finally, Christ is *king*. His kingship which was self-evident at times in his servant role, was suggested on Palm Sunday, indicated particularly at the ascension, and will be revealed fully at the *parousia* "when he delivers the kingdom to God the Father after destroying every rule and every authority and power . . . For God has put all things in subjection under his feet" (I Cor. 15:24, 27). Then the *Regnum gratiae* will make room for the *Regnum gloriae*. But *now already* Christ reigns: "All authority in heaven and on earth has been given to me" (Matt. 28:18). "God has made him to sit at his right hand in the heavenly places, far above all rule and authority and power and dominion . . . and *he has put all things under his feet*" (Eph. 1:20-22) and "God has delivered us from the dominion of darkness and transferred us to the kingdom of his beloved Son" (Col. 1:13-14). Therefore the church is not only the spokesman of Christ the Prophet, not only the organ of Christ the Sacrificer, it is also the army of Christ the King. And something of the royal majesty and glory of the Risen One who ascended to heaven has to come through in the worship of the church. Worship has to reveal partly in its liturgical forms

---

[3] "The liturgist, in the high sense of the word, is once and for all Christ the Lord. He has, as the only one for his people . . . brought a great sacrifice; he has made a sublime foundation: the λεῖτον ἔργον of our redemption. This ἔργον is as such something objective . . . an action embracing heaven and earth, which Christ wants to live anew in us." (Albert Hammenstede, *Die Liturgie als Erlebnis*, Freiburg-in-Brisgau: Herder, 1919, p. 25).

the royal glory of Christ, the triumph and present power of the Head of the church, who was once the crucified, and who is now the living, the conqueror. By its hymns, candles, the beauty of the ornaments of the sanctuary, and all the dignity and fullness of the divine service, the church makes known to the world that its Lord reigns in the midst of it in his divine beauty. It is not, however, mere estheticism, but a witness. Without confusing itself with the kingdom that is coming, the church fulfills simply its mission as a prophetic *sign* of the kingdom and by using symbolism which Revelation, this scriptural authority, does not judge to be contrary to worship "in spirit and in truth" (Rev. 1:13; 2:1; 3:5; 4:4-5, 10; 5:8, etc.).

To summarize, then, the worship of the church is *prophetic*, for the Lord who is present there proclaims the gospel. It is *priestly*, because Christ who is present there offers to God the sacrifice of praise, with the living and holy sacrifice of those who are members of his body. It is *royal*, because Christ who is present there manifests the power and splendor of his reign. Worship must have enough radiancy to reveal the glory of Christ, the Son of God, but keep, at the same time, enough simplicity to remember the humble submission of Christ who was the simple man and suffering servant of the Eternal.

Worship which is celebrated by the new people of God— that community of Christ kept for the age to come—is already, therefore, an eschatological event since Christ in glory is actually present there. He really comes among his assembled people with his *prophetic* word, his gospel of the kingdom, "which will judge men on the last day" (John 12:48). He comes there as the *sacrificer* who stands forever in the heavenly sanctuary to intercede and to present there our prayers. He is there in our midst as the *king*, reigning effectively over the new creation. In worship his presence means, therefore, an irruption here below of the world to come: heaven on earth (or, as the theologians of the Eastern church like to say, "The joy of heaven on earth;" and we, in a more subtle way along with a reformed theologian, Max Thurian, who gave this suggestive title to a work on liturgics). For the world to come, by drawing near to us in worship, does not abolish the present world; the heaven which descends does not yet do away with earthly realities.

As Peter Brunner says, the divine service is described as an interim between the mystical death and resurrection of baptism on the one hand, and the actual and corporal death and resurrection at the last day, on the other. Worship is a periodic reverberation of what is signified by baptism: our death to the present world and our birth and resurrection into a new order of things, our real participation in the Kingdom of Heaven, inaugurated by Christ on the day of his ascension. Therefore, humiliation, repentance, pardon, and reconciliation have to be declared and lived anew always in our worship which is set on this earth, in this world that is under judgment and destined to disappear. But the adoration, joy, and triumphant praises of the heavenly city where the Lord permits himself to be beheld face to face, penetrate and assimilate this earthly worship which the Lord honors with his invisible yet real presence. The divine worship of the church militant is, at the same time, the worship of pilgrims on earth who pursue their painful and perilous march down here, and the worship of the citizens of heaven who have arrived at the end of a limited world and are at rest. Already the boundary of the two ages has been surmounted. We have crossed the borderline which holds us normally to this passing world. "We lift our hearts unto the Lord,"[4] and he comes down and approaches us in the worship event.[5]

We have said that the presence of the Lord is given to the church by the Holy Spirit. Indeed it is only when the risen Lord breathes upon the assembled believers and says, "Receive the Holy Spirit" (John 20:22), that he is recognized as being present and the worship dialogue becomes a real encounter. It is only then that the assembly makes itself known as the body of Christ, through which the Holy Spirit imparts the presence of the Lord with reality and persuasiveness. It is essential that "the love of God [be] poured out into our hearts through the Holy Spirit" (Rom. 5:5) and that the be-

---

[4] Characteristic beginning of the traditional eucharistic liturgy in the opening dialogue of the preface.

[5] Peter Brunner, in *Zur Lehre vom Gottesdienst der im Namen Jesu versammelten Gemeinde* (*Leiturgia, Handbuch des evangelischen Gottesdiensttes*), I, pp. 166-169 & 213-214.

lievers know and recognize themselves as one in Christ Jesus, so that the worship witnesses effectively to the presence of the Lord in the midst of his people. Without the Holy Spirit who creates the κοινωνία of the brethren, there is no real presence of the Lord. It is questionable to speak of the real presence of Christ in juxtaposition to individuals who are strange and indifferent to each other and who come there on their own to listen to a preacher or to hear a Mass. The outward marks of the divine presence must be authenticated by what one might call "pneumatic" signs, namely the essential *fruits of the Spirit* and the *additional gifts of the Spirit.* The fruits of the Spirit are "love, joy, peace, patience, kindness, goodness, and faithfulness" (Gal. 5:22). These fruits are drawn from the three great things that abide: faith, hope, and charity (I Cor. 13:13). They are indispensable to the worship assembly in order for the presence of God the Savior to be revealed. This is worship "in Spirit and in truth," of which the fourth Gospel speaks; worship inspired by the Holy Spirit and harmonized with the truth of the life that is in Christ. As for the gifts of the Spirit of which the first letter to the Corinthians speaks especially (12:8-11), it is necessary that they exist in the church, but it is not essential that all of them find expression or use in the worship. This is why in chapter 14 of the same letter Paul takes great care to limit the importance and significance of speaking in tongues. When we read the text carefully, however, we notice that he tolerates it more than he encourages or recommends it. In return, the apostle makes a great case for prophecy and longs for the exercise of this gift even by all believers within the framework of worship. "But if all prophesy, and an unbeliever or outsider enters, he is convicted by all, he is called to account by all . . . so, falling on his face, he will worship God and declare that *God is really among you*" (14:24, 25). We must conclude at least that the active and explicit participation of all the members of the community in the act of public worship is a necessary sign and convincing witness of the divine presence in the worship.

4

Word and Sacrament

As we have seen, Christ who is the living and vital center of worship unites in himself both word and vision with the permanent sign. These elements, when joined in the unique person of our Lord and reflected anew in the worship of his church, are, as it were, proofs of his presence. For God, who willed the incarnation in order to come down to the level and measure of human beings such as we are, knows that although this was realized totally and once for all in Christ, yet it must be extended in a certain way as long as the present order lasts, and as long as there are human beings to reach and save for the world to come. Consequently, the mystery of the incarnation has its vibrations and reflection in the worship of the church. The hidden and unseen presence of God the Savior in the man Jesus has its continuation and extension in the presence of the Lord of glory in his community which hears the word and celebrates the sacraments.

Word and sacraments then are the two signs—one principally heard; the other chiefly seen—of the Lord present in worship. Through the words of Holy Scripture which come to us through the human voice of the celebrant and through the material substance of the sacraments and the manual acts that are involved in them, faith discerns its Lord; it listens to him who speaks in the Bible and gazes upon the one who administers the baptism or distributes the eucharistic elements. When the Bible is opened in order to be read in church, or the water of baptism flows, or the bread and wine of the Holy Communion are consecrated, the community possesses the distinctive and true signs of its Lord in their midst. Word and sacraments are the permanent signs of the divine presence grasped by faith. This presence is bound willingly to these signs which reflect and make real at different points in space and time the incarnation of the eternal Word. The word is already an incarnation; it is a physical tone expressed by the fleshy organs: the tongue, the palate, and the vocal cords. The sacramental elements are also, in their own way, a material concretion of a 'spiritual event. Sensible signs of the presence and action of the Lord: such are the word and sacraments. [1]

Since the divine presence in word and sacrament is a mystery, indeed a kind of miracle—a miracle of the Holy Spirit—we ought to make clear that it is necessary to guard against identifying the visible signs with the presence to which they witness as well as to avoid separating and isolating them mutually. The material elements (Bible, words of the preacher, water, bread and wine) remain intrinsically what they are and do not undergo a substantial transmutation. They are not deified, but remain created things. These created things, nevertheless, are there by right of a certain sign, divinely guaranteed, of a presence and power which is somewhat tangential to them, yet surpassing and transcending them infinitely. The sacramental elements are the point of

---

[1] On this subject see Max Thurian, in *Joie du ciel sur la terre*, Chap. 3, *Le Culte et l'Incarnation*, (Neuchâtel and Paris: Delachaux et Niestlé, 1946). Cf. *Leiturgia*, I, p. 217: "The mystery which pervades the whole worship and appears especially in the proclamation of the Word consists of this: into our human action which we perform in obedience to Christ's institution, God injects invisibly, yet in reality, his own action . . . To his human word there is joined in actuality the outpouring of the Holy Spirit, like the epiphany of the incarnate presence of God in Christ . . . There is an indissoluble and incomprehensible interpenetration of the human word and the saving presence of God in Jesus, through the Spirit. This *unio spiritualis* of the human word in history and of the Lord risen from the dead, makes the preaching of the gospel the *sacramentum* of the last days . . . between the incarnate presence of God during the earthly life of Jesus (John 1:14) and the same incarnate presence of God in the new world of the resurrection (Rev. 21:3)."

focus, for us and our human gaze, of a divine reality that cannot be enclosed, circumscribed, or limited in space. Therefore, to give to these signs the honor and adoration that belong only to the Lord himself is forbidden. But it does not follow, however, that we should fall short in our respect for these signs, any more than in the secular realm we would treat disgracefully or with contempt any object closely associated with or belonging to a respected and beloved individual. The holy book and the sacramental elements have a right to the respect we owe to "consecrated" things, that is, those withdrawn from the worldly realm in order to fulfill a particular and personal service of the Lord. Thus, in the Catholic liturgies the celebrant kisses the book of the gospel after he reads the prescribed pericope; and Zwingli, in his liturgy of the Holy Communion, 1525, continued this custom. In some Reformed circles the practice still exists of bowing slightly while receiving the bread and the cup. But neither the Bible nor the eucharistic elements should be the focus of acts of adoration or be objects of worship. To wipe out virtually the sign by confusing it with the divine reality is to fall into docetism or monophysitism; whereas to separate the sign from this reality and to deny all functional relationship between them is to enter an idealistic dualism (Nestorianism). In either case we eliminate both the mystery of the incarnation and the cultic mystery and inherit a doctrinaire rationalism.[2] This is to overlook the fact that the relation of the *signum* and the *res* does not enter our rational concepts or categories, but is a "pneumatic" order related to the Holy Spirit. It is by and through the Holy Spirit that the signs proclaim and represent the Lord. These signs which may be called "institutional" become the penetrable and transparent indications of the presence of Christ, using those "pneumatic" tokens which are the fruits of the Holy Spirit. Otherwise they remain obscure and ineffective; they are merely warning signs of the Judge who is at the door (I Cor. 10:1-12; 11:23-12:2, Jas. 5:9). The signs which are word and

---

[2] Robert Will calls *mystical realism* that intermediate and well-balanced position represented in the New Testament by the writings of Paul and John (*op. cit.*, I, pp. 161-163 and II, pp. 100-104). On the relationship between word and sacrament, see II, pp. 450-455.

sacraments are inseparable then from the Holy Spirit. The
Johannine Christ says, "The *words* that I have spoken to you
are *spirit* and life" (6:63). "Unless one is born of *water* and
Spirit (by baptism), he cannot enter the kingdom of God"
(3:5); and with reference to the eucharist, "It is the *spirit*
that gives life, the *flesh* is of no avail" (6:63). The early
church being sensitive to this correlation invoked the Holy
Spirit (epiclesis) in consecrating the baptismal water and the
elements of the Lord's Supper.

The deviations of medieval theology in the West have
raised a problem with the Reformation which did not present
itself explicitly to the early church and which has remained
until this day outside the perspective of the Eastern Orthodox
church: namely, the problem of the mutual relationships
and respective value of the institutional signs—word and
sacraments.[3] It is true that Augustine said, *Accedit verbum ad
elementum, et fit sacramentum,* but in this instance these were
not the same terms of reference as those suggested by the
Lutheran formula: *Wort und Sakrament.* In fact, through its
reaction against a solid and condensed sacramentalism, the
Reformation has found itself, *volens nolens,* with a one-sided
exaltation of the word to the detriment of the sacraments;
and the Reformed churches have often lost sight of their
organic link, and, therefore, of the specific character of ·
the sacrament.

Word and sacraments, therefore, are equally an integral
part of divine revelation and of the worship life of the church.
Christ preached the word of God and the gospel of the
kingdom to his hearers in order to enlighten them. But, he
also gave his person and his life to men in order to deliver
them from the power of darkness. He preached numerous
parables, but he touched the sick with his fingers; he laid
hands on them. He used even his saliva to anoint blind eyes.

[3] On the relationship between word and sacraments, from the broader Reformed viewpoint, consult useful readings in Max Thurian, *op. cit.,* pp. 126-133, and from the
Lutheran viewpoint in Theodore Süss, *Parole et Sacrement (Études Luthériennes,* No. 4)
Ed. Oberlin, (Paris-Strasbourg, 1946). Süss defines the difference as follows: "The
Reformed are possessed with the idea that everything in Christianity should be according to the operation of the word, without diluting, however, the sacrament entirely in the word. The Lutherans, on the other hand, are led by the deeply rooted
personal feeling that the sacrament encloses a particular reality which must not be
neglected when one does not wish to be false to Christian truth" (*op. cit.,* pp. 7-8).

He allowed himself to be approached and touched by those who had faith in the value of these contacts, and he believed his blood shed on the cross was for the expiation of our sins. "Power came forth from him and healed them all" (Mark 3:10; Luke 6:19). His word inspired faith, but it was contact with his person that saved. This distinction, however, is in a sense formal because his person is the Word or Voice of God. But this Word has reached and saved us as *incarnated*, that is, *incorporated in the substance of a life of man and in the event of a death of man*. The word which regenerates is not an abstract word, a doctrine which only the intellect has to assimilate, a word about God or on the subject of Christ. The Word of salvation is the Word-God made flesh, made blood, made human soul in Christ. If, according to the usual definition, a sacrament is "the visible sign of an invisible grace," then Christ is himself the great and living Sacrament, and we may speak of the sacrament of the incarnation.

The often established antithesis between word and sacrament is, therefore, artificial. Upon analysis the difference between these two media of God's approach to us is more modal than essential. It is a question of accent. Both in their proper place are complementary expressions of the saving presence of God in Jesus Christ and in the church, and they involve each other reciprocally. The word of God then has been revealed to us sacramentally only in the incarnation, and the sacraments are such, and valid as such, only through the divine word which affects and determines them. A word which is only read or preached; a sacrament celebrated in silence, or with words in a foreign language unintelligible to the community, give a truncated picture of the divine action in the church. These are two misrepresentations, the one as serious as the other, of the fullness of salvation, and which include equally the fullness of the presence and of the saving action of the Lord.[4]

There is no predominance of the word over the sacrament, nor of the sacrament over the word. From one point of view

---

[4] It is interesting to note, in the same order of thought, that a Roman Catholic who was unable to be present at the Mass will ask readily someone returning from it: Did you pray well? Whereas a Protestant will ask in the same case: Did the minister lead a fine act of worship? (that is, give a fine sermon).

the word has precedence over the sacrament for it arouses the faith of the unbeliever and influences him to join the church. "But how are men to call upon him in whom they have not believed? And how are they to believe in him of whom they have never heard? And who are they to hear without a preacher? And how can men preach unless they are sent?" (Rom. 10:14-15). Also it is always the word which calls to mind afresh the demands of faith. Moreover, it constitutes the sacraments by conferring upon the material elements their "new" sense (that is, in the eschatological sense) and that "pneumatic" value which the Lord has assigned to them. Theoretically, the word can be without the sacrament and bear fruit, whereas the sacrament itself cannot be without the word. Worship may consist of the simple reading and preaching of the word, whereas a sacrament cannot be celebrated without at least the sacramental words being pronounced. On the other hand, however, we should note that the word reaches the community only when it is incarnated in a lecturer and preacher. The isolated believer is reached only when the word is written on paper, in the substance of a book, in some ways sacramentally then in the larger meaning of the term.

From another point of view, the sacraments have something more than the word in that they are more *synthetic, unifying,* and *community* directed.

They are more synthetic because they unite word, vision and sign, similar in their relationship in the person of Jesus Christ. They touch the whole man, in his corporal nature as well as his intellect and feelings. They reach him through all his senses and not through hearing alone. They make the Lord present in his whole person and in all his work, while the word, because it is analytical and argumentative, can only present at any given time one or some particular aspects of Christ and his salvation.[5]

[5] Cf. Alexander Vinet, *Pastoral Theology.* (New York: Ivison, Blakeman, Taylor, 1880): "Worship consisting of rites and words is more distinctive than pure contemplation and less than word or discourse. Contemplation is a synthesis, the discourse is an analysis. Worship which participates in contemplation and word unites the synthesis and analysis and cannot, without mutilating itself, exclude the one or the other" (p. 180). "Every hour of worship must present the whole Jesus Christ to the soul of the believer" (p. 184). In other words, only the sacrament of the Lord's Supper can answer fully this legitimate demand.

The sacraments are more unifying than the word for they put every believer—body and soul—personally into a covenant and grace relationship with the Lord. Through the sacrament the Lord takes possession of his redeemed and joins himself mystically to them, that is, in "a life hid with Christ in God" (Col. 3:3). He lives in him, and the believer is able to live in his Lord.[6] Most texts in the New Testament which deal explicitly with the intimate union and interpenetration of our Lord and his own are in relation to baptism and the eucharist.[7]

Finally, the sacraments are a more community-centered aspect than the word because they integrate concretely the believers not only with their head, but with his body also— the church. They incorporate them visibly into the people of God. Baptism celebrated in the worshiping congregation, as it ought to be done normally, makes the baptized a member of the body of Christ, and the Holy Communion renews and nourishes this relationship.

In the Reformed churches it is scarcely necessary to insist on the essential value of the word which is generally recognized. "How could God address himself to man if the church does not acknowledge the central and essential function of preaching?"[8] It is more necessary to underline the not less essential character of the sacraments. The sacraments are in line with redemptive incarnation. They declare that God not only speaks but acts, or better said, that the divine Word is action and incarnation.[9] They protect faith from intellectual and rational deviation.[10] The isolated word may give the

---

[6] "The essential character of the Christian sacrament according to the unanimous teaching of the apostles and of Romans 6 in particular, is to unite us in Jesus Christ . . . the mystical union established in the sacrament is not an hypothesis, but a reality" (Theodore Süss, *op. cit.*, pp. 20-21).

[7] Romans 6; John 6 and 15. The only exception is John 14:23, where the word of Christ is the instrument of the union.

[8] Cf. J. L. Leuba, *Résumé Analytique de la Dogmatique Ecclésiastique de Barth* (Neuchâtel and Paris: Delachaux et Niestlé, 1945), p. 22.

[9] "The sacrament is added to the word as a new and indispensable element which completes the action of the word and realizes what the word declares . . . These are two different gifts which cannot be reduced the one from the other, but which call for one another and have each its true significance when associated intimately in the work of our salvation" (Theodore Süss, *op. cit.*, pp. 44-45).

[10] "The effect of the Lord's Supper instituted in the Ecclesia is certainly to prevent the church from becoming a 'school' with a 'doctrine,' after the manner of an ancient school of philosophy, or of a Jewish sect, or of a modern association, in order to oblige a certain religious conception of the world" (*Leiturgia*, I, p. 184).

hearer the illusion of understanding God, and thereby induce him to confuse the gospel with an intellectual system (*Weltanschauung*) together with a group of moral precepts and good feelings.[11] The sacraments recall and safeguard the supra-rational and mysterious character of the Lord of the church and of the faith which unites us to him.[12] They are some of the joint actions between the Lord and the church, some perceptible gestures, some visible events, which at the same time reveal and hide the word of God invisibly present, while they are actualizing it.[13]

The Catholic temptation certainly is a sacramental magic or theurgy that presumes to handle grace as a thing, and that sometimes loses sight of the fact that through the material of the sacraments is revealed the direct intervention of the living Word of God and of his Spirit, who "blows where it wills" (John 3:8). But the Reformed temptation is to disincarnate the word of God, even as the man who receives it, and reduce faith to a cerebral act or emotional shock so that instead of laying hold of the real presence of the Lord, we discuss and argue rationally and carp without end about somebody absent. Under the pretext of "religion in the spirit,"[14] we reduce worship to cerebral activity and confuse spiritualism with intellectualism and idealism. Only a balanced synthesis of the word and the sacraments is able to prevent both Catholic and Reformed deviations.

* * * * *

With the word declared and heard and with the sacramental elements administered and received, the real presence of the Lord is witnessed to in the worship and community of be-

---

[11] One thinks of the words of Tersteegen: "A God understood would not be a God."

[12] Cf. Wilhelm Stählin, *Vom göttlichen Geheimnis*, (Kassel: J. Stauda-Verlag, 1936)' p. 35. "The New Testament concept *mysterion* . . . belongs, unfortunately until to-day, to those biblical concepts which Protestant theology thinks with some embarrassment it may bypass. But actually, when the Reformers spoke about Word they meant precisely what the concept *mysterion* means: God enters into a concrete earthly body, and when we encounter this body, we meet the living God and participate in the salvation which he has put in this body."

[13] "What happens in worship is a hidden mystery . . . The subject of this event is God alone. That God himself acts upon men in the cultic actions performed by men makes worship a mystery" (*Leiturgia*, I, p. 181).

[14] Cf. Robert Will, *op. cit.*, I, p. 163, and II, pp. 99-100.

lievers through the help of the Holy Spirit. This authentic presence which, however, remains veiled, raises the matter of mystery—more precisely, eschatological mystery. It is not within the power of rational analysis to define the relation between the sign and the divine reality signified. It is impossible to explain how the Lord can draw near to us through the resonance of some human words and in the material substance of a little water, bread, wine, or oil. In the church, in its worship and the elements of this worship, as in the human life of Jesus of Nazareth, we are before the mystery of God hidden and revealed, *Deus absconditus et revelatus*.[15] In the weak flesh and humble life of Jesus, and also in the poor human words of the Bible and the material elements of the sacraments, this occurs: something which on its own is poor or deficient, points to and at the same time conceals the splendor and power of Almighty God and the glory of the world to come. In the earthly ministry of Christ and in the cultic acts which his church performs from age to age, the *clare-obscure* of the living God reigns, which can only be found in faith (I Kings 8:12; II Chron. 6:1). Still more immediately than the word, the sacraments are given in the service of the eschatological mystery.[16] With good reason the theology of the Greek fathers called *mysterion* what in the West had been named sacraments, even though the eschatological point of the sacraments had generally escaped them. The sacraments are prophetic signs of the definitive salvation of the entire man—body and soul—and of the whole creation in the kingdom of God. Baptism is the pledge or token of our death to the present world and of our new birth in Christ, and the declaration of our inclusion in the coming renewal of all things. The material eucharistic elements, taken hold of by the divine spirit, are like the first fruits of the final transfiguration of this present world into a new heaven and a new earth: they

[15] "The sacred action or cultic message is always supposed to represent the action of God or to reproduce his word. The Eternal veils himself in a terrifying mystery or he unveils himself in a radiant revelation" (Robert Will, *op. cit.*, I, p. 335; cf. also II, p. 154.)

[16] Theodore Süss, in order to describe the sacramental realism of St. Paul, speaks of *eschatological realism*, "in order to avoid the ambiguity of the word *spiritual* and because this reality is nothing else than the anticipated manifestation of the ultimate reality which we hope for and which is the Kingdom of God" (*op. cit.*, p. 27).

34

give us a part in the crucified and risen Christ, and are a sign in anticipation of our resurrection in the last day. The sacraments illustrate and make actual and concrete the word concerning last things, and thus contribute to the preservation in worship of that mysterious tension between what is already given and what is not yet accomplished; between what *is* in grace and faith and what *will be* in glory and sight; between the Savior already come and the Lord who will come.[17] They keep the ears of the church open for eschatological prophecy and sensitive to the mystery of God "who was, who is, and is to come." This is the mystery of an invisible presence and continuous imminent manifestation in a real and spiritual encounter between the Lord and his community which calls upon him and adores him.[18] The Lord is there and he comes in, with, and under the sensible things (*in, cum, sub*)[19]: *in* the church which is his people and his body (in spite of all the deficiencies of the church); *with* the words of the biblical word; and *under* the cover of the sacramental elements: *mysterium tremendum, mysterium fidei*. "Be silent, all flesh, before the Lord; for he has roused himself from his holy dwelling" (Zech. 2:13) in order to come and act in the midst of his people at prayer.

If the word and sacraments are the only means of communicating the grace of God, *silence* is an important condition in order that the encounter between God and his assembled people will actually take place.[20] Rudolph Otto wanted to

[17] Cf. Max Thurian, *op. cit.*, pp. 131-132: "The sacrament is not the word of God which one has to believe to receive it. Nor is it the vision of Jesus Christ himself: the sacrament is between the word and the kingdom, between the economy of faith and that of heavenly vision. If we want to give a name to this way of perception by means of the sacrament, we would call it *contemplation*, giving to this term a particular meaning . . . Contemplation is truly reached in the sacrament, which prevents it from becoming a mystical reverie."

[18] We can mention only in passing the theology of the liturgical mystery of which Dom Odo Casel, Benedictine monk of Maria-Laach, has become the protagonist and which is treated in his principal works: *Die Liturgie als Mysterienfeier* (Collection *Ecclesia orans*, No. 9, Freiburg-in-Brisgau: Herder, 1923); *Das christliche Kultusmysterium*, (Regensburg 1935), French translation under the title *Le Mystere du culte dans le Christianisme*, (Éditions du Cerf, Paris, 1946). Starting from the mystery of Christ in Pauline theology and from the relation to the eucharist, the author sees Christian worship as sacramental and mystical. This thesis, though one-sided, contains an important element of truth which for the Reformed, who went too far in the opposite direction, could be of advantage to consider and appropriate.

[19] Cf. W. Stählin, *op. cit.*, pp. 14-17 and pp. 130-136.

[20] Cf. Odo Casel, *Die Liturgie als Mysterienfeier*, (Freiburg-in-Brisgau: Herder, 1923), chap. 4, entitled *Das mystische Schweigen*, espec. pp. 148-157.

make of the cultic silence a sort of sacrament. We must be cautious about following him on a dangerous and slippery path which is without biblical justification. However, there is what we might call a *liturgical silence*, which is a silence of waiting. In this momentous suspension of all exterior activity, in the absence of all articulated words, the unmoving and sovereign majesty of the Eternal and the nothingness of the creature are reflected. This silence prepares the community to receive the Lord who comes and to hear his word: "O Lord, come to help us! Speak, Lord, thy servants listen." Before the reading of the word and before the sacramental communion, the liturgical silence is there "to empty and sweep out" (Matt. 12:44) the premises and to leave the Lord completely master of the place. "Let all mortal creatures keep silence and remain still, with fear and trembling without thinking any bigger about things of the earth; for the King of kings comes." So says a hymn of the Greek liturgy of St. James, sung in the midst of the eucharistic celebration. As Robert Will says, "It is regrettable that Protestant worship, based on the principle of revelation, has lost almost entirely this silence of waiting which is truly prayer. The word which one proclaims as the cultic center of Protestantism lacks a necessary intensity when its message is not preceded by the silence of recollection; when revelation is poured out upon souls which do not expect it . . . Hence this sometimes breathless, sometimes boring character of Protestant worship. It is music without rests and pauses."[21] Our church must recover the cultic value of silence, the silence of waiting for God, the silence of the eschatological expectation. "When the Lamb opened the seventh seal, there was silence in heaven for about a half hour. Then I saw the seven angels who stand before God, and seven trumpets were given them. And another angel came and stood at the altar with a golden censer; and he was given much incense to mingle with the prayers of all the saints upon the golden altar before the throne; and the smoke of the incense rose with the prayers of the saints from the hand of the angel before God" (Rev. 8:1-4): Silence is a wholesome antidote for the churches

[21] *Op. cit.*, I, p. 378.

when the *word* is in danger of being drowned often in words and phrases.[22]

[22] See also André Schlemmer, *En Esprit et en Vérité*, (Paris: Messageries évangéliques, 1947), pp. 30-31.

5

The Lord Present in His House

The human situation requires our being limited to the dimensions of space and all our activities are subject to the local. Worship does not escape this same necessity. The community must be in a certain place to hear the word and to celebrate the sacraments. Whether it be in a building or in the open air, the encounter between the Lord and his people takes place at a fixed point in space and in this place there is his real presence.

From its opening pages onwards, the Bible discloses the paradox of God everywhere present with his own, and at the same time present with them in certain predetermined locations, places of his own choice. He is present in his whole creation, but it was in the Garden of Eden that "they heard the voice of the Lord God walking in the garden in the cool of the day" (Gen. 3:8). Abraham and his descendınts heard God speaking to them and they were able to call upon him wherever they happened to be, but whenever they constructed an altar, it was because God had appeared to them in this place and there they returned more readily to seek the divine presence. God appeared to them there again and again and spoke more willingly, too (Gen. 12:8-9; 13:14, 18; 18:1; 21:33; 28:16, 19; and 35:1, 3). Jacob recognized the presence

38

of God in the place where he had a vision and he called this place *Bethel*, that is, the house of God. But even in this vision he heard God making a promise to him: "Behold, I am with you and will keep you wherever you go" (Gen. 28:15-19). God appeared for the first time to Moses on Horeb (Ex. 3:1) and later on the same mountain he gave him the law (Ex. 19). Once the people settled in Canaan the tabernacle of God was set at Shiloh and only there could sacrifices be offered (Josh. 18:1). But the tribes which had their territory on the upper side of the Jordan built for themselves their own altar which the rest of the people finally recognized as legitimate and which "is a witness between us that the Lord is God" (Josh. 22:10-14). Solomon, having built the temple in Jerusalem, said, "I have built thee an exalted house, a place for thee to dwell in forever." But immediately he adds, "But will God indeed dwell on the earth? Behold, heaven and the highest heaven cannot contain thee; how much less this house which I have built" (I Kings 8:13, 27).

In the New Testament Christ himself said, "I tell you, something greater than the temple is here" (Matt. 12:6), therefore suggesting that he is himself the true temple, the living temple of the divine presence here below. But he chased the merchants out of the temple at Jerusalem because this building was the house of God, a house of prayer (Mark 11:17). He participated in the Jewish religious festivals in the temple, while announcing the destruction of the building and the hour when divine worship would no longer be localized in Jerusalem, nor anywhere else (Mark 13:2; John 4:21).

The first Christians still frequented the temple at Jerusalem (Acts 3:1) because they thought they should find God there, but they broke the bread of Christ in a private home (Acts 2:46). Paul prayed in the temple and it was even there he received his call to be an apostle to the Gentiles (Acts 17:24). The seer of Revelation noticed a temple in heaven (Rev. 7:15; 11:19; 14:17), but in the final consummation there is no temple any more, for "its temple is the Lord God the Almighty and the Lamb" (Rev. 21:22).

The apostolic community, however, possessed a sort of permanent sanctuary—the upper room, where the first Communion was celebrated and where the first believers "habitually gathered," for "devoting themselves with one accord to prayer" (Acts 1:13-14). In this upper room they had spent the vigil of the crucifixion with their Lord; there the Risen One had appeared to them on that Easter evening; there probably they had received the Holy Spirit on the day of Pentecost. Also, this room had become to them a privileged place for the presence of Christ, a center of assembly and a symbol of unity.[1] Nevertheless, this did not prevent their gathering somewhere else also to pray (Acts 12:12).

We see, therefore, in the scriptures a dialectical tension between the omnipresence of the Lord without respect to places and the localization of his presence, especially in a consecrated building (I Kings 9:3; cf. 8:27, 29). These are two complementary sides of the one reality. If we neglect the first, we slip into spatialization and simple magic that ties the divine presence to material conditions essentially human. If we forget or scorn the second, we fall into a disincarnate spiritualism which is contrary to biblical revelation and may lead to idealistic immanentism or even to an actual crypto-pantheism.

Strictly speaking then, the Lord is present only in a cultic building when the community is gathered there with the signs and symbols of that presence—word and sacrament validated by the Holy Spirit. It is not by accident, therefore, that the Christian cultic buildings have been called *ecclesiae*, churches—that is, places where the community gathered. The word *temple* is less proper in designating the place of Christian worship; it is more specific for the pre-Christian religions so to characterize a sacred building where the divinity is residing locally marked by his statue, image, or monument.[2] But if the church, properly speaking, is not a temple and if it has no intrinsic sanctity, it has an extrinsic holy value by virtue of its purpose. For when a building is

---

[1] Cf. Oscar Cullmann, *Le Culte dans l'Eglise primitive*, (Neuchâtel-Paris: Delachaux & Niestle, 1944), English trans. A. S. Todd, & J. B. Torrance. (London: SCM Press, 1953) pp 8-9.

[2] From the examination of the great French authors of the seventeenth and eighteenth centuries, it appears that the Roman Catholics have given to the Reformed places of worship the name of temples, as an injurious and scornful term, in order to liken to pagan religions that "religion which presumes to be reformed."

especially and uniquely intended for an encounter between the Lord and his people, it is likewise the customary location of the divine presence; it is the symbol of the divine presence in the secular life of the city.[3] There as nowhere else, the holy word re-echoes regularly; there the sacraments are celebrated. From one Sunday to another, from one divine service to the next, the place of worship is in a state of anticipation. Even its emptiness between times declares its special destination and readiness for the divine presence.

In the same sense the Bible, as a book, is not by itself the Word of God, but this word is continually available for those who know to find it there and hear it. In the same way the church is not the divine presence as such, but this presence is there constantly at the disposition of those who know how to recognize and perceive it. It takes on all the value of the "house of God" when a man enters it in a reverent frame of mind. God is able then to use this house where "his name is invoked" (Jer. 7:11, 30; 23:24; 34:15) to touch the indifferent visitor by his grace and to bring him to faith. What God proclaimed regarding Solomon's temple still holds for the building of the new covenent: "I have consecrated this house which you have built, and put my name there forever; my eyes and my heart will be there for all time" (I Kings 9:3; cf. 8:27, 29). It is true as Paul declared, "Do you not know that you are God's temple and that God's Spirit dwells in you?" (I Cor. 3:16). Peter wrote, "Like living stones *be yourselves built into a spiritual house*" (I Peter 2:5). But the presence of the Lord in the community ought not to be emphasized in a one-sided manner to the point of depreciating this same presence in the house where the community gathers regularly, and only the community.[4] The old established order of the temple of Jerusalem is not purely and simply abolished; it is

---

[3] "If the church is the house of God, it is not permissible that it serve purely human ends, even were they ecclesiastical: synod assemblies, pastoral conferences, or presbyterial elections; and especially not those secular aims, as in Switzerland where churches serve sometimes for musical festivals and where one saw Jean Jaures climb into the pulpit of the cathedral in Basle on the occasion of the pacifist Congress in 1913" Robert Will, *op. cit.*, II, p. 539.

[4] Cf. Yves M.J. Congar, *Vraie et Fausse Réforme dans l'Eglise* (Paris: Editions du Cerf, 1950), pp. 136-141, a remarkable survey of this dialectic and of the process of indwelling or "interiorization" to which the biblical plan of salvation bears witness. Developed in *Le mysteré du Temple*, (Paris, Editions du Cerf, 1958).

transcended and fulfilled in the sense that its high privilege
has been extended and made universal. When Christ said that
"the hour is coming when neither on this mountain nor in
Jerusalem will you worship the Father" (John 4:21), this did
not mean that from now on there would not be any special
places for the encounter between God and his children. It
meant that the presence could be given to all appointed places
where a community or congregation of believers celebrated
each Sunday the worship of the Lord.[5]

In order to fulfill its purpose the church ought to be open
constantly and its interior arrangements adequate for its aims.
A closed church is the negation of the words of Christ: "Come
to me, all who labor and are heavy-laden" (Matt. 11:28).
"Him who comes to me I will not cast out" (John 6:37). It
discharges only imperfectly its mission as a symbol of the
presence and action of Christ in the world. It fails to offer to
men today, deafened and wearied by the noise and agitation of
this century, the asylum of silence and peace which Christ
himself sought in the desert.[6]

The architecture of churches poses many problems we cannot discuss here.[7] Suffice it to say that the building has to be
conceived and furnished first of all in such a way as to indicate
the grandeur, majesty, and beauty of God and his Christ. A
church in which there is nothing, or almost nothing, to distinguish it from a classroom or conference room, from a university auditorium or parliamentary amphitheater, misses its
goal. It is necessary that from the very beginning everything
should give the impression of the glory of God and of the
grace of Christ the Savior and that silence and respect spring
up spontaneously in the visitor, whether he be believer or indifferent. "Guard your steps when you go to the house of
God; to draw near to listen . . . be not rash with your mouth
. . . before God, for God is in heaven, and you upon earth;

[5] "Is it not an unheard thing that God of whom it is said he does not live in buildings
made by human hands is pleased in his sovereign freedom to reveal his *presence* in our
poor sanctuaries?" Robert Will, *L'Espirit du Culte Protestant*, p. 37.

[6] "The tormented soul which longs to find, outside the house and the daily miseries, a
place of prayer and peace, does not know where to go." Henri-Frédéric Amiel,
Fragments d'un Journal intime, ed. Scherer (Geneva: Georg & Co., 1905), I, 14.

[7] Robert Will, *op. cit.* Vol. II, pp. 526-550; *Leiturgia*, I, pp. 365-433, and many English
and American books.

therefore let your words be few" (Eccles. 5:1, 2). The character of our places of worship depends naturally upon one's conception of worship and on the factor one considers to be central to the service. As Vinet has said, "Our worship, to us, is too much a confession of faith, a discourse; everything is articulated, everything is made precise, everything is explained. The effect of this tendency has gone so far as to determine the notion we hold concerning our churches. For us they are auditoriums; we enter to hear speaking there."[8] Respect for places of worship is more difficult to require from adults, as well as from children, if there is nothing that evokes the divine presence. The dimensions of the building enter only secondarily into consideration. A modest chapel with simple but well-chosen architectural lines, and furnished on the inside in an appropriate manner, may—better than a vast and gloomy cathedral—point to and make known the event of the Lord's presence. Then, "the Lord whom you seek will suddenly come to his temple; the messenger of the covenant in whom you delight, behold, he is coming," that is, Christ (Mal. 3:1).

Another important condition a place of worship ought to fulfill is to further, as much as possible, the coordination of the community. For it is in the cohesion of a congregation of brothers that the Lord reveals his presence in his house, as much and more than through the material character of these places.[9] In this regard, the side balconies which disfigure so many Reformed churches, do much more damage to the architectural design and liken the church to a theater. They reduce the worshipping community to fragments. Only a balcony for the organ is justified, such being possibly the place for the choir also. Side balconies must disappear for they are generally the vantage spot for those people who resist the involvement of worship, keep their distance, and look from above upon the leader and the rest of the congregation. This

---

[8] Alexander Vinet, *op. cit.*, p. 180.

[9] Cf. P. Romane Musculus, *La Prière des Mains*, (Paris-Gèneve: Editions Je Sers, 1938), p. 83: "The Reformed churches do not need to borrow the traditional forms of the Catholic nave, chancel, and transept. Their plans must be conceived in order to assemble the faithful as much as possible around the communion table and the pulpit. These churches can be rectangular, square, octagonal, round or oval, and have neither side chapels nor wide side aisles."

feeling is not always realized consciously, nevertheless it exists in a latent state.

When the place of worship is arranged properly, reserved for the only use to which it has been solemnly consecrated, ready to welcome on the stated occasions the assembled congregation—being "the church," which is itself the true "temple of God" in which the Spirit dwells (I Cor. 3:16 & Eph. 2:20-22)—then it is legitimate and true to say of the stone building: "The Lord God is present in his holy temple; let all the earth keep silence before him" (Hab. 2:20).

Part Two

The Response of Man

6

Liturgy: the Divine Service
of the Church

It is in the book of Acts that we find the word "liturgy" used for the first time in the sense and with the meaning it has had ever since in the Christian vocabulary. "Now in the church of Antioch there were prophets and teachers . . . While they were worshiping the Lord (λειτουργούντων αὐτῶν τῷ κυρίῳ) the Holy Spirit said: 'Set apart for me Barnabas and Saul for the work to which I have called them.' Then after fasting and praying they laid their hands on them and sent them off" (Acts 13:1-3). Out of this text emerges the outline of what we call liturgy: the church or community is gathered, and as such it gives homage to its Lord who is present. The Holy Spirit speaks and acts in worship through the agency of recognized and accredited "ministers."

In the Septuagint (the Greek version of the Old Testament), the word *leitourgeia* and the corresponding verb *leitourgein* mean the cultic service of priests and levites in the temple at Jerusalem, particularly the offering of sacrifices. This same meaning is found again in the New Testament (Luke 1:23; Heb. 9:21; 10:11); but since the sacrifices and the whole ceremonial cult and system of the Mosaic Law are out-of-date and abolished as far as new believers are concerned, the terminology which designated them are transferred significantly to Jesus, the Messiah, the Christ, who accomplished in himself all the symbols of the old covenant. The outmoded worship of the ancient people of God survives and continues in an entirely new form, in the transcendent and eternal service the glorified Messiah renders to God in heaven. This is the central theme of the letter to the Hebrews: Christ is *"minister* (liturgist) in the sanctuary and true tabernacle" (8:2); "he has obtained a *ministry* (liturgy) which is more excellent than the old, for the covenant he mediates is better" (8:6). The new community, therefore, has no longer to offer to God any propitiatory payment; it simply allies itself in faith with the heavenly *liturgy* of its head, by presenting to God its praise and active obedience. Paul speaks to the Philippians of the sacrifice of the *liturgy* of their faith (2:17), and calls himself "a *minister* (liturgist) of Christ Jesus to the Gentiles in the priestly service (ιερουργοῦντα) of the Gospel" in the hope of converting the pagans and of being able to lead them to Christ "that the offering of the Gentiles may be acceptable" (Rom. 15:16).

The New Testament has another word to describe the ceremonial and sacrificial worship of the old covenant: λατρεία and the corresponding verb λατρεύειν (Rom. 9:4; Heb. 9:1, 6), which refer not only to the priestly service, strictly speaking, but also to the perpetual prayer of the pious Israelites who wait for the Messiah (Luke 2:37; Acts 26:7). The same terminology is transferred also to Christian service in the broader sense of the obedient and consecrated life (Luke 1:75; Acts 24:14; Phil. 3:3; Heb. 9:14); and on the other hand to the perfect worship the elect offer to the Lord in the heavenly Jerusalem (Rev. 7:15; 22:3).

We notice, moreover, a certain fluctuation and lack of precision in the New Testament use of terminology regarding the worship of the new community. No Old Testament word qualified because none could express exactly what happened when Christians gathered for worship; there was actually something entirely new, something that was already a sign and portent of "the renewal of all things" (Acts 3:21). The Christian divine service is above all "to gather in the name of Jesus"; the verb συνάγεσθαι in Matt. 18:20 has given us the word συνάξισ, the *synaxis*, used originally but later fallen into disuse (Heb. 10:25 and James 2:2 use the same word). It is, however, this word which would qualify perhaps most adequately for the description of the worship of the last days, the time of "the gathering into one the children of God who are scattered abroad" (John 11:52).[1]

In a roundabout way we are led back to the word *liturgy*, because it connotes the collective and communal sense included in the term *synaxis*. Indeed in classical Greek the word *leitourgia*—a combination of λῆτος or λεῖτος, public, and ἔργον, work—meant a public service of artistic presentations (e.g. theatre), sport (games), or military, with a great popular meal for which the rich citizens had to pay the costs. The verb *leitourgein* meant, therefore, to assure a public service by paying with one's person and money. Passing through the Jewish religious vocabulary, and then the Christian, this word took on a new meaning: it is no longer the people who are the beneficiary of the public service, but the Lord. The people, on the contrary, assume responsibility for it. The civil "liturgy" of the Greek cities was the profane or secular service of one or several for the public. The liturgy of the Christian church is a religious service offered by the public to the Lord.[2]

We see at first sight then that liturgy is a collective act. It is not an individual activity, but a service of the community. It is not the private and subjective prayer of one or some individuals; but it is the prayer which is "together" and in common with the church. The people of God perform collectively the service to their Lord. It is, therefore, a throwback to the pre-Christian and civil meaning of the word to make worship out to be the action of one man before the people; the personal discourse and individual prayer of one individual in the presence of others who would represent a passive audience. Liturgy is a service of all for the one, the Lord. It is the unanimous prayer of the community, the organized cultic action of the church. Church and liturgy are, therefore, integral and interdependent.

[1] For this whole question of terminology it is worth while to consult the article *Leitourgia* in the *Theologisches Wörterbuch zum Neuen Testament*, *IV*, pp. 232-235; and *Leitourgia*, I, p. 83f., the useful article by Peter Brunner entitled *Zur Lehre vom Gottesdienst der im Namen Jesu versammelten Gemeinde*. See also *The Apostolic Ministry*, (London: Hodder & Stoughton, 1946), pp. 194-196, article by G. Dix, *The Ministry in the Early Church*.

[2] Cf. in *L'Esprit du Culte Protestant*, pp. 169-170, comment by H. Clavier.

Worship celebrated by the church has its own specific character which is distinct from individual piety. It is liturgical, that is, organized to be the sign of unity and fullness of the body of Christ, to be witness of a κοινωνία, of a common and unanimous life of the faithful, in time and space. This worship is the business of all the members of the body. This does not mean, however, that everyone ought to be permitted to give full play to his own individual state of soul; but the piety of each one should be disciplined in order to be brought forward as the common denominator of all, and as the means of expressing what can gather together all feelings, unite all hearts and suit all situations.[3] Life in Christ demands renunciation of oneself for the love of God and the brethren. Worship is one of the elements of this life and consequently does not escape this demand. It asks from everyone a certain renunciation of his subjectivity in order enter into the prayer and action of the community and therefore to reveal fully the unity of the church.[4]

[3] Calvin said: "In summary, all our prayers must be so common that they always concern the community which our Lord has placed in his community and in his house" (*Institutes of the Christian Religion*. Philadelphia: Presbyterian Board of Christian Education, 1936, Chap. 9).

[4] With regard to these points one can read to advantage the first class and complete analysis by R. Guardini in chapters 1-3 of his classic work on this subject *L'Esprit de la Liturgie* (Paris: Plon, 1929). We shall limit ourselves to some quotations: "These institutions (the liturgy) are not presented objectively in order to express some particular, individual state of soul; it is with the average life, the daily life, that they propose to correspond. What they intend to express is by no means the inner life of such and such a man in particular with his specific temperament; it is the inner life of a community, composed of the most diverse spiritual temperaments" (pp. 98-99). "The liturgy is mastered emotion (p. 116). "The prayer of the church does not exhibit nor expose the secrets of the heart; it can evoke the most intimate, the most profound, the most tender inner impulses, but at the same time leave them in secrecy . . . The liturgy has brought this masterpiece into being and this feat of strength of permitting the creature to express in all its depth and fullness the most intimate things of his inner life and at the same time to know his secret will be kept" (p. 120). "To the degree he acts as a member of the community the individual will have to renounce everything which is only for himself and excludes others. He will have to deny himself and sacrifice to the community part of his autonomy and independence . . . He will be asked to make his own that infinitely bigger and well-balanced content of life, which is the life of the community" (pp. 143-14). "He will have to get out of his circle of customary ideas and appropriate a whole world of thoughts infinitely broader and richer. He will have to leave and go beyond the horizon of his own little interests, of small private and personal profits . . . he will have to address to heaven some of the requests that do not touch nor interest him directly; he will have to hold up before God these requests with as much devotion as if they were his own, even though they are far from his interests and dictated only by common concern" (pp. 145-146). "This does not mean that this prayer does not include sacrifice; everybody among us must know how to impose constraint upon themselves. A man must get out of himself. But by leaving himself he does not lose himself. On the contrary, his life rejoices in freedom and riches" (pp. 176-177).

The Barthian orientation in theology has brought back to us an awareness of the divine and sovereign transcendence. It has raised the Most High up from the limitations of our experiences and emotions. It has made us suddenly aware of the acts of grace, and of our duty of adoration, of praise, and of supplication—duties which devolve upon dependent and sinful man who is nothing before a holy God who said, "I am who I am" (Ex. 3:14). Our prayer cannot be merely an intermittent outburst of our subjectivity towards a God who is really in ourselves, or according to the state of our souls and individual needs of the moment. It is service which is due; an "office" or duty which is right and necessary to perform regularly with utmost faith and love already given to us. Prayer thus understood is a constant reminder of our state of subjection and obligation to the Lord of our life, the indication of our humble condition as servants under orders from their Master.[5]

Liturgy is the public prayer of the church, the voice of the body of Christ, the expression of the collective praise and supplication of the people of God as a unity in space and time. It avoids the danger of narrowing and constricting the prayer of the whole group to become merely the outpouring of the heart of the officiant, and the worship of the church as such being only the personal devotion of a particular individual done in public.[6] It liberates the community or congregation from the personal limitations of its spiritual leaders and makes actual the union of the local community with all the congregations of the church now as well as of centuries gone by. The liturgy is a sign and indication of "the communion of saints" through the whole length of time and across the reaches of space. It constitutes one of the marks of the catholicity and ecumenicity of the church.[7]

[5] Cf. R. Guardini, *Ibid.*, "Liturgy cannot be understood and grasped from merely the viewpoint of being 'useful' . . . it is because its *raison d'être* is God and not man. In liturgy man focuses his view on God and not on himself. He does not think of moulding and perfecting himself; his whole gaze is towards the splendor of God" (pp. 211-212).

[6] "The minister is bound to the liturgy, which does not belong to him, which is the voice of the flock itself, and to which he lends his individual voice" (Alexander Vinet, *op. cit.*, p. 192).

[7] Cf. André Schlemmer, *op. cit.*, "All liturgical reform must lead to ecumenicity" (p. 48).

Liturgical unity, which is a sign of ecclesiastical unity, is not the same thing as uniformity and conservatism. The orders of worship and the forms of prayer may vary in detail, and necessarily so, according to traditions and local circumstances and according to the particular genius of various races and peoples. Some revisions, readjustments and readaptations are necessary with the evolution of language and habits. There is a history, very complex however, of the development of the worship and of the growth of the liturgy of the Christian church. Certain diversities existed from the beginning: usages were not strictly identical in Jerusalem, Antioch, Corinth, or Rome. But this variety on many particular points did not exclude—on the contrary, it assumed—a solid basic unity, especially regarding these orders of services, in the principal elements which constitute them, and even in certain liturgico-dogmatic formulas which were like keywords of the new faith over against Judaism and paganism, or of ecclesiastical orthodoxy in the face of Marcionite, Gnostic, Arian, or other heresies. The sixteenth century Reformation decided upon some drastic revisions of the old liturgy, but the majority of the churches of the Reformation have been able to preserve the framework and the fundamental elements received from ecclesiastical tradition. In Wittenberg, Upsala, and Canterbury, particularly, they were able to avoid confusing reformation with demolition and they tried to disengage the major lines of the traditional liturgy and to free them from the excesses and changes which had been made in it during fifteen centuries of history. Therefore, they have not only retained, but have emphasized and put in better light the catholicity of the worship of the church. Unfortunately one is not able to say as much about the Geneva of John Calvin.[8] But it is precisely for this reason that the liturgical problem now presents itself sharply in the Reformed churches. Contact with other churches, brought about by the ecumenical movement, has exposed a deficiency which has to be remedied.[9]

[8] Already Osterwald complained "about the beautiful piece of work made out of the Reformation: instead of repairing the house, one destroys it and turns it upside down" (quoted in J. J. von Allmen, *L'Eglise et ses fonctions d'apres Jean-Frédéric Ostervald*, Neuchâtel and Paris: Delachaux et Niestlé, 1947, p. 53).

[9] All narrow confessionalism and all complacency in any local ecclesiastical tradition must hear the apostolic judgment: "What! Did the word of God originate with you, or are you the only ones it has reached?" (I Cor. 14:36).

For the ecumenicity of the church must be indicated also in a certain liturgical unity.[10]

Through its liturgy the church turns to its Lord to praise him, to offer its supplications to him, and to adore him. All that the Bible reveals to us about the subject of the cultic service which men owe to God, sheds light upon the theocentric and Christocentric nature of worship. The Old Testament worship in the temple was a continuous offering of sacrifices of expiation and thanksgiving, accompanied by the singing of psalms. The worship of the primitive church was a service of prayer accompanied by the breaking of bread. The heavenly worship of Revelation, at the same time the projection and archetype of the one of the church on earth, is perpetual adoration and praise of "him who sits on the throne and to the Lamb" (Rev. 4 & 5; 7:9-12; 11:15-19; 14:1-5; 15:2-4; 19:1-4). The preaching and exhortation by the apostles in the book of Acts are addressed to people on the outside; they are missionary addresses—"evangelical meetings"—intended for the conversion of unbelievers. But when the believers gather, it is for the purpose of praying to the Lord, singing his praises and breaking bread together. No doubt the exhortation has had its legitimate place from the beginning; the first communities read during the *synaxis* the letters received from Paul or another apostle; these letters had not yet acquired the value of Holy Scripture and of a sacred text. In the second century, Justin acknowledges the usual occurrence of a homily in the act of worship. Today, just as it was yesterday, preaching is as necessary for believers as for those outside. But the paradox of our time is that the church preaches the word almost solely to believers and does not know how or does not have the means to do it for others, while the apostolic church addressed its preaching essentially to unbelievers and only secondarily to its members. If preaching has its place in worship, it is not itself the

---

[10] Cf. Max Thurian, *op. cit.*, pp. 22-23: "As one recognizes all the insufficiencies of his own tradition and the authentically spiritual value of numerous practices and forms strange to himself, he yearns for the realization of all this for his own community and rejoices in it without any mental reservation. So, little by little, through the rediscovery of the common treasure, which is dispersed, he has the same spiritual experiences and lives with the same realities and forms: the way toward unity is cleared."

worship.[11] A misuse of words currently among the Reformers applies the word *worship* or service principally, not to say uniquely, to preaching, whereas the proper meaning of this word is "honor and service rendered to someone." Worship addresses itself to God in order to honor him, while preaching is directed to men to instruct and exhort or admonish them. Preaching is part of worship, but not by virtue of being essential and necessary. One may offer or celebrate worship without having preaching at all. The liturgical order of worship may include and call for preaching, but worship, in its essence, is liturgy—that is, the offering of our service to the Lord in adoration by prayer, either spoken or sung, and by sacramental communion. These are the elements which constitute the act of worship, the elements properly called "liturgical," directed towards God in order to confess and honor him. To speak of "liturgical worship" is an improper use of terms because an act of worship, public and organized in advance, is necessarily liturgical. If there are no prayers and no well-ordered acts of worship, it is a preaching or revival meeting, and not worship. If there is no preaching but only prayer, reading, singing and sacrament, it is not "liturgical worship" but a worship purely and simply, a divine service.[12]

It is to the extent that worship conforms to its theocentric essence that it is a sacrifice of praise, the homage of our lips confessing the name of our Lord (Heb. 13:15); that it expresses and promotes at the same time a true conception of the Christian way of life. As Paul phrased it, "I appeal to you therefore, brethren, by the mercies of God, to present your bodies as a living sacrifice, holy and acceptable to God, which is your spiritual worship" (Rom. 12:1). Christian morality proceeds entirely from the gift of self to God, in union with

---

[11] Cf. Alexander Vinet, *op. cit.*; "Worship consists also of exhortation or instruction or explanation of the word of God, although this act is set within the act of worship more than being itself an integral part of it. It is only by generalizing the idea of worship and including in it everything that has God for its object . . . are we able to call preaching worship" (pp. 178-179). "Preaching is added to worship; it is not worship" (p. 181).

[12] In the preface to the Liturgie of Neuchâtel of 1713, Ostervald is rather extreme in his criticism of the primacy of preaching: "In the beginning sermons were only an interruption of the worship and an accessory to the reading of Scripture, whereas today in many places preaching is considered as the most important part of the public service and as the principal reason for which the people assemble together."

Christ "who gave himself up for us, a fragrant offering and sacrifice to God" (Eph. 5:2). If "worship" is too anthropocentric, or if it consists entirely of preaching that is didactic or admonishing, the Christian life will tend to deviate towards moralism, or even towards a new legalism regarding our duties which can come close to the legalism of meritorious works.

The service of divine worship is the point of departure for the divine practical life.[13] The first is not a convenient and easy substitute for the second. The "sacrifice of praise" (Heb. 13:15) produces and sustains the offering of the "body as a living sacrifice." Our whole life ought to be divine service, and, consequently, comprise and involve cultic value. It is this very offering of our living being in the service of the Lord which counts finally in the eyes of God. But if we carry this truth unilaterally to its furthest consequences, we shall end up denying and doing away with worship in the ceremonial sense. Now with the disappearance of worship, living religion and the inspiration it gives disappear equally. All that remains is a sort of philosophical theosophy that is never free from pride or banal natural morality. Worship in the liturgical sense is indispensable if the "reasonable service" (or worship), Paul speaks about, is to be possible.[14]

The offering of prayer and praise along with sacramental communion is the source of the inspiration and stimulus of the active love of the believer in the service of him who "first loved him" (I John 4:19). The celebration of Holy Communion is, at the same time, the most complete expression and most fruitful spring of the living and spiritual offering that is Christian worship. This offering, which the "eucharistic prayer" develops with unequalled breadth, was made actual

---

[13] Cf. André Schlemmer, *op. cit.*, "The essence of worship is in the offering . . . To go to the Sunday worship means to bring to God the offering of a week of one's life" (p. 7).

[14] Cf. Odo Casel, *Die Liturgie als Mysterienfeier*, (Freiburg-in-Brisgau: Herder, 1923), the entire third chapter entitled "Das Opfer im Geiste," especially pp. 106-118. Robert Will has a stern yet fair section (*op. cit.*, I, p. 115) on the lack—indeed, the elimination—of the spirit of sacrifice from Protestant worship as compared with Catholicism. He notes with equal relevance to the subject of Reformed worship that "its verbalism, sometimes didactic, sometimes stimulating, does not allow any place for contemplative adoration" (II, p. 131).

in the early church through the offering of bread and wine in which every believer present took part. The material elements of the sacrament were provided by the communicants themselves as a visible proof of their involvement with the Master and of the consecration of their goods and themselves to his service. The same meaning applies to the offering of money: "On the first day of the week (Sunday), each of you is to put something aside and store it up, as he may prosper" (I Cor. 16:2). In our time it is difficult, though not impossible in certain cases, to accomplish the offering of bread and wine; but the collection of money during the service and its presentation at the holy table may be done without difficulty every Sunday and does emphasize clearly the "liturgical" character of worship—in other words, its meaning or significance is the offering of ourselves, our strength and our goods to the Lord. The same word of God which says, "Let us continually offer up a sacrifice of praise to God, that is, the fruit of lips that acknowledge his name," adds immediately, "Do not neglect to do good and to share what you have, for such sacrifices are pleasing to God" (Heb. 13:15-16).

The universal ecclesiastical community is, in this world, the privileged voice of praise and the instrument of service through our Lord God, Creator and Savior. Its mission is "to render highest honor to God" by exercising the priesthood of continual praise. It is in this high sense that we must hear the word *liturgy* and not in the narrow concept of an order of worship. The entire creation is one liturgy to the glory of God: "The heavens are telling the glory of God; and the firmament proclaims his handiwork . . . Nor are there words; their voice is not heard; yet their voice goes out through all the earth, and their words to the end of the world" (Psalm 19:2-5). The church of Christ, the first fruit of the new creation, expresses in articulate and intelligible words the silent sighing of nature subjected to corruption and waiting for deliverance (Rom. 8:19-23). Its "liturgy" of gratitude for the deliverance received through Christ and for the hope of the manifestation of the glory to come, lends a voice to the entire world. Christian worship carries to the throne of God, through Christ the supreme liturgist, the praise and supplication of all humanity and of the whole creation.[15] This is the meaning and *raison d'être* of liturgy.[16]

[15] Cf. Max Thurian, *op. cit.*, p. 35: "As new creatures, we must enter into the life of creation and try to give back to it its earliest role: the proclamation of the glory and splendor of God. Does not the story of creation indicate as the chief end of all creatures the praise of the Creator who rests on the seventh day? . . . To consider the world as the setting for a great liturgy and to see in the liturgy of the church the extension of this great drama of the world, of this great drama of children, the children of God." Cf. also *Leiturgia*, I, pp. 178-180, where Peter Brunner shows how the worship of the church is set between the heavenly worship of the angels and the silent praise of nature and of all subhuman creatures.

[16] From the point of view of his own theology of the liturgical mystery, Odo Casel is able to write: "If one does not wish to hear through liturgy either showy ritualism, preoccupied with esthetics, or stately and deliberate ostentation, but better—and according to the old and only true sense of the word—the realization and accomplishment of the mystery of Christ, as revealed in the New Testament and continued through the centuries in the church to sanctify it and bring it out from what is common, then the Liturgy of the holy mysteries is the central and vital activity of the Christian religion." (*Le Mystère du Culte dans le Christianisme*. Paris: Editions du Cerf, 1946, p. 53).

7

Worship:
the Service of the Community

With the gospel a new element, especially in relation to Judaism, appears in the transfer of the priesthood from one particular category of individuals to the whole of the new people of God. The cultic functions, formerly reserved strictly to the priestly class of the Levites, come now under the jurisdiction of the whole community (compare, however, Exod. 19:6). This is the people in its entirety, the *laos*, which is "a chosen race, a royal priesthood, a holy nation" (I Pet. 2:9). This is the complete body of the redeemed which is "a holy priesthood, to offer spiritual sacrifices acceptable to God through Jesus Christ" (I Pet. 2:5). The word "laity" then in its original meaning is not in opposition to priesthood or clergy, but it expresses precisely the priestly character of all the believing people.[1] It is the church as the body of Christ and as a spiritual house that possesses and exercises now the office of priest formerly vested in the race of the descendants of Levi. The exclusive privilege of being a closed caste is extended from now on to the entirety of the believers; it is transferred to the community as such. The church possesses now collectively the

[1] Cf. *L'Esprit du Culte Protestant*, pp. 29-32.

functions of a priesthood which is essentially spiritual (Rev. 1:6; 5:10; 20:6).

Two errors threaten this community idea of worship and priesthood: clericalism and secularization. Both, in fact, have appeared in the history of the church. As soon as we cease to think in terms of the body of Christ and to look upon the church as a whole, seeing only the individuals who compose it, and when the problem of worship is put in an individualistic perspective, the priesthood becomes a matter of an individual or group of individuals set apart for this purpose and distinguished in this way from the mass of the faithful. Or, on the other hand, we attribute this same prerogative to all the faithful, taken individually or equally. "Clerical sacerdotalism" or "universal sacerdotalism" are the two misrepresentations of the biblical notion of the collective priesthood of the body of Christ. These are two over-simplified and geometric views of a reality which is fundamentally organic. "Catholicism" has often fallen back to the Old Testament system of a priestly caste and "Protestantism" has frequently destroyed the cohesiveness of the body in the confusion of the very distinct offices that comprise it. [2]

The biblical image of the body of Christ, as St. Paul presents it, is that of a compact, though diversified, unity. "For just as the body is one and has many members, and all the members of the body, though many, are one body, so it is with Christ . . . For the body does not consist of one member but of many . . . God arranged the organs in the body, each one of them, as he chose . . . Now you are the body of Christ and individually members of it" (I Cor. 12:12, 14, 18, and 27). The life of the church is not then a monolithic, but a "corporate" unity in which everyone has received his own call to manifest better the unity of all. This truth must find expression in worship since worship is the heart of the life of the

---

[2] It is, however, paradoxical to notice that in a clerical church such as the Roman, we often see in remote mountain parishes how the faithful gather for evening prayer and saying together the rosary *without the presence of a priest*. A layman, even a woman, may lead the responsive prayer. By contrast we do not see in our churches which are denoted as a "universal priesthood," the faithful gathering in church to pray together unless the minister invites them and soliloquizes the prayer! J. J. von Allmen notes also in *Verbum Caro*, 1949, p. 113, n. 2: "Is it not rather pointed to say that in this 'church of priests,' which is the Roman, all the faithful have their missal; whereas in our 'churches with the universal priesthood,' practically only the ministers possess the *liturgy* of the church?"

church. It is not by mere chance or coincidence that chapter 12 of I Corinthians is followed closely in chapter 14 by rules concerning the worship of the early assemblies. In the "pneumatic" climate of the apostolic church, a climate perhaps more characteristic of the community in Corinth, the apostle sets forth the principle of "corporate" worship in which everybody has his own role and function, his own particular service, his own special liturgy. Some pray, others prophesy, and some others sing in order to demonstrate that God is really in their midst (I Cor. 14:25). And everything is done "decently and in order" (v. 40) because "God is not a God of confusion, but of peace" (v. 33).

One can count upon the fact that the collective or "corporate" character of worship appears principally in the church's act of the breaking of bread. The Lord has said: Do this (in the plural) and share this among you. This is then a collective action in which everyone participates personally in order to maintain and demonstrate the unity of the body with its head. "Because there is one loaf, we who are many are one body, for we all partake of the same loaf" (I Cor. 10:17).[3]

Fifty years after this letter from Paul which taught the Corinthian church the doctrine of the body of Christ, they received another one from Bishop Clement, the presumed head of the community in Rome, regarding a particularly critical moment when their church was torn by factions. This letter also reminded them emphatically of the unity of the body of Christ amid the diversity of callings and gifts. Paragraphs 37 and 38 are merely a paraphrase of Chapter 12 of Paul's letter. In paragraphs 40 and 41, Clement draws from it liturgical conclusions. Using as images some Old Testament cultic terminology, he writes: "The Master has ordered the sacrifices ($\pi\rho o\sigma\phi o\rho\acute{a}s$) and the divine services ($\lambda\epsilon\iota\tau o\upsilon\rho\gamma\acute{a}s$) be performed not at random and without order but at fixed times and seasons. He has, moreover, determined by himself through his sovereign will where and by whom he wants

---

[3] Cf. *Ways of Worship*, pp. 60-61, the remarks of the Orthodox theologian Georges Florovsky, and p. 194, the same point of view summarized by the Anglican theologian A. H. Couratin: "There is no question here of a priest offering sacrifices instead of the people or instead of Christ. It is rather that Christ, embodied in people—deacon and bishop alike—performs the various actions of the eucharistic rite."

them to be carried out. Therefore, all things are done religiously, acceptable to his good pleasure, and dependent upon his will . . . Special functions (λειτουργίαι) are assigned to the high priest; a special office is given to priests; and special ministrations (διακονίαι) fall to the Levites. The layman (ὁ λαικὸς ἄνθρωπος) is bound by the rules laid down for the laity (λαικοῖς προστάγμασιν). Each of you, brethren, must in his own place present his thanksgiving to God in good conscience and taking care not to deviate from the established rule of service" (τὸν ὡρισμένον τῆς λειτουργίας αὐτοῦ κανώνα).[4] In the high priest we recognize without difficulty the bishop; in the priests, the presbyters; and in the Levites, the deacons; that is, the three degrees of the ministry which began to take shape in the apostolic age, and the structure which Ignatius of Antioch outlines so accurately in his letters.[5]

This is not the place to deduce from this information a doctrine of the ministry. Let us note, however, the liturgical implications of this important text. In the worship of the church all of these have their active share according to their own office or function. There are different "liturgies," those of the ministers and those of the people, which altogether constitute *the* liturgy. The celebration of the liturgy is not centralized in one single person, nor even a single class of persons. The functions of worship are decentralized; they are divided among all, according to an order fixed beforehand. The "corporate" worship or divine service of the body of Christ excludes both monopoly and monologue.[6]

Let us transpose this "corporate" principle now to the present condition of our churches, with the fourteenth chapter of the first letter of Paul to the Corinthians and the letter of Clement of Rome to the same Corinthians as special applications. We shall guard against worship that presents only *one*

---

[4] Clement of Rome, *The Epistles of St. Clement of Rome and St. Ignatius of Antioch* trans. J. A. Kleist, (Westminster, Md.: Newman, 1946), pp. 33-34 (§40 & 41 of Epistle to Corinthians).

[5] Ignatius of Antioch, *ibid.*, p. 76 (§ 3 of Epistle to the Trallians); pp. 70-71 (§ 6 of Epistle to the Magnesians).

[6] Alexander Vinet, after he had reviewed the New Testament data on the worship of the first church, concludes: "It must be noticed in all this that one sees the community more than its head. One does not see that in these assemblies one man was all and did all" (*op. cit.*, p. 184).

active officiant and an almost passive assembly; one "preacher" before an "audience." It is the whole body of believers which celebrates its liturgy through the instrument of its diverse members. There will be the principal officiant who will lead in the prayers and be the celebrant at the eucharist; then the readers, each of whom will be charged with the reading of one of the biblical passages; the preacher (in a small community or rural parish he may be the principal officiant); the collectors of the offerings; the "deacons" (who may be the officials of the parish), who prepare and set up the sacramental elements and may assist in their distribution; the choristers, who sustain and complement the singing of the congregation, and all other believers present who ratify the readings and prayers by spoken or sung responses and who come to the holy table to take Communion.[7] Therefore, passivity in worship is excluded; everybody according to his rank does something, according to the function that has been given to him. Each plays his active role so that the community may give its unanimous witness.[8] The plurality of the officiants is essential for demonstrating the fraternal and community life of the church of Jesus Christ. Moreover, this avoids the use of some of those popular and regrettable sayings that suggest a false concept of the church and its worship, such as, the minister leads *his* worship or the priest says his Mass.[9]

The whole congregation must express itself, because it is the body of Christ which acts and prays *in persona Christi*. It does this first of all by saying, "Amen through him (Christ), to the glory of God" (II Cor. 1:20). The word *Amen* ("so be it") is the proper word for the congregation; it is this word which permits them to take upon themselves and make their own the prayers which the principal officiant pronounces in

---

[7] Cf. A. G. Hebert, *Liturgy and Society*, (London: Faber & Faber, 1935) p. 75: "In the early church the deliberate effort was made to divide up the functions of worship among as many people as possible."

[8] Notice that the Lutherans call *Agende* the book containing the official liturgical order of a church, and that one formerly called *Action* the principal service of the Sunday morning worship in our French-speaking Reformed churches.

[9] Cf. A. G. Hebert, *op. cit.*, pp. 172-174, a survey of the struggle the English reformer Cranmer had to wage in order to establish community use of *The Book of Common Prayer* against those who upheld liturgical medievalism and who wanted to maintain the passivity and silence of the congregation.

their name.[10] It is abnormal, not to say absurd, that this word is always said precisely by the one who does not need to say it, because he has expressed everything personally in the prayer entrusted to him.[11] It is abnormal that the congregation, which has only this means of making it known that the prayer is theirs also and not that of the officiant only, abdicates its right. Many texts in the Old Testament show that the *Amen* constitutes the explicit approbation of the people to the words of the Levites or the singers.[12] It is the most frequent and adequate word of the "liturgy" of the man in the group and it completes the "liturgy" of the ministers of worship. But the most relevant text of the New Testament in this regard is in the fourteenth chapter of First Corinthians where we read: "Otherwise, if you bless with the spirit, how can any one in the position of an outsider say 'Amen' to your thanksgiving when he does not know what you are saying?" (v. 16). The apostle expresses himself here in such a way that we have to admit that for him prayer, in order to possess its full value, must be ratified by the *Amen* of the congregation. The heavenly liturgy of Revelation, which reflects without doubt certain ecclesiastical usages, gives equal value to the *Amen* (5:14 & 7:12). In the second century Justin judges it worthy of mention, even to the pagans to whom his Apology is addresssed, that the consecration prayer of the eucharist is concluded by the *Amen* of the congregation.[13]

[10] A Catholic observer of Reformed worship in Lausanne in 1553-1554, said that "the preacher . . . offers a prayer composed according to his own whim or fancy, concluding it with the Our Father, without Ave Maria, everything in French, and the people respond quietly: So be it. (H. Vuilleumier, *Historie de l'Eglise réformée de Pays de Vaud sous le régime Bernois*, Lausanne: Editions de la Concorde, 1927, I, p. 324). This good habit must have fallen into disuse soon to judge from the preface of Osterwald to the liturgy of Neuchâtel (1713): "The people must not be present at worship only in the capacity of hearer and spectator, nor even merely to follow in thought what is pronounced by the minister of the church, but they must also speak from their side and at least they must respond *Amen* to what is said in the name of the congregation."

[11] "The Amen of the congregation has been retained by all the churches of the Reformation, but in many Reformed churches today it has disappeared from popular use and is said only by the officiant in order to indicate that the prayer is finished. Such sacerdotalism is unjustifiable as much for history as for reason. It is not only an impoverishment of worship but a real perversion that should be stopped" (W. D. Maxwell, *An Outline of Christian Worship*, London: Oxford University Press, 1955, p. 181).

[12] Deut. 27:15-26; I Chron. 16:36; Neh. 8:6; Ps. 41:13; 72:19; 89:52; 106:48.

[13] *First Apology of Justin Martyr*, Ante-Nicene Christian Library, II, 65:3; trans. A. Roberts & J. Donaldson (Edinburgh: T. & T. Clark, 1867).

Other responses than *Amen* are possible, and indeed necessary, in order to give a voice to the individuals in the worshiping congregation. It may be *Alleluia*, the *Maranatha* (I Cor. 16:22), the *Deo gratias*, the *Gloria tibi Domine*, the *Laus tibi Christe*—all these biblical responses are only variations of the *Amen*.

The Lord's Prayer is by its very nature a communal prayer. It was taught by Christ to his own as the prayer of the great spiritual family of the children of God. To this end he gave it a rhythm suitable for corporate recitation. At the conclusion of a service of the word, at the end of the intercessions presented by the officiating clergyman, or at the close of the eucharistic prayer given by the celebrant, is the occasion for the community to "lift its voice together ὁμοθυμαδόν to God" (Acts 4:24), and to join explicitly in all that has been said in his name. For the Lord's Prayer summarizes every possible Christian request.[14]

The confession of faith was not originally used in regular acts of public worship. It was the personal confession of the candidate for baptism, which explains why it was formulated in the singular. From the fourth century in the East, and a little later in the West, the church decided for good reasons to make its confession of faith every Sunday at the main service of worship. From this time it was normal then that this confession of faith be made by the entire assembly. It befits the whole body, the community in its entirety, to confess before the world that "Jesus Christ is Lord, to the glory of God the Father" (Phil. 2:11). A confession of faith said in monologue by the officiating clergyman is nonsense, just as it would be for one person to say the Lord's Prayer alone in public. On the other hand, nothing is more impressive than to hear the Nicene Creed sung by a great congregation during the solemn Roman or Anglican service.[15] It is precisely

---

[14] See in André Schlemmer, *op. cit.*, pp. 25-28, the extended discussion of the meaning of the petitions of the Lord's Prayer and of the necessity for a single and adequate version of it. We shall indicate further the different possible ways of saying together the Lord's Prayer. Granting the addition of the doxology which is characteristic of the most recent manuscripts of Matthew 6:13, it is possible that in the early church the prayer had been given generally by one person and ratified by the congregation saying the doxology together.

[15] "The creed is, so to speak, an expanded Amen of the congregation in response to the prophetic and apostolic word, just as each Amen contains and conceals a confession of faith" (*Leiturgia*, p. 260).

in view of the recitation or singing the creed in unison that some Eastern liturgies have changed to the first person plural: *We believe* in one God . . . and that Luther did the same in the paraphrase he made of it in the choral work *Wir glauben all' an einen Gott.*

A great number of psalms are biblical prayers composed for corporate recitation. Their poetic character lies in the alliteration of two couplets, the second of which repeats generally in different words the thought expressed in the first. This calls quite naturally, and indeed sometimes necessarily, for the antiphonal method; for in this manner the congregation takes up in its turn with other words the request spoken before it and in its name by the officiating clergyman. Therefore, dialogically the psalms become the occasion for the congregation to externalize its prayer more fully than simply by the *Amen.* In the early church,[16] where many of the faithful could not read, the congregation was content generally to repeat the same single couplet, as in the case of Psalm 136. Monastic communities and cathedral chapters have sung the complete text antiphonally with a divided choir.[17] In Anglicanism and in several American Protestant churches it is the congregation, with either Bible or prayer book in hand that responds antiphonally with the officiant. Not all the psalms, however, lend themselves to this, and one can criticize the old tradition of reading in dialogue all 150 psalms in the Psalter. On the other hand, through wise selection one can put into the hands of the congregation a choice of psalms that lend themselves easily to antiphonal use, especially those that are real prayers, with the exception, for example, of narrative psalms, such as 78, 105, or 106, or the reproachful, such as Psalm 50.[18]

---

[16] It is possible that the ἑαυτοῖ of Col. 3:16 and Eph. 5:19 includes a responsive chant (cf. *Theologisches Wörterbuch zum Neuen Testament,* I, pp. 164 ff). Cf. Isaiah 6:3. In the letter sent to Trajan in the year 110 by Plinius, proconsul of Bithynia, the subject of Christian assemblies is dealt with: *carmenque Christo quasi deo dicere secum invicem.* F. J. Dölger has shown that it is a question there of a chant in responsive form (*Sol salutis, Gebet und Gesang im christlichen Altertum,* Münster: Aschendorff, 1920, ch. 3).

[17] The practice of singing antiphonally between two choirs may appear to us as less appropriate than the dialogue between the officiating clergyman and the congregation. It can become monotonous and give the impression of confusion.

[18] There is a version of the Psalms in French, in which the text and the typographical format permit antiphonal singing without groping or hesitation. *Les Psaumes Pries en Commun,* Lausanne 1964.

The responses (*Amen, Alleluia*, and their derivatives), as well as the confession of faith, may be sung or spoken according to whether one wishes to give more or less solemnity to the service. Sometimes, however, one objects that the prayer spoken by a whole congregation runs the risk of being disorganized, and the anxiety each person feels in trying to synchronize his own recitation with the others hinders his inner devotion.[19] This objection is valid only in those churches where the feeling of community has been lost and the devotion has become highly individualistic. In such cases, in order to regain the rhythm of praying corporately and to surrender oneself effortlessly to it without uneasiness or embarrassment, some re-education is necessary, which is not always as easy with an adult generation as it is with young people. In the worship of churches where the tradition of common prayer has been continued without interruption, this custom has become so natural to believers that the recitation flows without any formal preoccupation disturbing spiritual concentration. Let us note also that common spoken prayer is within the grasp and scope of all members of the congregation, which is not the case with singing. If singing were the only channel of expression offered to the congregation, all those who cannot sing or do not know how are sentenced to silence. In any case, prayer recited in unison is limited to the Lord's Prayer, the psalms antiphonally, the confession of faith, and possibly the confession of sin. All other prayers are necessarily by the officiating clergyman, in which the role of the congregation is limited to the concluding *Amen*.[20]

Nothing expresses better the beauty of corporate prayer than the words of Ignatius of Antioch: "It is necessary for you to have one and the same thought with the bishop as you do in other instances. The venerable body of your presbyters, which is worthy before God, is united with the bishop like the strings of a lyre. This is why, from your perfect unanimity (ὁμονοία) and your harmonious charity (συμφώνῳ

---

[19] This is the objection of André Schlemmer, *op. cit.*, pp. 24-25.

[20] Cf. Robert Will, *op. cit.*, II, p. 384: "In this collective prayer, the congregation experiences on the one hand the gracious strength of the fraternal community, and on the other hand the joy of exercising the priestly prerogative."

'αγάπη) rises a hymn to Jesus Christ. Each of you, according to his part, enters the choir, in order to harmonize one with the other in perfect accord; through your unity itself you take on the accent of God. And you sing with one voice through Jesus Christ, the praises of the Father.''[21]

Worship is a living dialogue between the Lord who addresses himself to his community, and the community which responds fully to its Lord. The Lord speaks through the reading of the Holy Scripture and communicates himself to his own through the sacramental acts. And the entire body of the church, in every one of its members and according to the functions of each of them, answers through prayer, spoken or sung, with the same heart and voice.[22] Thus there is confirmed and takes shape, in the horizontal sense as well as the vertical, that κοινωνία which is the common life with God and the brethren and is the essence itself of the new life in Jesus Christ.[23]

[21] *Ad. Eph.* 4.

[22] R. Guardini, *op. cit.*, pp. 127-130, has some remarkable pages on prayer in dialogue and the *dramatic* movement it implies. We may add that worship in dialogue is the only remedy for the proverbial sleepiness that frequently overtakes the "listeners" in Reformed worship.

[23] In conclusion, one must discredit here the unfortunate error that prevails in parishes with two or more ministers, where one sees those who do not preach on a certain Sunday and who are not occupied somewhere else, present at worship presided over by their colleague and lost as simple individuals in the congregation. Actually *all* ministers of a parish community (the parish team) who are present at the divine service must be there and act as *ministers*, gowned, taking some part of the liturgical action, in order to assist their colleague who is responsible for the preaching and manifesting the communal and non-individualistic character of the divine service.

8

Liturgical Prayer

The liturgy being the order of the collective prayer of the church and not the personal prayer of the officiant or of such and such a member of the congregation, it must have its own proper style, its special language, independent as much as possible from the individual feelings or changing modes of expression of the centuries and generations, a language which is dated as little as possible but which remains constant throughout time. Liturgical prayer avoids, therefore, what is too peculiar or intimate. It guards against novelty or originality as ends in themselves. It settles upon an average which suits different feelings and is accessible to the various levels of intelligence of the members of the congregation. Liturgical style must be "classical," that is, of universal and permanent value. There is only one Christian language which answers these conditions: it is that of the Bible. The liturgy itself speaks to God in the style of the words of God; it is nourished on biblical content and imbued with the spirit of the Bible.[1]

This is the only way it can be protected from becoming old, at least to the extent the church succeeds in preserving the clarity of biblical language for believers. It may be said in pas-

[1] "God alone speaks well of God" (Pascal).

sing that this is why the movement towards liturgical renewal is consonant with the renewal of biblical studies; one conditions the other. Liturgical style is appreciated and understood by all believers who have been instructed in the Bible and influenced by it. In this way there is a link between the different churches. Schleiermacher, though an innovator in dogmatic theology in his own time, said that the greatest failure of a liturgy is to be modern.[2] This is true, if we mean by "modern" a creation done entirely by one person or a "Liturgical Commission" or a "Congregation of Rites" which starts from zero without taking any historical data into account.

The Bible provides numerous liturgical texts and themes. In the Old Testament there are, in the first place, many Psalms, such as 24, 29, 42, 43, 47, 48, 65, 66, 67, 68, 76, 84, 92, 93, 95 to 100, 103, 104, 107, 118, 121, 122, 126, 134, 136, 145, 147, 148, 149 and 150. There are also the prayers of David (II Sam. 7:18-29 and II Chron. 29:10-19), the prayer of Solomon for the dedication of the temple (1 Kings 8:15 f. or II Chron. 6:14 f.), the prayer of Nehemiah (Neh. 5:9-17), and the prayer of Daniel (Dan. 9:14-19). In the New Testament the model for liturgical prayer is, of course, the Lord's Prayer.[3] Several Pauline texts are reminiscent of liturgical usage, such as, Phil. 2:5-11; Eph. 1; 1 Tim. 3:16. So also in the book of Revelation and in Acts, especially 4:24-30.

From the outset the early church prayed instinctively in a style inspired by biblical language. One is convinced of this when one reads the great prayer of the Epistle of Clement of Rome to the Corinthians (Chaps. 59-61); the eucharistic prayers of the Didaché (Chaps. 9 and 10); the Acts of the Martyrdom of Polycarp (14); the prayer of Irenaeus (*Adv. Haer*, 3:6), and all the Ante-Nicean liturgical texts, without speaking of the hymnological texts such as the *Hymn of Oxyrhynchus*, the *Phòs hilaron*, the *Te Deum*, and the *Gloria in excel-*

---

[2] *Praktische Theologie*, (Berlin: G. Reimer, 1850), p. 166.

[3] In *L'Esprit du Culte Protestant*, Henri Clavier infers from the structure and style of the Lord's Prayer the normative characteristics of liturgical prayer: "The simple and pure style of Jesus is radically incompatible with complex pantheistic and magical structures . . . Here prayer is *clear*, without incomprehensible mumblings, without archaic terms and without the dialect of Canaan. Here prayer is *simple*, without lace and embroidery of courtiers, without artificial or farfetched words, without flattery or affectation. Here prayer is brief, without endless reeling off titles, sentiments, or requests, and without spinning out vain repetitions" (p. 191).

sis. For anyone who has even a little acquaintance with the more ancient forms of Christian prayer, the existence of a common liturgical language of the church is an obvious reality. Robert Will defines in an excellent way the rules of liturgical style: "As to its form, liturgical prayer must defer to the rules of cultic style. One does not pray in worship as one does in his room . . . Neither modern nor archaic, liturgical prayer, especially intended to prepare souls for communion with God, must be within the grasp of every mind and congenial to all tastes . . . In order to be understood by all, liturgical prayer will not appropriate or effect a stiff gravity or seriousness, nor a familiarity that is unbecoming, neither vain pomposity nor didactic insistence. It will avoid heavy sentences and ambiguities . . . prayers so long that they exhaust attention, theological or philosophical themes whose subtleties are not within the grasp of the simple believer, descriptions of states of soul of which God is aware without laying them bare before him, rhetorical padding, pathetic exclamations and hysterical spasms. The style of liturgical prayer must be brief and forceful. It will find its classical model in the language of the Bible (which is not to say that prayer must be a "rosary" of Biblical quotations). At the same time that it is the basis and stimulus of sincere fervor, it will have an attraction in its majesty, simplicity in its grandeur, tenderness in its solemnity, and soberness in its enthusiasm."[4]

From the theological point of view, this prayer is always theocentric and Christocentric. From the formal and literary point of view, it is marked by a lyricism that grows in fullness and dimension. Liturgical prayer is focused entirely upon the divine object of faith, which it contemplates and entreats. It is the voice of the bride waiting to admire the glory of her divine bridegroom.[5] It is the impetus and thrust of the body of Christ toward him who is its Head and from whom it ex-

[4] Robert Will, *op. cit.*, I, pp. 226-227.

[5] This is what the Roman Catholic liturgists mean when they speak about prayed truth or dogma. Cf. Romano Guardini, *op. cit.*, p. 112: "The liturgy is the truth in the vestment of prayer" (*gebete Wahrheit*). Cf. also Albert Hammenstede, *Die Liturgie als Erlebnis:* "Das lebendige Dogma ist die Liturgie" (p. 12). "Die Liturgie lebt aus dem Dogma, d. h. aus den Wahrheiten des Glaubens, und vertieft deren Verstandnis" (p. 35). "Sie spricht und denkt immer nur gross von Gott, nicht mit unwürdiger Sentimentalitat" (p. 38).

pects everything for living. Liturgical prayer is not "psychological" in the sense that it does not examine the subject who prays in order to analyze his feelings, frame of mind, or the disposition and status of his soul; it contemplates the Lord in serene objectivity. It does not permit its thrust to falter while questioning the value and sincerity of its own action. An anthropocentric and introverted prayer, colored by subjectivism and the psychological, does not meet the demands of the collective prayer of the church. It is anti-liturgical because it is interested in the experiences of an individual subject and not in the splendor of the transcendent object of faith. Nothing is more contrary to the objectivity of the liturgy and of liturgical style than giving undue attention to the emotions of the pray-er, than introspective pseudo-prayers which are an examination of the hidden conscience or a poorly disguised moral exhortation. From a more formal point of view, the subjunctives in the first person are one of the revealing signs of this emotional or ethical subjectivism which is the negation of the liturgical spirit and style: "May we have the feeling . . . May we sense . . . May we know . . . May we be informed . . .!" They indicate the intrusion of the sermonic style into prayer, a frequent phenomenon in Reformed worship in which nearly all is dominated and determined by didactic and moralistic preoccupation. Newman gave an apt description of this oddity: "Even more than on Christ, the object of faith, reliance is on faith itself, and on the conviction and comfort which come with it. No longer are we told to look at Christ, but to assure ourselves that we are looking at him . . . Instead of giving us a direct impression of the Savior, we are invited to reflect upon the actions of our own mind. Instead of concentrating ourselves upon the unique Reality, we are taken up with eloquent words or flaming tirades."[6] These are very often the prayers "from the heart" or "of the overflow," which, while feasible in family gatherings, are clearly out of place in the public service of the church, with the exception probably of certain objects of intercession necessitated by peculiar circumstances of time or place.[7]

[6] Selected from *Lectures on the Doctrine of Justification*, (New York: Charles Scribner's Sons, 1874).

[7] Cf. in *Ways of Worship*, pp. 98-99, remarks made by Herbert Goltzen.

When practiced systematically, improvised prayers are an annoyance because generally they go round in a circle with ideas that are always the same, according to the thoughts and feelings of the one who expresses them and even according to the complexion of the setting surrounding them. Experience has shown us that nothing slips more quickly into vain repetition than prayers "of the heart." This type of prayer, moreover, offers another distraction which is well described by André Schlemmer: "The improvised prayer in public is a spurious type because it can hardly ever be prayed by the faithful. It is contrived; one does not know in advance the improvised sentences. It is necessary therefore to wait until each one is finished in order to be able to say it internally to God. It is necessary to conclude two actions successively to place oneself in two spiritual attitudes: "to hear and to understand, first of all, that is, to take in the thoughts of the pastor in order to make them one's own; and then to turn toward God to offer him one's own prayer. But the continuation of the dialogue which follows and which demands attention prevents this second attitude from being realized. It would be necessary in such a situation to pray what one had just heard while listening for what should be prayed for."[8] We concede also that the same objection could be made about liturgical prayers unknown to the congregation. Always the impersonal style of liturgical prayer makes it more rapidly assimilable, and the officiant can arrange for sufficient silence between each sentence, with a regularity that is not possible to the same degree in a spontaneous prayer.

Spontaneous prayer after the sermon generally offers the disadvantage also of repeating to God what the sermon has just said to the faithful. This is a trap from which few pastors who practice this type of prayer escape. Thus, "God is favored with edifying reflections, and there is something bothersome in these explanations that are given to him."[9]

The style of liturgical prayer as we have defined it calls for a certain liturgical tone that one might describe as impersonal. For liturgical prayer is not personal in the sense that it is not

[8] André Schlemmer, *op. cit.*, pp. 16-17.

[9] *Ibid.*, p. 17.

the expression of the individual faith and piety of the officiant. But it is not impersonal either; for, being the expression of the faith and piety of the church, it is supra-personal. The officiant must avoid imprinting upon it the intonations of his private religious sentiments by an exaggerated emphasis upon any one word more than another, in causing his voice to vibrate with emotion, or in slowing down or speeding up his delivery according to his own feelings. The early church inherited from the synagogue and the temple of the old covenant the tradition of using the monotone in the recitation of prayers, a sort of chant that lies between speech and singing.[10] It is almost certain that Jesus himself practiced it, because it was prevalent in his time. Particularly useful for the reading of biblical pericopes as well as for prayers, it has remained the rule in the Roman and Eastern churches, and has been kept or restored also in certain churches coming out of the Reformation. This method has the advantage of disindividualizing the liturgy by dissociating it from the subjectivity of the officiant, and thus expresses adequately its suprapersonal character. Too many prejudices in the Reformed churches oppose taking this usage up again; for the rest, in the de-Christianized world of today, this would not be understood anymore and the church would be criticized still further for losing contact with the world it has to evangelize. The real need is for the officiant in his delivery to impose upon himself voluntarily a certain restraint; he must keep in mind that he should not give free rein to his personal feelings, but ought to be sensitive to the average responsiveness of an assembled group, and remember that he is the spokesman of the Lord and of the church in its universality and timelessness. Still less will he attempt by means of a pathetic swelling of this tone to arouse in himself feelings which ordinarily he would not experience or infuse into the community.

The tone of the liturgical prayer ought to be marked by gravity and serenity. At the same time, it must guard itself on the one hand against that heavy emphasis which might give rise to a tragic and funereal resonance; and on the other hand,

---

[10] "For antiquity in general the transition from spoken language to singing is fluid." *Leiturgia*, I. p. 294.

it should eschew that carefree lightness which, in attempting to be natural and joyful, gives the impression of frivolity. The delivery should be regular: not too slow, in order to avoid a drowsy effect; nor too fast, in order that the congregation may assimilate and live the prayer gradually. The liturgical tone is the result of a balance for which there is no recipe, but which is given naturally to the officiant who is conscious of what is truly the church and the worship of the church. Moreover, the liturgical tone excludes any outburst of the voice. Prayers shouted like a harangue or a military command destroy the meditation and take away from the faithful every possibility of their praying inwardly themselves. Even in the large building with little favorable acoustics, prayer may be heard without forcing the voice, provided that every word is pronounced slowly and distinctly. And when the acoustic conditions allow it, nothing is more favorable for the fellowship of prayer of an entire congregation than the moderate voice of the officiant (with the exception to some extent of prayers of praise and thanksgiving, such as the eucharistic preface or the *Te Deum*).

We are led, therefore, to distinguish between the different types of liturgical prayer. In the first letter to Timothy we read, "First of all, then, I urge that supplications, prayers, intercessions, and thanksgivings be made for all men" (2.1). The same sequence of terms is found in Philippians 4:6, which is probably not mere chance. One can hardly force the sense of these different words in order to differentiate among them. Perhaps while writing the apostle threw them together without any systematic classification in mind; however, while the first, δέησις, has only a very general meaning — a request for what we lack and what we need — the three following may be given a more precise interpretation, and may be considered as being in explanatory apposition to the first. προσευχή means vow or wish, and corresponds rather closely with the first type of liturgical prayer, the *collect*. 'Εντευξις means supplication, solicitation, and intercession. It corresponds to a second type of church prayer, the *litany*. Finally εὐχαριστία, thanksgiving, coincides exactly with the *preface* type, the prayer of praise and thanksgiving. The collect (from *colligere*, to gather or summarize) is a form of prayer which unites and summarizes the wishes and needs of the community.[11] In the *Apostolic Constitutions* it appears as the conclusion presented by the officiant to the different requests of the deacon's litany. The collect is a brief prayer. In the East it may contain two or three distinct objects of request; whereas in the West, especially in the Roman liturgy, it has taken a brief, concise, and concentrated form. One single request is made which depends upon a divine attribute or the recollection of a redemptive act of God, and which is concluded by the formula of the mediation of Christ, "through Jesus Christ our Lord," motivating the hearing of that for which we hope. Thus conceived the collect is perhaps the most characteristic and fruitful liturgical creation of the West; it avoids all the dangers of verbosity and redundancy, and it is the antidote *par excellence* to the flowing, haranguing, or sermonizing prayer. It focuses the attention of the congregation upon one single object at a time, and by means of a moment of silence observed when the prayer is said, it permits the faithful to live the prayer inwardly in the most favorable conditions. The collect still exists in the Lutheran and Anglican churches and in certain early Reformed liturgies, such as the one of Neuchâtel.

Here is an example of an early Latin collect:

O God, who hast prepared such good things for those who love Thee, penetrate our hearts with the gentleness of Thy love, so that by loving Thee in all and above all, we may obtain what Thou hast promised for us and which surpass all our desires, through Jesus Christ, our Lord, Thy Son. *Amen.*[12]

Here is an example of an Anglican collect:

Blessed Lord, who hast caused all holy Scriptures to be written for our learning; Grant that we may in such wise hear them, read, mark, learn, and inwardly digest them, that by patience and comfort of thy holy Word we may embrace, and ever hold fast, the blessed hope of everlasting life, which Thou hast given us in our Saviour, Jesus Christ. *Amen.*[13]

[11] See Robert Will, *op. cit.*, I, pp. 269-272.

[12] *Gelasian Sacramentary* and *Gregorian Sacramentary*, Seventh Sunday after Pentecost. Still used in the Roman liturgy on the Fifth Sunday after Pentecost, and in the Anglican liturgy on the Sixth Sunday after Trinity.

[13] *Book of Common Prayer*, Second Sunday in Advent. (Composed by Cranmer for the Prayer Book of 1549).

The following collect is a Reformed composition:

Heavenly Father, creator of heaven and earth, who hast received us into Thy keeping, do not allow affliction to overcome us to the point of abandoning the trust we have in Thee; but rather direct all our enterprises in such a way that we may be more and more assured of belonging to the number of those Thou hast chosen for salvation, in Jesus Christ our Lord. *Amen.*

The second type of church prayer is the *litany* (from the Greek word λιτανεύειν, meaning "to make repeated supplications"). It is of Oriental origin and consists of a series of invocations or short requests of the officiant, punctuated by the same response which is always repeated by the congregation, such as "Lord, have mercy," or "Lord, hear us," and so forth. Actually, though within a different context, the Bible contains some antecedents of the litany prayer (Deut. 27:15-26; Ps. 118:1-4; 136). In spite of this, the Reformed church alone among all other Christian churches, has rejected this form of prayer;[14] whereas it has been conserved in Lutheranism and Anglicanism as a valuable heritage of the early and medieval church. For, "the evangelical spirit is precisely asserted (in this form of prayer), whether it be the congregation, dividing itself up in two choirs and sharing the two elements of the litany—the object of intercession and the response; or whether it be the alternation established between liturgist and congregation. In any case in the litany the priestly act of the congregation, which Luther in his treatise of 1520 recognized as the most sublime function of Christian freedom, is expressed better than in any other liturgical practices."[15] A. Vinet also says about the liturgy: "There is something in it which rep-

---

[14] "It would be a strange misunderstanding of the needs of the human soul to pretend in a preconceived way to reject this form of prayer . . . Such prayer will be more likely than all others to interpret a burning impetuous and heartfelt request, the total gift of the soul to God . . . [Nevertheless] this form of prayer conceals the danger of putting to sleep the movement of the soul." Romano Guardini, *op. cit.*, pp. 126-127.

[15] Robert Will, *op. cit.*, I, p. 275. See also II, pp. 384-385. In a sermon dated December 4, 1530, Luther declared: *Ego fidelissime credo quod his litaniis omnes Satanae technas et iram Dei depelleremus. Ideo alacres sitis in oratione.* The *Deutsche Litanei* has appeared for the first time with musical annotations in the beginning of 1529. It was sung in the church of Wittenberg every Wednesday; a double boys' choir led the congregation. The medieval litany in Latin, revised and amended in a more scriptural way, was sung every Sunday by the same boys' choir. (See Paul Drews, *Luther's Liturgische Reformen*, Tübingen: J. C. B. Mohr, 1910.)

resents the normal state of a soul meditating before God. The Christian must be child-like and consequently speak the language of a child . . . the litany has something childish about it; this is precisely its excellence and truth."[16]

Before the litany took its specific form in the fourth century the prayer of intercession had a similar form. The officiant stated the object of the request in a declarative form: "Let us pray for such a person or such a thing," then the congregation prayed a moment in silence, and the officiant concluded with a brief collect summarizing everybody's silent prayer. It was like this for every successive request of the intercession. The litany form, properly called, gave a voice to the congregation so that it was able to express its agreement; but this progression has now been sacrificed. It is possible, however, to combine the two advantages by arranging a short period of silence after every response of the congregation.

Here is an example of a litany prayer used in Rome in the fifth century (somewhat abbreviated):

> Lord, hear us, have mercy on us.
> With all faithful souls we pray the Father of the only Son, and the Son of the eternal God, and the Holy Spirit.
> *Lord, have mercy.*
> For the holy Church of God, extended through the whole universe, let us ask the full richness of the divine goodness.
> *Lord, have mercy.*
> For the holy priests of the great God and the ministers of the altar, for all the people who adore the true God, let us pray Christ, the Lord.
> *Lord, have mercy.*
> For all those who are proclaimers of the Word of truth, let us ask the manifold wisdom of the Word of God.
> *Lord, have mercy.*
> For those who master their minds and their bodies for the sake of the Kingdom of heaven and give themselves to spiritual works, let us pray to him who gives the gifts of the Spirit.
> *Lord, have mercy.*

[16] Alexander Vinet, *op. cit.*, p. 191.

For Christian princes and their armies, those who love justice and uprightness, let us ask the power of God.
Lord, have mercy.

For calm periods, favorable rains, and life-giving breezes; for the beneficent alternation of the different seasons, let us pray the Lord who governs the world.
Lord, have mercy.

For the dispersed Jews, for the erring heretics, for pagans who worship idols, let us implore the Lord of truth.
Lord, have mercy.

For the workmen of God, who make themselves the servants of others in brotherly love, let us pray to the God of mercies.
Lord, have mercy.

Ourselves and all that is ours, of which the Lord is the principle and the increase, the giver and the keeper, we offer ourselves to his mercy and providence.
Lord, have mercy.[17]

The third type of church prayer is thanksgiving and praise. This type could be called "eucharistic," if that term were not generally reserved for the sacrament of the bread and wine. We might use more readily the term *preface* (from the Latin *praefari*, to proclaim or to invite in an urgent manner).[18] In fact the dialogue which introduces it ordinarily: "Lift up your hearts . . . Let us give thanks to the Lord our God," is an invitation to praise, and the prayer itself is an ample proclamation of the perfection and benefits of God in Jesus Christ, a declaration in a lyric mode of the "acts" of God in the history of salvation. The preface had Jewish antecedents, of which Nehemiah 9 is the most marked biblical example. In the early church this form of prayer was reserved for solemn acts in the sacramental category, especially for the consecration of the baptismal water. But it is in the eucharistic prayer, above all, that the preface has had its proper and superior place. More precisely, in that ceremony the essential act, the great eucha-

---

[17] *Deprecatio Gelasi.* See Bernard Capelle, "Le Kyrie de la messe et le pape Gélase," (Révue Bénédictine, 1934), pp. 126-144. See also Josef Andreas Jungmann, *Missarum solemnia,* (Paris: Aubier, 1952), II, pp. 91-92; and Adalbert Hamman, *Prieres des Premiers Chrétiens,* (Paris: Fayard, 1952), pp. 349-352.

[18] See F. J. Dölger, *Sol salutis,* in Chap. 7: *Praefatio et Actio.*

ristic prayer, bears the name preface. In practice, however, the Latin liturgy restricts the usage of the word "preface" to that section of the eucharistic prayer which precedes and introduces the *Sanctus*, and denotes as the canon, (i.e. Rule) that which follows the *Sanctus* and which has lost all eucharistic significance (i.e. of thanksgiving) to the gain of the sacrificial element which has become predominant.[19]

The heavenly liturgy of Revelation sketches already the style and form of the preface: "Worthy are thou, our Lord and God, to receive glory and honor and power, for Thou didst create all things, and by thy will they existed and were created . . . Worthy is the Lamb who was slain, to receive power and wealth and wisdom and might and honor and glory and blessing . . . Day and night they never cease to sing, 'Holy, holy, holy, is the Lord God Almighty, who was and is and is to come!' "[20]

Here is an example of an Eastern preface which may be dated approximately in the 4th century:

Lift up your hearts
We turn them toward the Lord
Let us give thanks to the Lord.
That is right and necessary.
It is right and necessary to adore Thee and glorify Thee, because Thou art the true God, with Thine only Son and Thy Holy Spirit. Thou hast brought us from nothingness into existence. From the fall Thou hast raised us up, and Thou wilt not cease until Thou hast lifted us into heaven to make us participants in the kingdom to come. For all these things we give Thee thanks, to Thee, and to Thine only Son and to the Holy Spirit.

Before and around Thee stand the cherubim with many eyes and the seraphim with six wings. With all other heavenly powers, they glorify and praise Thy majesty, with one voice which is never silent and with sounds which never

---

[19] On the question of the preface, a useful source to consult is *Liturgies de Communion*, Eglise et Liturgie, Lausanne, 1952, pp. 10-12; René Blanc, *Etudes liturgiques sur le service divin* (Etudes luthériennes, No. 5, Paris-Strasbourg: Editions Luthériennes, 1948) pp. 24-33.

[20] Rev. 4:11; 5:12; 4:8; see also 11:17.

end. They proclaim and sing, *Holy, holy, holy is the Lord God of Hosts.*[21]

Here is an example of a Latin preface for the Feast of the Ascension:

Lift up your hearts.
We lift them to the Lord.
Let us give thanks to the Lord our God.
That is worthy and right.
It is truly worthy and right, it is necessary and salutary to give Thee thanks, holy Lord, Father Almighty, eternal God: for rightly we are overflowing with joy and gladness in the glorious feast of this day. In ascending into heaven, Jesus Christ, the mediator between God and men, has not abandoned our human condition, but in the glory that he has always possessed with Thee, he retains the nature that he received from us. He has deigned to become man in order to make us participants in his divinity.

Therefore with angels and archangels, with thrones and dominions, with all the hosts of heaven, we sing a hymn to Thy glory without ceasing: *Holy, holy, holy is the Lord.*[22]

Since the Reformation the preface type of prayer in the church, which was reserved until then for the liturgy of the sacraments, has been transposed into the service of the word, but deprived of its introductory dialogue. It has become the prayer of adoration and of thanksgiving in our Reformed liturgies, which has its indispensable place in worship without the Lord's Supper as a substitute for the eucharistic preface.

These three types of prayer mutually complement one another and must have their place in worship so that the voice of the church be heard in its fullness.

Having said all this, a very delicate problem remains for the whole church which takes seriously the liberty we have in Christ. For the word and the sacraments stem essentially from the resurrected Christ, who liberated himself and has freed us from all the constraints of this present passing age. The litur-

---

[21] Found in the *Anaphora*, called *The Twelve Apostles*, a Syriac liturgy, whose original text and a Latin recension are given in Alfred Raes, *Anaphorae Syriacae*, Rome, 1940. French translation in Adalbert Hamman, *op. cit.*, p. 336.

[22] Found in the Leonine Sacramentary. See Adalbert Hamman, *ibid.*, p. 355.

gical form is definitely not linked with the question of salvation. We are no longer under the Law, but under the law of liberty (Jas. 1:25; 2:12). As in the Augsburg Confession: "The true unity of the Christian church does not demand that one observes everywhere the same ceremonies instituted by men, nor for even stronger reason, that prayers be word for word the same." [23] The form of worship is not linked to an order of ritual-legalism, but it stems from the eschatological liberty of Christ and his kingdom. The liturgical order is always merely a sign destined to manifest Jesus Christ. But this sign must be aware of its insufficiency and its inadequate character. It must remain open to the Spirit as a provisional container, while awaiting the *parousia*. [24] It is essential then "to link the necessary tension between freedom and liturgical order, between inspiration and tradition, between spontaneity and discipline." [25] Consequently the officiants in the worship are not bound to the slightest syllable and the smallest iota of liturgical prayers. According to the general or local circumstances and according to the Holy Spirit suggesting to them in the *hic et nunc*, some words or even a sentence may be modified or omitted or, on the contrary, added. But the exercise of this liberty is without danger for only the celebrant who is impressed by a communal sense and by the living reality of the church. There must be no changes, omissions, or additions which cry out in a discordant way or which alter the unity of the cultic style. Liberty must not, in any case, be a pretext for disorder or bad taste. The first virtue of the officiant is humility; he must not substitute coarse forms of his own for those received and prescribed by the church without really feeling himself *spiritually* constrained; and he must watch lest he confuse the fantasies of his own spirit with the inspirations of the Holy Spirit. Moreover, it is above all in the prayer of intercession that this liberty can be exercised most fully if the fraternal prayer of the body of Christ is not intended to remain on the level of generalities without existential meaning. Outside of

---

[23] *Augustana Confession, VII* (Philadelphia: Lutheran Publication Society, 1888), pp. 22-23.

[24] See *Litourgia*, I. pp. 270-280.

[25] J. J. von Allmen, *Inventaire des problèmes d'une révision liturgique*, in *Verbum Caro*, No. 11-12, December 1949.

that the forms of the church have the greatest likelihood and possibility of being superior to all individual improvisations.

To tell the truth, the ideal would be perhaps for the officiant to be able to pray from the heart and by heart — *de pectore*, as Tertullian said — following the traditional kerygmatic scheme of the prayer, as in the early church. Thus, it would be necessary to be pervaded by biblical style and content, be familiar with the early liturgies, and demonstrate respect for the apostolic *kerygma* which formed the warp of the common prayer of the universal church. It is necessary *sentire cum Ecclesia* truly and deeply. Since these conditions are united only rarely in one man, liturgical formularies are practically indispensable for avoiding the pitfalls of liturgical ineptness, and at the same time for insuring the essential unity of the church in prayer.

Liturgical Responses and Acclamations

1. *Kyrie eleison* ("Lord, have mercy")

This supplication in Greek, the result of a union of a typically biblical prayer and an invocation of Hellenistic paganism to the sun god, passed as such without translation, into the Latin church of the West after the second century. The Lutherans also have retained it in Greek and use it with the same easiness as we of the Reformed tradition do with such words as *Amen, Hallelujah*, and *Hosanna*. The *Kyrie eleison* in the Lutheran liturgy is normally said or sung at the altar by the officiant, to which the congregation answers in popular language (*Herr, erbarme dich*) "Lord, have mercy". Originally the *Kyrie* was Christological. The later arrangement (sixth to seventh century) of the Roman Mass (*Kyrie eleison, Christe eleison, Kyrie eleison*) put it into a trinitarian frame which is not in accord with the original intention and comprehension of the *Kyrie*; apart from this the Eastern church has not had this transposition.

The *Kyrie* is linked basically with intercession. It was the Reformation that attached it to the abasement of repentance, together with the confession of sins. It was not without good reason that in the Reformed church its usage has been made more explicit: "Have mercy *upon us*."

For the supplication part of the intercession we dispose of

the *Kyrie* as such (Lord, have mercy) and of those responses that are diversifications of it: *paraschou kyrie*, *Exaudi nos Domine*, or *Te rogamus audi nos* (Hear us, Lord), or *Libera nos Domine* (Deliver us, Lord). These responses are literally biblical and were part of the liturgy from the beginning of the church.

2. *Gloria Patri*, or *Small Doxology*

The trinitarian doxology is considered to have been in use at least from the second century. The Greek form, so also the Eastern, is the oldest: *Doxa toi patri kai toi Uioi kai toi pneumati hagioi, nun kai aeis kai eis tous aionas ton aionon* ("Glory to the Father and to the Son and *to the Holy Ghost*, now and for ever and ever"). The Latin Western formula that passed into the popular language of the churches of the Reformation, is more recent: *Gloria Patri et Filio et Spiritui Sancto, sicut erat in principio, et nunc et semper et in saecula saeculorum*, i.e., "Glory be to the Father and to the Son and to the Holy Ghost, as it was in the beginning, is now, and ever shall be, world without end."

Originally the trinitarian doxology expressed, in a sense, the preeminence of the Father, the supreme Principle of the Divine. The oldest form we know, certified to in the *Acts of the Martyrium of Polycarp*, dated A.D. 155, is: "To the Father, with the Son and the Holy Ghost, be the glory now and in the ages to come." According to Justin we have, "glory to the Father, through the Son, and through the Holy Ghost" (*Apology, I.* 65:3 and 67:2). According to Clement of Alexandria and Hippolytus of Rome (third century), we glorify "the Father and the Son with the Holy Spirit." Origen puts the principle in this way: we must "praise the Father through the Son in the Holy Spirit."

Unfortunately these different doxologies came under the suspicion of heresy, or at least were considered suspect, when Arianism exploited them for its own advantage. Moreover, the church also kept the shorter and more weighty formula as indicated in the baptismal formula and institution in Matthew 28:19 and that marked already the trinitarian doxology in Syriac Christianity. To underline the eternity of the Son against Arian negativism, there was added in the West: *Sicut erat in principio*, that is say, "as he (the Son) was from the beginning." The Synod of Vaison (France) in A.D. 529 made this usage official and general, and it has remained specifically Western. The Christological point of *sicut erat* has dimmed somewhat; today the *Gloria Patri* is practically said or sung as a doxology to the eternal Trinity.

The early church stopped, therefore, at an "egalitarian" formula of the trinitarian doxology, at the price of more differentiated ante-Nicene formulas, which were open to subordinate interpretations. Nevertheless, it kept firmly to the principle of liturgical prayer being addressed to the Father through the Son, particularly in relationship to the specifics of the eucharistic prayer. The synods of Hippone (A.D. 393) and Carthage (A.D. 397) decreed: *Nemo in precibus vel Patrem pro Filio, vel Filium pro Patre nominet; et cum altari assistitur semper ad Patrem dirigatur oratio.* Thus, even if the trinitarian doxology hails the Father *and* the Son *and* the Holy Spirit, the liturgical prayer addresses itself in general to the Father alone, *through* the mediation of the Son, *in* the power of the Holy Spirit.

The *Gloria Patri* finds its proper place at the end of the psalms; this "Christianizes" the act in a certain way. The *introit* psalm of Sunday worship and the psalms of the Divine Office are concluded with the "small doxology." It may be sung, also, at the conclusion of the prayer of adoration and thanksgiving of a service of the word without the celebration of the eucharist; but it should not be used as a response to the Bible reading. The *Gloria Patri* is omitted in the liturgy of Holy Week, as a sign of sadness. It bursts out again triumphantly during the service of Easter evening.

3. *Gloria in excelsis* (Luke 2:14) or *Great Gloria*

This biblical *Gloria* must not be confused with the preceding one. It is surprising that it only exists, in its biblical simplicity, in the eucharistic liturgy of the *Apostolic Constitutions*, which reflects approximately the usage at Antioch in the fourth century: it is found among the final acclamations immediately before the communion. Except for this instance, the *Gloria in excelsis*, in the Eastern Divine Office as well as in the Roman Mass, is always accompanied by its long paraphrase: "We praise thee, we bless thee...[etc.]," which gave it the name of Great Doxology and which makes it into a hymn or complete song. In Reformed worship, the simple *Gloria in excelsis* has its appointed place as a shout of thanksgiving after the words of grace and absolution: one gives glory to God for his benevolence towards men and for the peace and covenant he has made with us through his Son. At Christmas we might use more freely the *Gloria in excelsis* by singing it, for example, in conclusion to the Gospel of the Nativity.

4. *Hallelujah* (Praise God)

This Hebrew acclamation was taken over by the church from the synagogue and temple without translating it, and it serves as a conclusion to a certain number of psalms in the Old Testament: therefore, Psalms 104, 105, 113-117, 135, 146-150 are sometimes called the "hallelujah psalms". The fourth book of the psalms is concluded as follows: let all the people say–*Amen, Hallelujah* (Ps. 106:48). The heavenly liturgy in Revelation gives it a definite place: Chapter 19:1,3,4, and 6. The *Hallelujah* may be sung at different locations in the worship; for example, as a response of the congregation to the confession of faith when there is one formula pronounced by the officiant alone, or after the absolution as a variant of the *Gloria in excelsis*. Still, the traditonal place of the *Hallelujah*, in its threefold form, in the Western as well as in the Eastern liturgy, is between the epistle and the gospel. Most Lutheran liturgies have kept it in this place; and as Reformed, we should set it here too.

The Eastern church sings the *Hallelujah* every Sunday of the year. In the West it is usually omitted during the Sundays of Passion and Holy Weeks. It must be sung during the entire season of Easter. If an *Amen* is joined with it, the *Amen* must precede and never follow the *Hallelujah* (Ps. 106:48; Rev. 19:4).

5. *Deo gratias* (Thanks be to God)

The response is originally Pauline: *chairoi toi theoi* is found in 1 Corinthians 15:57; 2 Corinthians 2:14 and 9:15. Paradoxically, it has found a place only in the Western liturgy in Latin translation; it is in this form that it is found in the inscriptions in the Roman catacombs. In principle it may serve as a response to any biblical pericope whatsoever. We should avoid, however, using it after the gospel which has its own specific response. It will be sung normally after the reading of the Old Testament, or after the epistles or the Acts, if there has not been a pericope of the Old Testament. The *Deo gratias* concludes as well the "Little Chapters" of the divine office.

6. *Laus tibi, Christe* (Praise be to thee, O Christ)

In this form this response seems to be of medieval redaction. In the Middle Ages it found its place after the gospel in the Latin Mass, from where it passed into the Lutheran liturgies (*Lob sei dir, O Christe*). But we may find the context of this response by attaching it to the *Christe laudes* of the ante-Nicene inscriptions. It is the most adequate response of the congregation to the proclamation of the gospel.

7. *Gloria tibi, Domine* (Glory be to thee, O Lord)

Basic to this acclamation are numerous biblical texts that invite us *to give glory to* or to *glorify God:* such as Josh. 7:19; 1 Kings 8:35; Ps. 115:1; Isa. 42:12; Luke 17:18; Rev. 14:7; 19:7. It is of Eastern origin (*doxa soi kurioi*) and had been distributed widely in the fourth century in all the churches. In the Orthodox liturgy it appears before *and* after the gospel—before, as response to the announcement of the reading and as an acclamation to the Lord who comes to his own in his gospel; after, as response to the reading that has been done. The Latin liturgy prescribes it only before the reading of the gospel, the *Laus tibi, Christe* serving as a conclusion. In our Reformed worship, the *Gloria tibi, Domine* may be used as a variant of the *Laus tibi*; notably in the case where the evangelical pericope does not deal with the person of Christ (like Luke 1 and 2; Mark 6:14-29). Normally it is put after the epistle.

8. *Trisagion* (Holy God . . .)

This Eastern response, typical of Orthodox liturgy, must not be confused with the biblical *Sanctus*, about which something will be said later. Its text is as follows: *Hagios ho theos, hagios ischuros, hagios athanatos, eleison hemas;* this means: "*Holy God, Holy and strong God, Holy and immortal God, have mercy upon us.*" The *Trisagion* dates from the first half of the fifth century; it is mentioned for the first time at the Council of Chalcedon in 451. It seems that in its early acceptance this supplication did not deal with the three persons of the Trinity, but with the exalted Christ in his holy, omnipotent and eternal divinity. The addition, *crucified for us,* made at Antioch, in a monophysitic sense is a precise indication of it. This interpolation of the early invocation has remained until today in the Jacobite Syrian liturgy; analogous additions in the Coptic Abyssinian and Armenian liturgies confirm this fact. The transposition the Lutherans have made of the *Trisagion* indicates a similar point of view: *Heiliger Herre Gott, heiliger starker Gott, heiliger barmherziger Heiland, erbarme dich unser.*

The Byzantine liturgy omits the *Trisagion* at Christmas, Epiphany, Easter and Pentecost. The Roman liturgy borrowed it from the East through the medium of Gallican liturgies, but only for the canonical service of *Prime* and for the ceremony of the veneration of the cross on Good Friday. In the Sunday liturgy, the Reformed church may give a place to it during Passiontide on account of its suggestion of humble supplication to Christ, who is victorious through his cross. It will be sung after the reading of the Old Testament, or after the confession of sins, instead of the *Kyrie*. On Holy Friday it has its place in the *Improperia* or *Reproaches*.

9. *Sursum Corda* (Lift up your hearts)
Reference was made earlier to this liturgical response in Chapter XVII, but we may add here the biblical reference in Lam. 3:41 where the gesture of the hands is indicated also. We should note also that Cyprian was the first who quotes explicity the *Sursum Corda* (*De dominica oratione,* 31). Cf. also Col. 3:1.

10. *Sanctus* (Holy, holy . . .)
This acclamation of the seraphim in the vision of Isaiah (6:2-3) reaches almost to the border line separating a simple acclamation from a real hymn. The *Sanctus* has passed from the synagogal liturgy into the church liturgy, first in the service of the word, and then it appeared to settle definitely in the third

century at the heart of the eucharistic prayer. The biblical text has: the whole earth is full of his glory. The Christian liturgy has added *the heavens* before the earth. It is intended to indicate what the new covenant and the mystery of the incarnation have added to the old realities. The victorious Christ is the King of Glory who has penetrated heaven (Ps. 24:7-10). "He who descended is he who also ascended far above all the heavens, that he might fill all things" (Eph. 4:10). This Christological note, particularly at its place in the eucharistic prayer, is accentuated also when the enlarged *Sanctus* is completed with "Hosanna in the highest!" just as the crowd shouted during the royal entrance of Christ in the holy town (Mark 11:10). This complementary acclamation to the *Sanctus* has been introduced in all the ancient liturgies, except in the Egyptian-Coptic group.

11. *Benedictus* (Blessed is he that comes in the name of the Lord)

This acclamation has been included in all the liturgies with the Hosanna of Palm Sunday. It has been linked with the *Sanctus*, which gives to the whole a very marked Christological significance. There is a tendency today, however, to separate the *Benedictus* from the *Sanctus*, to give it a place it had earlier at the conclusion of the great eucharistic prayer. From a Reformed point of view this location has the advantage of underlining the coming of the Lord to us in the very act of taking communion.

We have to take care in the translation of *en onomati kurion* that it be, "in the name of the Lord God," for the word "Lord" is generally applied to Christ. Moreover, we must not confuse the *Benedictus qui venit* with the biblical song of Zechariah (Luke 1:68-79), also called sometimes *Benedictus* because of the same opening word.

12. *Maranatha* (Our Lord, come!)

This acclamation with its eschatological overtones, calling for the *parousia*, mentioned in 1 Cor. 16:22 and the *Didaché* 10:6, translated into Greek in Rev. 22:20, did not survive beyond the second century. It fell into disuse with the weakening of the eschatological hope. However, another acclamation, certified during the whole ante-Nicene period, has had probably the value of an approximate replacement of the *Maranatha*. It is the *Exsurge Domine* or *Exsurge Christe, adjuva nos:* Get up, Lord! Get up, Christ, and come to our help! The biblical warrant for it may be found in Pss. 3:8; 21:12, and especially 44:26. We must recover the *Maranatha* in the eucharistic liturgy, to emphasize the eschatological aspect of the feast.

13. *Eis Hagios*

In almost all Eastern liturgies, at the moment of the communion, the officiant proclaims: "The holy things are for the saints" (*ta hagia tois hagiois*). This liturgical phrase is one of the oldest, for we find it already in the Roman liturgy of Hippolytus (beginning of the third century) and also in the liturgy of the *Apostolic Constitutions*, thus simultaneously in both West and East. We may identify it with Matt. 7:6. In all the liturgies this proclamation calls for a response of the congregation. The original substance of it was: *eis Hagios, eis Kyrios, Jesus Christos, eis doxan Theou patros*, that is, "One only is holy, one only is Lord, Jesus Christ, to the glory of God the Father." We could also translate it: "There is only one Holy, there is only one Lord . . . etc." This acclamation recalls textually the end of the *Gloria in excelsis* or great doxology: *Tu solus sanctus, tu solus Dominus . . . Jesu Christe, in gloria Dei Patri.*

In the ulterior liturgical development, the *eis hagios* has taken most of the time a trinitarian form. In the normal usage of the Reformed church, the original form of the *eis hagios* is preferable, being more biblical (1 Cor. 8:6; Phil. 2:11; Rev. 15:4).

14. *The Easter Dialogue*

"The Lord has risen, Hallelujah. He has really risen, Hallelujah!" It is in Luke 24:34 we must find the origin of what became very early the Easter greeting in the whole of the Christian East. It figures in the conclusion of the office of the daybreak of the Byzantine liturgy. The Orthodox who greet each other on Easter Day and during the whole of Easter week exchange these words: "Christ has risen—He is risen indeed!" The matins of Easter Day and of the following Sunday, in the West, start with: *Surrexit Dominus vere, Hallelujah.* The Easter dialogue is the best possible introduction to the great worship of Easter morning: on that day it must replace the usual initial invocation.

15. *Agnus Dei (Lamb of God)*

This invocation to Christ, the "offered Lamb," is of Eastern origin and refers to John 1:29. It was introduced in the seventh century to underline the liturgical act of the breaking of bread; it points to Christ "as offered" (Rev. 5:6) in the eucharist. Originally the *Agnus Dei* was reduced to: *Agnus Dei, qui tollis peccata mundi, miserere nobis,* repeated several times. Then, from the ninth and tenth centuries, the third *miserere nobis* was replaced little by little by *dona nobis pacem,* probably in connection with the kiss of peace which, in the Roman liturgy, preceded the fraction. Thus the actual significance of this response, which has almost become a hymn, is as follows: *Lamb of God, that takes away the sins of the world, have mercy upon us, give us peace.* Its normal use is, therefore, in the liturgy of Holy Communion between the fraction and the communion. Luther kept it at this place in his *Deutsche Messe;* all Lutheran liturgies have done so also. This is the place we ought normally to give to it in Reformed worship. We may allow it instead and in the place of the *Kyrie* in Lent and Passiontide, after the confession of sins.

Apart from these responses in the traditional liturgy that belong to our ecumenical heritage, there are others in the Holy Scripture that may be used as substitutes or variants during special services. Here are some:

(i) *Lord, be among us.* Inspired by Matt. 18:20, this response figured in the old Mozarabic liturgy; it was taken up by Bersier as a response to the initial invocation of the act of worship.

(ii) *Father, we have sinned against thee, we are not worthy to be called thy children* (Luke 15:21), as a response to the confession of sin.

(iii) *Speak, Lord, thy servants hear* (I Sam. 3:9-10), as an introduction to the reading of the Bible.

(iv) These three responses may serve at the conclusion of the Bible reading:

(a) *Blessed are those who hear the word of God and keep it* (Luke 11:28).

(b) *Blessed are those who have not seen and yet believe* (John 20-29).

(c) *Sanctify us in the truth; thy word is truth* (John 17:17).

(v) These various acclamations are confessions of faith and may be used as such:

(a) *You are truly the Son of God; you are the Christ, the Son of the living God* (Matt. 14:33 and 16:16).

(b) *We have heard for ourselves, and now we know that this is indeed the Savior of the world* (John 4:42).

(c) *Lord, to whom shall we go? You have the words of eternal life* John 6:68).

(d) *We have believed and we have come to know that you are the Holy One of God* (John 6:69).

(e) *Lord, we believe that you are the Christ, the Son of God, he who is coming into the world* (John 11:27).

9

Spirituality and Corporality

It is well known that biblical anthropology is very different from that of Greek philosophy. According to the Bible, man constitutes a whole, body and soul. As proof, the Old Testament knows almost nothing of a survival beyond the tomb; physical death leads inevitably to obliteration, or what is actually the disappearance of the individual. The Greek man of Socrates and Plato, however, is an immortal soul temporarily enclosed in a body. Though very different, these two perspectives have often been confused and sometimes the realistic spiritualism of the Bible has had to give precedence, even in the church, to the idealistic spiritualism of the Greeks. For the New Testament message of the incarnation of the only Son and of his bodily resurrection would apparently have had to hinder such a misunderstanding. Biblical religion is clearly an incarnate spirituality, and the orthodoxy of the church has always understood it in this way, against docetism and gnosticism.[1]

Corporality, with all its sensitivities and its necessary frame of reference in space and time, conditions the religious life just

[1] See Romano Guardini, *L'Esprit de la Liturgie*, (Paris: Plon, 1929), pp. 179-189. See also the reflections of Robert d'Harcourt in the introduction to the French translation of this work, pp. 47-57.

as do the other aspects of human activity.[2] The spiritual life of man is the life of a soul intrinsically united with a body. It follows from this that the various movements of the believing soul have direct and natural correlation with bodily attitudes. In this regard the fear of the Protestant Christian of external-izing his religious feelings through bodily expression is an in-hibition against nature and results from either a hereditary throwback, or education that contradicts biblical truth. It is a symptom of a deep psychological cleavage.[3] He who is able to sing, "Prostrate before Thee, we adore Thee, O great King," while remaining standing in a completely rigid posture, is un-aware of an obvious contradiction, or if he is aware of it, he is prevented by false modesty in not matching his gesture with his words. To say "spirituality" does not mean pure "interior-ness."[4] St. Augustine was correct in saying, "By the exterior and visible movements of the body, the internal movement which has produced them grows, and the feeling of the heart which preceded them gains in intensity."[5]

In the Old Testament, the congregation of Israel bows and prostrates itself (I Chron. 29:20); the people bow to adore (Exod. 4:31 and 12:27). This is summarized in a significant text in Nehemiah: "And Ezra blessed the Lord, the great God; and all the people answered, 'Amen, Amen,' lifting up their

---

[2] On this subject see the interesting chapter entitled, "L'Esprit et la matière," in the book of Paul Romane Musculus, *La Prière des mains*, (Paris: Editions Je sers, 1938), pp. 196-206, which gives the theological justification for the value of corporality and, by consequence, of religious art. This justification rests on the three dogmas of creation, incarnation, and the resurrection of the body, which are fundamental in the thought of the Fathers of the church and of the sixteenth century Reformers. See also Anders Nygren, *Erôs et Agapé*, II, *op. cit.*, pp. 56-69.

[3] See Robert Will, *op. cit.*, II: "Protestant churches, and above all Reformed puritanism, have unbalanced the equilibrium between the two spheres, the outer and inner, for the benefit of the latter. The spiritual poverty which results from this meets neither the postulates of our dual nature, nor the needs of popular piety, nor the tendencies of our generation which is so eager for reality, objectivity, and for strenuous life" (p. 9). "To renounce the resources of corporality would not be to spiritualize worship, but to volatalize religion... In worship man wants to be able to give himself totally to God, in the entirety of body and soul" (p. 14).

[4] On the whole question of sacred attitudes and gestures, see Robert Will, *op. cit.*, pp. 437-447.

[5] Neither is Luther an "angelizing" hyper-spiritualist: "Anbeten . . . ist nicht Mund-verk, sondern des ganzen Leibes Werk: mit dem Haupt neigen, sich bücken mit dem Leibe, auf die Knie fallen, auf die Erden fallen, und solches tun zum Zeichen und Bekenntnis der Oberkeit und Gewalt (Gottes)... Wo das herzlich Anbeten ist, da folgen gar fein auch das ausserlich Neigen, Bücken, Knien und Ehrhbieten mit dem Leibe" (*Vom Anbeten des Sakraments des Heiligen Leichnams Christi, 1523*. Weimar Ausgabe, 11, pp. 445-446 (Spelling is modernized).

hands; and they bowed their heads and worshiped the Lord with their faces to the ground" (Neh. 8:6).[6]

In the gospels, worship "in Spirit and in truth," about which Christ spoke to the Samaritan woman in John 4:23-24, is not exclusively an interior religion which prohibits every gesture and attitude that would give form and shape to one's intimate feelings. This would be an exegetical misreading to interpret the Johannine text in this way, since the fourth Gospel is dominated entirely by the theme of the incarnation. It is well known that the *pneuma* in Paul is not contrasted with the body, but with sinful flesh; the *pneuma* animates both the body and soul of the believing man who has been redeemed in Christ.

Christ himself prayed either standing or prostrate, depending upon the circumstances, or 'with his eyes raised to heaven. He raised his hand to bless his own. Those who came to entreat him prostrated themselves at his feet. In the primitive community the custom, derived from Jewish tradition, was to pray with raised hands, or on the knees in certain circumstances.[7] On Sunday in the early church they prayed standing as a sign of the victory and joy of the resurrection of the Lord, and similarly on weekdays during the Paschal season. The remainder of the year they prayed on their knees during the week, especially on fast days. And they bowed deeply for the prayer of humility preceding the act of communion.[8] The great eucharistic prayer was pronounced by the officiant with his arms extended, a posture engrained in the graphic representations of the "orantes" in the Roman catacombs and in which one saw a reminder of the cross. From early ages the gospel was heard standing, as a sign of respect, because it was the voice of the Master himself and the guarantee of his presence in the community.

In our Reformed churches the problem of bodily posture of the faithful has never found a satisfactory solution; therefore, confusion reigns. It is discussed periodically whether or not the congregation should pray standing and sing seated, or vice

---

[6] Cf. Ps. 63:5; 28:2; 88:9; 143:6; Lam. 3:41.

[7] Acts 20:36; Eph. 3:14; I Tim. 2:8; Acts 21:5.

[8] It was called "the prayer of bowing." The deacon announced it with these words, "You are standing; bow your heads."

versa. On this point there cannot be any primary solution, whereas any practical solution is made all the more difficult by our lack of a third possibility: kneeling. It is true that the early church prayed standing at the Sunday service (Mark 11:25), but the structure of this service differed somewhat from that of ours. Moreover, during the week the services offered the faithful the possibility of praying in the kneeling posture so appropriate for humility and so useful for overcoming natural pride. The early Sunday worship, full of Easter and eschatological joy, did not include the confession of sin as an introduction, as is the case in our services. Today conditions are quite different: the majority of our parish congregations have services only on Sunday, or if a service on weekdays does exist, it is attended by only a small group of the faithful. It is this matter of crowds, with the inevitable lowering of the average spiritual level that results from it, that makes the confession of sin necessary in principle every Sunday.[9] For it is normal for this act of worship to be performed kneeling. Calvin favored kneeling, and indeed demanded it for confession of sin.[10] If this discipline has fallen into disuse, there is no reason for surprise, since the officiant does not set the example; and since the pastors themselves seem riveted to the pulpit for the whole service—contrary to the first Reformed usage and against all reason—and, not being able to kneel there, the inevitable result is for the faithful also to give up this posture for prayer. While awaiting the possibility of reorientating our congregation to this clearly biblical posture, it is preferable for the people to remain seated and with bowed heads for the confession of sin rather than to remain standing. The Parable of the Pharisee and the Publican associates the standing pos-

[9] We must also take into account the fact that in the thought of Calvin and in average Protestant opinion this act must indicate that we have not given up "confession," but have given it public and communal form in place of private and auricular form.

[10] See André Schlemmer, *op. cit.*, p. 58, who quotes this regulation of the early Church Discipline of the Reformed Churches of France (Ch. X, article 1): "One will correct the irreverence that is seen in some people, when they are presented at public or domestic prayer, in no longer uncovering their head and of no longer *bending their knees*." From the observation of a Frenchman who lived in Lausanne from 1553 to 1554, and who described the new worship, he reported that "as soon as the preacher appears everyone knelt, except the preacher himself who was standing for prayer" (Quoted in H. Vuilleumier, *op. cit.*, I, pp. 323-324). In certain parishes of the Canton of Vaud in the seventeenth century the people knelt even for hearing the reading of the Decalogue (*ibid.*, II, p. 338).

ture and raised head with spiritual pride, while the humility and repentance of the publican are expressed with the head bowed toward the ground (Luke 18:9-14).[11]

The congregation should stand for the confession of faith, as well as for the prayers of adoration and thanksgiving, and the offertory also. This is the normal posture in all religions for the priest who offers the sacrifice; the Christian congregation is a priesthood, "to offer spiritual sacrifices acceptable to God through Jesus Christ" (I Pet. 2:5). For intercession, the congregation will be in a position for supplication, i.e. kneeling, or better still for practical reasons, seated and with heads bowed. In fact, in this way one can give as much time to the requests or petitions as desirable and provide sufficient silences between them, without having to be aware of the physical fatigue of too long a period of standing or kneeling; otherwise the celebrant will feel constrained either to shorten this important element of the service or to accelerate the delivery of his words to the great disadvantage of the inner concentration of the faithful. The Lord's Prayer can be said either standing or kneeling; standing, if it concludes the service as the culmination and summary of praise and petition.

For the singing of hymns it is impossible to make or form a general rule. One may sing standing or seated according to the nature of the hymn or the necessity for alternation in postures in the development of the service. In any case the congregation should rise with the entrance of the officiants, not as a sign of homage to them as individuals because they are merely servants as all the others, but in order to signify that the divine service is beginning and to honor the presence of the Lord who comes to his gathered community, as well as to sing the first hymn of the worship in this posture. The faithful may be seated or even kneeling for the sung responses which follow the confession of sin, but they should stand for the hymn of

---

[11] Gregory Dix, in *The Shape of the Liturgy*, (London: Dacre, 1947), p. 312, shows that the rejection of liturgical forms and ceremonies which characterized Puritanism is not linked intrinsically with the spirit of the Reformation, but that there was a collusion, if not fortuitous, at least contingent. Thus the first Cistercian monks were profoundly Puritan without their ever having been Protestant. On the opposite side, the High Church Anglicans of the seventeenth century and the Swedish Lutherans who used candles, crucifix, and sacerdotal vestments had a Protestant theology and were not at all Puritans. Puritanism maintains that worship is purely a mental activity and that only words can express or stimulate the attitude of worship.

praise after the absolution. They will stand also for the final hymn preceding or following the benediction.

If the church wishes to demonstrate before the world and remind itself always that it is a community of brothers, the body of Christ, it is important that the faithful gather together as closely as possible in the sanctuary. They must fill the places in the front and in the middle of the building. And anyone who isolates himself in a corner or hides behind a pillar reveals his own lack of a sense of community and his tendency to want to worship by himself and on his own, which is really contemptuous of the apostolic concept of "togetherness" (Acts 2:24-27). Such a person disrupts the community and instead of contributing to "edifying" the church in order to make it a body or a congregation, he creates diffusion. He weakens considerably the possibility of singing totally in unison and renders incoherent the prayers or responses said in common.

From corporality proceeds also the justification of certain cultic or ceremonial acts. In social life and other human relations everyone will admit that a certain mode of behavior is required. Every organized public event, whether it be civil, military, or sports, includes a certain number of gestures and postures that are arranged in advance. Before a head of state or military leader, any man — even one most enamored with the democratic ideal—feels obliged, nevertheless, to behave civilly and to make gestures of respect. Should there be an exception to these elementary rules when it is a case of Almighty God or Christ the Lord and Savior? Disorder and laxity are not necessarily a sign of the purest and sincerest spirituality, which even Puritan prejudice with its emphasis upon bareness would admit. Without going as far as the synchronized genuflections of the officiants in the Roman Pontifical Mass, nevertheless, it is only natural to express through bodily actions, soberly and with dignity, the feeling we have towards God as we honor and serve in his presence.[12] When worship is con-

[12] "Quanto magis accedit cumulo rituum in ecclesia, tanto magis detrahitur non tantum libertati christianae, sed et Christo et ejus fidei: dum vulgus eas quaererit in ritibus quae quaererit in solo Dei Filio Jesu Christo per fidem. Sufficiunt itaque pii pauci, moderati, simplices, nec alieni a verbo Dei ritus" (*Confessio helvetica posterior*, 1562, article 27). "In the Christian community, there ought to be great, elevated, and serious actions" (*In der Gemeine Christi grosse, hohe, ernste Handlungen vorhanden seien*). (*Ordonnance ecclésiastique, Strasbourg, 1598*).

ceived of as a discussion about the subject of God and not as a real encounter with God personally, a relaxed form of bearing and behavior is the inevitable result. On the other hand, anyone who knows and feels that God is invisibly present in his word and in the sacrament instinctively adopts an attitude and posture of complete respect. And when several officiants celebrate worship together, it is normal that their movements and postures be harmonized, instead of each one acting according to his whim in a disorganized manner. The ceremonials in the temple at Jerusalem and of the triumphal church in the Book of Revelation, even if they do not give us precise and compulsory rules, are nevertheless useful guides and they provide us with a measure of orientation so that the divine service is not unworthy of the majesty of God.[13] For "The Eternal reigns... He sits enthroned upon the cherubim . . . Holy is he! . . . Extol the Lord our God, worship at his footstool!" (Ps. 99:1, 3, 5, & 9).

Spirituality must express itself in a manner of corporality that is adequate to the biblical data on God's transcendence and holiness. The Holy has its own claims which, when observed and respected in worship and liturgy, develop in the faithful that intimate feeling of the awful holiness and sovereign greatness of the Lord. The Holy postulates a certain style or manner of worship, which may suggest to believers the majesty and beauty of the Lord God shining in the face of Christ (II Cor. 4:6).[14] Holiness and beauty complement each other; ethics and esthetics do not exclude but sustain one another.[15] Ugliness and uncouthness are not destined to be the necessary accompaniment of faith and virtue.[16] In this respect,

[13] See in Max Thurian, *op. cit.*, all of Chap. 4: "La liturgie céleste de l'Apocalypse."

[14] "Protestantism as such possesses no style of worship, which does not prevent certain Protestant forms from having style ... Perhaps the ecumenical movement, of which we are the witnesses, will some day give to Protestant worship the style it needs." Robert Will, *op. cit.*, II, p. 232.

[15] See Max Thurian, *op. cit.*, pp. 25-26.

[16] But, as Romano Guardini says, "One danger threatens us: that here, too, estheticism comes to exercise its havoc; that liturgy succeeds in being appreciated, enjoyed esthetically in the details of its richness; that the holy beauty of the house of God is devaluated in order to serve the pleasures of the connoisseurs of art... It is only by beginning from the *truth* of liturgy that our gaze will be open for its *beauty*." (*L'Esprit de la Liturgie*, pp. 242 and 252). Cf. as well Albert Hammenstede, *op. cit.*, pp. 30-31. "Kunstgenuss ist nie als solcher Gotterleben oder Religion." So also the same in Robert Will, *op. cit.*, II, p. 490: "A confusion of the whole idea of inner beauty and of esthetic beauty would depreciate the beauty as well as the sincerity. Worship can be beautiful if there is no preoccupation to be so."

Protestant worship often agrees very little with such biblical declarations as: "That I may dwell in the house of the Lord all the days of my life, to behold the beauty of the Lord the glory of his name; worship the Lord in holy array" (Ps. 29:2b).

During the service the officiants must always remember that they are servants of God who are in the real presence of their Lord and are not merely speakers before the public. Their posture will be marked, therefore, by seriousness and respect, but without sacerdotal stiffness. At the same time they must avoid everything that would give the impression of *laissez-faire* or familiarity and neglect. Their physical behavior should express their intimate feelings in the divine presence and help to communicate the same to the congregation.[17] On entering the church at the beginning of the worship, the officiant will come forward with dignity to the holy table and will bow there a moment in silent prayer. If he is accompanied by assistants, they will lead the procession by coming forward by twos, in front, and the principal celebrant will follow them alone. Having arrived in the chancel they will gather together before the holy table. This is not a sign of respect for the table as such, which is only a material object; but is a matter of witness given to the presence of God in his house and his community, a presence of which the holy table is the symbol: This gesture will not be repeated during the service every time one passes in front of the table, as is done in other Christian confessions; this would give the impression that the table itself is venerated. But from the moment the officiant enters and stands in the presence of the congregation until the moment the worship begins, all will agree that it is more appropriate that this moment of personal prayer be done in front of the table and the cross, than in front of a banister of the pulpit or against a corner or pillar!

The principal celebrant will stand during the whole liturgy, just as the high priest must do before the Lord God. Near the holy table or at the pulpit, even when the congregation is singing seated or when the organ is being played, he will stand as the watchful sentry before the Master who is there. If the

---

[17] See Robert Will, *op. cit.*, II, p. 240. "All worship, which conveys to the celebrants this feeling of the divine presence, gives particular attention to these precepts. Many Protestants deplore the lack of deportment among their ministers."

sermon is delivered by another celebrant than the liturgist, the liturgist and the other officiants would be seated, of course, during the preaching and readings.[18]

Christian worship in its original and essential character is like an anticipated wake for the *parousia*, an appeal and a wake for the appearance of the Lord. "But who can endure the day of his coming?" (Mal. 3:2). "But watch at all times, praying that you may have strength to escape all these things that will take place, and to *stand* before the Son of Man" (Luke 21:36). Any celebrant who is seated comfortably, who leans on his elbows and eventually crosses his legs, in the pulpit or in his stall, or rests against the holy table as a balustrade, or turns his head in every direction, shows clearly that he is forgetting the presence of divine Majesty and is not conscious of the eschatological moment which is the worship.

[18] Oscar J. Mehl, *Das liturgische Verhalten*, (Göttingen: Vandenhoeck und Ruprecht, 1927), pp. 66-68. It is evident that if kneeling can be restored, the celebrant will be kneeling on his *prie-dieu* for the confession of sin and for the intercession. See also pp. 112 and 118.

10

Liturgical Time

Corporality links us not only to space but also to time. Time systematizes our existence. God has willed it and given it a positive value by unfolding in time the redemptive plan of which the Bible is the witness. In the human creature, who is set in the stream of time, there is placed a spirituality that moves according to the rhythm of natural time: day and night; morning and evening; the seasons of the year; and through the period of salvation relived figuratively in the cycle of a year. If Paul reproached the Galatians about observing "days, and months, and seasons, and years" (4:10), it was a matter of a *legalistic* interpretation of these factors in our human life; in other words, it was a question of distinguishing before God their supposed intrinsic value and meritorious character. But the apostle is very well aware of the fact that the times and years exist, and he urges the Corinthians to celebrate the feast of Easter (I Cor. 5:8). The church also is situated in the stream of time; it is a fact of history and it stands between the time of the incarnation and the moment of the *parousia*. The works of the Holy Spirit in the church give value and permanence to spiritual experiences and to the prayers offered by successive generations of believers. It is the task of the liturgy to gather up these valuable contributions and preserve their benefits for the centuries that follow. The man "in Christ" is the first-born of the new creation to praise in his name the God who is his creator and redeemer; in this praise he assumes the constitutive elements of actual creation, the times and seasons and the hourly stages of the day, which in their turn lend their rhythm to the praise. God himself commanded his ancient people to set apart one day in seven to be consecrated to him. "The seventh day is sabbath to the Lord your God . . . the Lord blessed the sabbath day and hallowed it" (Exod. 20:10-11; Deut. 5:14-15). In the book of Exodus this day recalls the finishing or completion of the creative work of God. In the Deuteronomic interpretation of the Law, which is more recent, the sabbath recalls continually the event of the delivery of the people of God out of Egypt. There was, therefore, in a rudimentary sense a weekly Easter. The first Christian community in Palestine kept rigorously the celebration of the sabbath, but they did not seem to have been tempted to impose it on the Hellenistic Christian churches. Probably from the beginning these had come to set apart the next day after the sabbath, which was the first day of the week and has become "the day of the Lord" (I Cor. 16:2; Acts 20:7; Rev. 1:10). The vision of John on the Island of Patmos (Rev. 1:9-20) seems to indicate clearly that this "day of the Lord" called to mind the resurrection of Christ which the gospel set as occurring on the first day of the week. In fact the Lord shows himself to the seer of Patmos, clothed with heavenly glory, and declares, "I died, and behold I am alive for evermore" (Rev. 1:18). It is, however, only in the records and documents of the third generation of Christians that it is indicated explicitly why the church made the switch from the sabbath to *Sunday* (*Dies dominica*). Ignatius of Antioch wrote to the Magnesians: "Those who lived under the old order of things have entered upon a new hope; they do not observe the sabbath any longer, but they live under the rule of Sunday, the day on which the star of our life arose. Thanks be to him and to his death; it is a mystery, denied by many, but which is at the basis of our faith."[1] This newly consecrated day of the new people of God

---

[1] *Epistle to the Magnesians*, ix:1, Ante-Nicene Fathers, I, ed. A. Roberts and J. Donaldson, (New York: Chas. Scribner's Sons, 1925), p. 62.

has been, therefore, a sort of weekly Easter, marked by the celebration of the eucharist; in other words, the celebration of the sacramental mystery of the death and resurrection of the Lord.

The letter of Barnabas gives the same witness under a slightly different angle: "[The Lord] says to the Jews, I do not tolerate your new moons and your sabbaths. Watch well what this means: it is not the actual sabbaths that please me, but it is the one I have made and during which I shall inaugurate the eighth day, putting an end to all things, *i.e.*, the beginning of a new world. That is why we celebrate with joy the eighth day when Jesus rose from the dead and, after he had manifested himself, ascended to heaven."[2] The eschatalogical point of the Easter mystery, passing from one eon to another in Christ, dead and resurrected, is here clearly brought to light and confers on Sunday its full theological value and all its liturgical significance.[3]

The morning and evening hours call for prayer more naturally, for every day is like an abridged life, like the structure of a piece of work to be done for the Lord: a man invokes him at the beginning and then similarly at the end. "In the morning I prepare a sacrifice for thee, and watch" (Ps. 5:3). "Let the lifting up of my hands be as an evening sacrifice" (Ps. 141:2). From the beginning the church has marked the opening and closing of Sunday with a divine service. The letter from Pliny to Trajan dating from A.D. 112 shows the Christians gathered on Sunday at sunrise to sing the praise of Christ. The eucharist and agape were celebrated normally in the evening. In the Constantinian era a daily celebration of divine praise was developed in the East, in the morning and evening.

The year is a temporal unity which is essential for our life as earthly creatures. The unchanging order and succession of the

[2] *Epistle of Barnabas*, xv: 8, 9, *The Apostolic Fathers*, Vol. XV. Loeb Classical Library, ed. K. Lake, (Cambridge: Harvard University Press, 1959), p. 397.

[3] Justin (I Apol. 67:3) conforms to the Roman nomenclature and speaks of the day of the sun for the first day of the week or day of the Lord. Perhaps he is making implicitly a transposition of the sun god of the Roman pantheon to Christ, the real Sun. Ignatius of Antioch has perhaps preceded him in this way, when one judges it from Magnesians 9:1, quoted earlier. On this whole subject, see the excellent article *Fêtes N.T.*, by J. J. von Allmen in the *Vocabulaire biblique*, (Neuchâtel and Paris: Delachaux et Niestlé, 1954). The problem of the liturgical year is treated in a very complete way in *Leiturgia*, I, by Gehrhard Kunze, pp. 438 and 534, under the title *Die gottesdienstliche Zeit*.

seasons stamps upon our existence its fundamental rhythm: spring, summer, autumn, winter, with the alternation of day and night, shorter or longer, making us live and experience diverse plans and multiple moods and tones of human existence. In this way we taste successively the various gifts which the Creator gives us and in the framework where he has placed us. Upon the plan of creation and nature alone, already one could build up a song and tribute of praise which would change its tone with the seasons, a "liturgy" in which the accents would be modulated differently according to the time of the yearly cycle and the position of our earth on its orbit which it makes again and again around the sun.

But the church looks at another Sun. "When the day shall dawn upon us from on high to give light to those who sit in darkness and in the shadow of death" (Luke 1:78-79). Just as in the natural order the old earthly creation makes a tour each year around the physical sun, so in the order of grace, the church — the first fruit of the new creation — makes a cycle each year around its spiritual Sun, Christ, in order to experience successively all its beams and to contemplate the various aspects of it. There is therefore a church year, a liturgical year, which has to a large degree a certain parallelism with the cosmic year. Does not the light of Christmas, for example, coincide at least in the northern hemisphere with the winter solstice? And the feast of Easter with the rebirth of nature in the spring?

The liturgical year, with its distinctive dates and seasons, takes its shape beginning with the festival of Easter and inherits much from the old covenant. It is consecrated forever by the great event of the death and resurrection of Christ. The Easter solemnity included always the remembrance of the crucifixion (See I Cor. 5:8). The old Jewish feast of Pentecost, which the church has associated with every remembrance of the first outpouring of the Holy Spirit, was preserved naturally. The period in between became Eastertide, observed from the second century and considered and designated as an uninterrupted feast of the glorious Christ. The remembrance of the ascension was not initially the focus of any particular anniversary. It was included in the whole Easter commemoration.

Later it was separated from this whole and localized at Pentecost.[4] Therefore, Pentecost became at the same time the day of the exaltation of the Lord and of his gift of the Holy Spirit to his church. It was only with certain changes from the fourth to fifth centuries that the ascension became the object of a particular celebration, ten days before Pentecost, and thereby entered into conformity with the chronological data of the scripture. In the third century the winter solstice, fixed erroneously by the Easter astronomists on January 6, suggested the feast of Epiphany or Theophany, in order to commemorate the divine manifestation of Christ along with the remembrance of his birth and baptism. It did not take long for this feast of Egyptian origin to spread throughout the entire East.

At the same time the discipline of preparation of candidates for baptism (which took place *en masse* on the eve of Easter) produced the cycle of Lent (from *quadraginta*, forty, alluding to the forty days the Lord spent in the desert preparing himself for his ministry). Intended originally for the catechumens, by the fourth century this preparation concerned the whole of the faithful.

In this same century, around A.D. 340, the Church of Rome began to celebrate December 25 as the feast of the birth of Christ, *Natalis dies*, from which came Christmas, a season which has countered and absorbed many of the pagan sun festivals associated with this solstice. Was not Christ the real "rising Sun," "the Sun of righteousness with healing in [his] wings"? (Mal. 4:2). Then a kind of exchange occurred between West and East: the Latin church adopted Epiphany by changing the accent to the episode of the Magi and by adding the wedding of Cana to it, whereas around A.D. 380 the East added the festival of Christmas.

It was almost the sixth century before Advent became the season of preparation for Christmas. It started with taking six Sundays,[5] but later the number was reduced to four. It was not until A.D. 900 that the first Sunday after Pentecost was consecrated to the mystery of the Trinity, but no general and

---

[4] See *Itinerarum Aetheriae*, (Editions du Cerf, Sources Chrétiennes, 1948), p. 43.

[5] The choice of this season of six weeks, being forty days, was dictated by a concern for parallelism with Lent. Christmas demanded preparation with as much care as Lent.

official sanction was given to this festival until 1334. Thus the liturgical year has been marked by a very gradual development. [6] The two pillars of the liturgical year are Christmas and Easter. The first is celebrated particularly in the West; the second more so in the East. Without taking anything from the solemnity and character of Christmas, it is necessary that Western churches restore to Easter some of the splendor accorded to it by the Eastern Orthodox church. It is a matter of restoring proper balance. It is not normal that everything should be thrown into confusion in the parishes, schools, and families as they prepare with thoroughness for the festival of Christmas and that this one feast should have so many facets — notably the rather debatable Christmas tree — whereas Easter is taken up with only the one Sunday morning service on the day of the feast. Evangelical churches are being gradually won over to the custom of a midnight service on Christmas Eve in imitation of the midnight Mass of the Roman church. This kind of service may be justified biblically by reference to Luke 2:8, though it has not been stated precisely that the event, which is properly called the nativity, took place during the night. But it is feared that a certain amount of sentimentalism has become mixed up with it, and indeed the festival of Christmas can be said to be saturated with it, to the extent that for many people the Christmas tree is the real *ersatz* for worship. This symbol is now so much abused that we ought to face seriously the possibility of the church renouncing it for its own sake and abandoning it to the world.

The restoration of the Easter vigil which has taken place in various churches [7] is better authenticated historically and theologically. It was on this night that the ancient people of God realized the passing (this is the meaning of the word Easter) of the kind of death which enslaves the life of freedom in the service of their God (Exod. 12:8, 11, 12, 29, and 31). It was at the end of this night that the resurrection event took place

[6] See Odo Casel, *Le Mystère du Culte dans le Christianisme*, Chap. 4, entitled "Le mystère de l'année liturgique," pp. 127-142.

[7] In the Roman church a decree of the Sacred Congregation of Rites, dating from February 9, 1951, authorizes and recommends the reestablishment of the solemn vigil of Easter, hitherto fallen into disuse. This movement is related to theological renewal which gives back to the mystery of Easter the centrality it should have (Rom. 6; Phil. 3:10; II Tim. 2:11, etc).

(Matt. 28:1-4). Easter is the passing from the night of sin and death into the light of the life in Christ. The early church also consecrated as holy the night of the Saturday before Easter and designated it as a time for the baptism of the neophytes. Buried mystically with Christ in the baptismal water, where they drowned the "old man," they emerged from it regenerated into the light of a new life with the risen Christ. Easter eve, moreover, exemplifies clearly that splendid passage from Paul in chapter 6 of the Letter to the Romans (vs. 3-11). Upon these bases there are stronger reasons for a service on the night preceding Easter than we can give for midnight service on Christmas eve. What is more, the eschatalogical significance of Easter is more apparent than Christmas.[8] It is, therefore, more natural to prepare for Easter by a night service which emphasizes the attitude of watchful waiting for the appearance of the Lord who will return "in the evening, at midnight, or with the crowing of the cock, or in the morning" (Mark 13:29, 32-37). Let us not misunderstand this: we do not object to a service on Christmas eve, provided it is not tainted with liturgical "romanticism." But the service on Easter eve has priority, and if the first is reestablished, the second ought to be also, under penalty of emphasizing more the Western disequilibrium in favor of Christmas at the expense of Easter. Easter may be reevaluated also by a great service of praise in the evening of the festival itself, with readings from all the stories of the appearance of the Risen One and accompanied by the choir performing some of the numerous and splendid Easter chorales, still often overlooked in our hymnbooks. This would be a meaningful Easter counterpart of the traditional Christmas tree. The following Sunday which the liturgy calls Sunday *in albis* and in popular parlance is named "little Easter," must also be the occasion of prolonging the triumphant affirmation of the festival.[9]

---

[8] Christmas declares, with the mystery of the incarnation, the coming of "the last days" (Heb. 1:1-2), but Easter is already the actual passing and entrance into the age to come, in the person of the risen and transfigured Christ, the first fruits of the new creation. See O. Casel, *op. cit.*, p. 59: "The sacrifice of Christ has been the vesper sacrifice of the world and his resurrection was the sunrise of a new and eternal morning."

[9] One can only say that Robert Will is right in writing: "We deplore the fact that Protestantism is so poor in its store of symbols interpreting the mysteries of the Passion and Resurrection," *op. cit.*, II, p. 475.

The cycle of Christmas includes the weeks of Advent preceding the feast and the Epiphany period which follows it. Advent (from *adventus*, meaning "arrival") is the season of waiting and hope. It features readings from the Old Testament prophets and the messianic psalms, and then the first chapter of Luke's Gospel. Isaiah and John the Baptist occupy important places in it; both are oriented toward what the Bible calls the fulfillment and/or the fullness of time. The gradation of the four Sundays is very clear in the entire liturgy: it is seen in the candles of Advent which are lit progressively as the time of Christmas draws near. This custom, originally Lutheran, provides a further advantage in getting the Reformed tradition to become accustomed to the use of candles apart from the so-called Christmas tree.

The Sunday after Christmas should provide a place for the Virgin Mary because our churches have reserved no date for her. It is perhaps the most natural and favorable occasion for the Reformed churches to remember at least once a year the one who had predicted that "all generations will call her blessed."[10] New Year's Day unfortunately has swallowed up by its civic character the ancient commemoration of the circumcision of the Lord (Luke 2:21). Without stressing unduly the fact itself or sacrificing the date on the civil calendar, we can recall the day that "the Son of God was born under the Law to redeem those who were under the Law" (Gal. 4:5).

Epiphany, also called Theophany earlier, or divine manifestation of Christ, commemorated in the beginning the Lord's baptism — that occasion when the voice from heaven declared: "This is my beloved Son." The wedding at Cana also was associated with it, that time when Jesus "manifested his glory" (John 2:11). Finally, and first of all in the West, it was the incident of the three kings or Magi that prevailed, without superceding entirely the other two. In our churches Epiphany may be regarded as recalling or as a final echo of Christmas; after the episode of the shepherds which makes real the fact that salvation was brought to the humble and to the Jews, the incident of the Magi indicates that salvation was being de-

[10] Luke 1:48. By doing this, we would be in agreement with the Eastern Orthodox Church which, following the Byzantine and Syrian Jacobite rites, consecrates December 26 in honor of the Virgin Mother.

clared to the pagan and heathen. Epiphany is the universal and missionary radiation of the mystery of the incarnation.[11] Epiphany is celebrated on the Sunday closest to January 6, if the latter falls on a week day, and therefore cannot be earlier than January 4 or later than January 10. The Sundays after the feast of Epiphany make us relive the historical ministry of Christ. Unfortunately their number is restricted, especially when Easter comes at an early date. From a maximum number of six they can be reduced to two or three. Those which must be dropped are transferred then to the end of the annual cycle where they fill up an empty place. We hope that one day the Christian churches will reach some agreement on fixing an immovable date for Easter on the first or second Sunday in April. Unnecessary complications in the liturgical calendar could thereby be avoided.

When the cycle of Christmas or of the mystery of the incarnation is completed, the cycle of Easter or of the mystery of redemption begins with the date of Septuagesima, which is the transition from one to the other. Septuagesima, sexagesima, quinquagesima—rather ungraceful words—should be replaced by a term equivalent to the much more adequate German word: *Vorfastenzeit*. The church begins to withdraw with its Master who removes himself from the crowds opposed to his message and who permits his own faithful to feel beforehand a sense of the hard way which he must follow.

With the sixth Sunday before Easter, Lent begins—which the Reformed churches are more inclined to call Passiontide. The word Lent is inseparably linked also with the idea of fasting which is not practiced in our churches. The term Passion is, therefore, preferable although it tends to darken too early the slow gradation of these six weeks at the beginning of which there is not the immediate question of the suffering of the cross. In the early church forty days were consecrated for the preparation of candidates for baptism and biblical pericopes were arranged for every day. The purpose of these pericopes, therefore, was less for reliving the stages of the passion of our Lord than for teaching the catechumens some episodes of the Holy Scripture considered essential for their under-

[11] In the Reformed churches in France and Switzerland in the month of January there is a Missionary Sunday, to which the significance of Epiphany can be related.

standing of the meaning of baptism. They form in this way a whole, so that the traditional epistles and gospels of the five Sundays in Lent, separated from the context of those designated for the week days, have little significance. Without capitulating entirely to it, we cannot but appreciate, however, the enrichment which the triennial system gives, of which the two new series of pericopes correspond better with the idea we entertain regarding Passiontide, namely, our going again with Christ by the way of the Cross.

This period culminates in Holy Week, called Great Week in Eastern Orthodoxy, during which every parish community ought to celebrate a daily service. Holy Thursday should recall the institution of Holy Communion. Holy Friday has a great service in the morning and should end in the evening with an "office of the burial of the Lord," for which the Eastern Orthodox *Epitaphion* may serve to a certain degree as a model. It impresses upon us the truth that Christ descended in our death and that we have not only to die with him but must bury our "old man" with him (Rom. 6). Medieval devotion to the suffering humanity of Christ and to his bleeding passion, as well as the theology of the Reformation which was nourished in this specific Western and medieval climate, have wrought something of a disruption or cleavage of the "death-resurrection" link, which the early faith did not separate and which the Eastern church has always maintained to be organically united. We have been led, therefore, to give a dramatic and tragic complexion to the services on Holy Friday in order to emphasize, by contrast, the triumphant jubilation of Easter. Undoubtedly the difference is there and it should never be overlooked. But, we must not forget that in the fourth Gospel the hour in which our Lord is glorified is the hour of the cross. Patristic thought reminds us that Christ had his victory over the demonic powers when he was dying on the cross. Paul had already suggested this in writing, "He disarmed the principalities and powers and made a public example of them, triumphing over them in the cross" (Col. 2:15). It is time for us then to return to a more balanced point of view of these two aspects of the one and central event of our salvation.[12]

But the service on Easter eve, about which some question

has been raised already, joins very happily Friday and Sunday and produces the unity of the *triduum paschale*. Did not the early church speak of the *Easter of the Crucifixion* (Holy Friday) and the *Easter of the Resurrection* (Easter, properly called) as forming a whole—the Easter mystery?

Eastertide continues from Easter to the Sunday after Pentecost. It is marked by signs of the joy of the resurrection and of the new life in Christ. Indeed the Easter Alleluias do not cease resounding from Sunday to Sunday, and ring more triumphantly than ever on Ascension Day. The feast of Pentecost ends the cycle of redemption by beseeching for the church the gifts of the Holy Spirit. In ancient Christianity, the fifty days from Easter to Pentecost were festival times; one prayed only standing. The first Sunday after Pentecost gathers up the whole divine work of salvation in contemplation of God who is unique and three times holy, Father, Son and Holy Spirit: it is Trinity Sunday.

The cycle of Christ, moving from Advent to Pentecost with its two foci, Christmas and Easter, gives way then to the cycle of the church. The period after Pentecost places in perspective the various functions of the church, the bride and body of Christ, and the diverse functions of the Christian life. This very long period, which extends from the end of spring to the beginning of winter, has 24 to 27 Sundays, depending upon whether Easter is early or late. It does not present the clearly marked stages we find in the cycle of Christ. Various and tentative efforts had been made in former times, and even in our day, to give some structure to this long series of Sundays that was without any particular character, but no one was able to impose his own pattern.[13] In our Reformed churches, Holy

[12] Note the mood of victory in the old Passion hymns, such as *Pange linqua gloriosi lauream certaminis et super crucis trophaeo dic triumphum nobilem et le Vexilla regis prodeunt, fulget crucis mysterium*. An English adaptation is the hymns *Sing, my tongue, the glorious battle* and *The royal banners forward go* by J.M. Neale in *Hymns Ancient and Modern*. From the theological point of view, cf. G. Aulèn, *Christus Victor*, (London, S.P.C.K., 1931).

[13] Thus some of the sacramentaries of the Carolingian period divide this season into three parts, punctuated by the birthdays of Saints Peter and Paul on June 29, of Laurence on August 10, and of Michael on September 29. Recently German liturgical movements of the *Hochkirchliche Vereinigung* and of the *Michaelsbruderschaft* have also subdivided the period after Pentecost by means of the birthday of St. Laurence, or of St. John the Baptist, on August 29, or of St. Michael. In the Reformed traditions, St. Michael's and St. Martin's Day (the latter on November 11) have still played a role, if not liturgical, than at least social and economic, until the end of the eighteenth century.

Communion in September, and in Switzerland the federal Lent on the third Sunday in September, provide a division of the period after Pentecost into two parts. The second period is marked by Harvest Sunday, a date which varies according to local conditions, and by Reformation Sunday at the beginning of November.[14] The other Sundays in November are set apart for meditation upon last things: the return of our Lord, resurrection, judgment, eternal life in the new heaven and new earth. Then the cry of Christian hope: *Maranatha* (Lord, come!) joins again with the cry of the messianic expectation of Advent, and the annual cycle begins again.

All Saints' presents a problem because of the break which took place historically between this feast, fixed in the West as November 1, and All Souls' Day on November 2. Popular religious tradition has confused these two anniversaries freely. It is proper that the church should set apart one day to call upon the "great cloud of witnesses" by which we are surrounded (Heb. 12:1) and to thank the Lord for having created so many older brothers and sisters whose examples encourage and stimulate us. They are not dead but are now alive in God (Luke 20:38); they are the living crown of Christ the King. For us, all invocation to the "saints" is excluded, but to call upon their life and witness is a benediction of which the church cannot deprive itself with impunity.

Commemoration of the dead in the parish once a year may be justified also; its most normal place would be one of the Sundays in November, for the whole month focuses upon eschatology. The last Sunday of the Church year, according to a section of Lutheranism, is called *Totensonntag*.

The succession of times and festivals in the church calendar determines quite naturally a corresponding pattern in the liturgical texts: introit psalms, prayers, biblical pericopes and hymns change according to the proper character of the liturgical season. These variable elements are called the *proper of the time*, and, on the other hand, one designates as *common* or *ordi-*

---

[14] Luther posted his famous articles on October 31. It would be good for the Reformed churches, following some of the Lutheran churches, to observe the Reformation on the last Sunday in October and not the first Sunday in November, in order to allow the whole month of November to be free for the Last Things, particularly All Saints' Day and the commemoration of the dead. The celebration of the anniversary of the Reformation dates only from the eighteenth century.

nary the permanent structure and the unchanging formulas of the liturgy. The church year does not coincide or start with the civil year, but approximately one month before with the first Sunday of Advent. Without the liturgical year the Christian festivals are isolated from one another and rise side by side like obelisks in the desert. Why should it astonish us, under these conditions, that so many Protestants consider it sufficient to go to church only at Christmas or Easter?

The liturgical year is a means for the church to become conscious in the present of what God has already done "once and for all" in the history of salvation.[15] The Lord, who is present in worship, makes the redeemed of our day to be contemporary with what he accomplished earlier. The use of time for this purpose permits, therefore, the passage of time; the community of today may, by the Holy Spirit, live really the human birth, or the ministry, or sufferings, or triumph of its Lord.[16] "Each year, to go again with Christ the way he went while here, is this not to accomplish, from the spiritual and mystical point of view, what Paul demands on several occasions: 'Be my imitators, as I am myself Christ's imitator'?"[17] There is also pedagogical value in it which one should not underestimate. The church finds here in obedience to the word of God the possibility of and the occasion for its being "united

---

[15] See in Odo Casel, *op. cit.*, the whole of Chapter 4, the mystery of the liturgical year, especially these words: "When the liturgical year celebrates facts, successions of great deeds and historical events, it does not adhere to these as such, but to their spiritual content which they make explicit and recall. This content is the great work of God on behalf of humanity, the redemption of Christ who wants to pull man away from the narrowness of time and introduce him to eternity without end." (p. 136).

[16] This is the meaning of the biblical concept *memorial*, in the Greek *anamnesis*. The anamnesis is not a subjective mental act referring to a past event or an absent person. It evokes or recalls, that is to say, it calls anew to make present by its effects and consequences such an event or person. It is in this sense that worship, word as well as sacrament, is an anamnesis of Christ and of the great christological facts, and that the Sundays and feasts explain and diversify the memorial of the Lord. See Gregory Dix, *op. cit.*, pp. 244-247 and 259-266; *Leiturgia*, I, pp. 209-212, 358; Odo Casel, *Das Gedachtnis des Herrn in der altchristlichen Liturgie*, Ecclesia orans, (Freiburg-in-Brisgau, 1922); F.C.N. Hicks, *The Fullness of Sacrifice*, 3rd ed. (London: S.P.C.K., 1946), pp. 211-212; R. Paquier, "Sens et legitimite theologique des temps et des fêtes de l'annee chretienne," *Verbum Caro*, n. 31-32, 1954.

[17] Max Thurian, *op. cit.*, p. 107. "Preaching too finds great advantage in the liturgical year. Themes and texts are assigned to it one after the other, without option. The whole Word of God is gone through, therefore, each year, and the church is edified harmoniously instead of being taken on a promenade Sunday after Sunday, from one end of the Bible to the other, haphazardly and at the discretion of the preacher."

with Christ" (Rom. 6:5), assimilated with him, particularly in his death and resurrection.[18] Properly understood, to relive in worship the redemptive work of Christ by means of the rhythm of the liturgical year does not mean necessarily that a man is already reborn in Christ, but that this is a regular remembrance and a stimulus towards such an end. These are really external elements and factors which cannot be ignored nor neglected by the believer who lives here below "in his body" (II Cor. 5:10; 12:2-3).

[18] See Rom. 8:29; Phil. 3:10-11; II Cor. 3:18; I John 3:2. In Albert Hammenstede, *op. cit.*, pp. 82-84, there is a suggestive essay referring the successive stages of the liturgical year to the three traditional degrees of the ascetic life: *via purgativa, via illuminativa,* and *via unitiva.*

11

The Furnishing
of the House of God

We indicated earlier that God, who created us with bodies subject to time and space, consents to come near us more particularly in certain places and at certain moments. These places or moments are not sacred in and through themselves and are not thus by right either entirely or exclusively. God may be called upon and served in every place and at every moment. But since certain places—particularly buildings constructed and consecrated for this purpose—are designed more than others for housing and encouraging the encounter of the Lord with his people, it is the duty of believers to arrange everything, materially speaking, so that this meeting will be under the most favorable conditions. It is not a matter of "creating an atmosphere" by any skillful or subtle search for effect as in the case of the theatre. It is not man's prerogative to direct that current or to catch that fluid which is supposed to emanate from God and put the congregation into a trance. The liturgist is not a technician who can take advantage of all the more or less verified data of "religious psychology," and thereby play upon the senses and sensibilities of the faithful. He is concerned simply that the exterior conditioning of worship is in conformity with the data of biblical revelation and in harmony with the means of approach God has chosen to come to us.[1]

The house of God must possess certain signs of the divine presence.[2] Our view from the entrance should include something to suggest to us the word and sacraments: the pulpit, where the word is read and preached; the font and the holy table, where the two fundamental sacraments of the gospel are administered. Since the breaking of bread is the central and culminating act of the worship, the holy table ought to occupy the main location and be fully visible in the axis of the building.[3] Whether the choir be in an apse or not, it will be convenient for the table to be one step higher than the rest of the edifice, so that the communicants on their approach have the feeling, even bodily, of rising toward Christ who "sits on the right hand of God" (Col. 3:1). If the pulpit occupies the central place, that is, in the axis of the church, and moreover, if it has excessive dimensions and is occupied by the minister from the beginning to the end of the religious service, then there will be nothing to suggest the presence of God when the church is not used. Furthermore, during the worship the "speaker" in the pulpit will attract the attention of everyone. Man will be on view instead of God being glorified.[4]

It is true that in the ancient basilicas the seat of the bishop was placed at the center of the apse in the axis of the building: a typical example is the Cathedral of Torcello in the lagoon

[1] See Max Thurian: *Joie du ciel sur la terre* (Neuchâtel-Paris: Delachaux et Niestlé, 1946) pp. 91-102. Here, especially pp. 93-94, are found suggestions for the furnishing of the sacristy, which we may omit from our consideration now.

[2] "Certain ornaments suitable to the acts performed in the church will not be useless, if they influence believers to do holy things with humility, meditation, and veneration," wrote Calvin. In another place he specifies: "When I consider the proper end for which churches are erected, it appears to me more unbecoming their sacredness than I well can tell, to admit any other images than those living symbols which the Lord has consecrated by his own word: I mean Baptism and the Lord's Supper, with the other ceremonies. By these our eyes ought to be more steadily fixed, and more vividly impressed, than to require the aid of any images which the wit of man may advise." Henry Beveridge (trans.) John Calvin's *Institutes of the Christian Religion*, I, II, xiii. (Grand Rapids: Eerdmanns, 1953), p. 101.

[3] See P. Romane Musculus, *La Priere des mains*, (Paris-Geneva: Editions Je sers, 1938), p. 83.

[4] In *Ways of Worship*, G. van der Leeuw shows how discussions on the respective place of the pulpit and holy table, and on the fixed or mobile character of the latter, refer to the different theological positions about the relation between word and sacrament, p. 226.

of Venice. But the ancient seat was not merely a chair in the modern sense of the word. It was a seat with side arms, a sort of armchair of wood or stone, reminiscent of the English word *chair*, which has preserved the idea of seat or chair as related to the word *chairman* or president or the one who occupies a presidential seat. From this seat, which was on the main level or raised by two or three steps with reference to the *mensa*, the Lord's Table, the bishop or officiant who replaced him, preached generally seated (continuing the Jewish custom, Matt. 23:1). The preaching ended, he would rise and proceed several steps in order to occupy his place at the table and offer the great eucharistic prayer. There was no parallel between this basilical arrangement and that of numerous Reformed churches built with a monumental chair perched high, secured fast, topped with a sounding board, and so separated from the holy table that the officiant is obliged always to take a little journey in order to serve at the altar.

In the church the holy table is the visible memorial of the presence and sacrifice of Jesus Christ. This does not mean that it is itself this presence, nor the guarantee of it outside of or independently from the living community of believers, but is a permanent sign of it. It is not itself a sacramental sign, but outside of those hours when the sacrament is celebrated, it is the material indication of that spiritual event which is repeated, or should be repeated, every Sunday. Ordinarily the Reformed tradition avoids giving the Lord's table the name of altar, as they do without any reservations among other confessional sections of the church universal. This is the result of a reaction, which is somewhat simplified, against the Roman Catholic altar on which the sacrifice of Calvary is supposed to be repeated. It is clear that the holy table is not an altar on which Christ, the eternal victim, would be sacrificed every Sunday or even every day. But it is on the holy table that the bread and wine are placed, set apart for divine use as effective signs of the sacrifice of Christ. It is there that the alms and offerings are placed after the gifts are received. It is there, also, that the faithful, while taking communion, offer themselves to God as a living and holy sacrifice. There are, therefore, from the scriptural point of view some valid reasons for calling the Lord's table an *altar*. In the new covenant the piece of furniture that succeeded it is normally called *table*, but rarely altar.[5] But the words are permissible. We cannot enter here into details concerning the history of the Christian altar. Let it suffice us to say that its form must be rectangular or square, in no case oval, which would make it resemble a living room table. It may be of wood or stone, but black marble should be avoided because of its funereal character.[6]

During the celebration of the eucharist, the table is set with the plate bearing the bread and the cup containing the wine, with the flagon for the wine in reserve. The book of worship has its place there, too. But what is this table between occasions; that is, during a service without the sacrament or apart from the regular service? Recently in the Reformed churches of French-speaking Switzerland the habit has emerged of putting on the table a big open Bible above which stands a wooden cross. This custom indicates some progress beyond the old habit. Previously the table had no distinctive sign and from every perspective the place of worship resembled a conference or school room. But after some experience and reflection, it has occurred to us that the intention, excellent in itself, of giving to the church some signs of Christian identity, has produced results that are not always immune from criticism.

The cross has become the symbol of Christianity because it was the instrument of our salvation. Paul described "the crucified Christ" to the Galatians (3:1), and in his ministry in Corinth he wanted to know only "Jesus Christ crucified" (I Cor. 2:2). The cross represents adequately the essential message of Christianity. It is not the memorial of a defeat which

[5] 1 Cor. 10:21, 23; Heb. 13:10. See Ignatius of Antioch, *ad Philad.*, iv. Tertullian, *De Oratione*, 19. *The Ante-Nicene Fathers*, ed. A. Roberts and J. Donaldson. Vols. I & III. (New York: Chas. Scribner's Sons, 1899).

[6] Without making the holy table into a fetish or placing it under taboo, we have the right to expect from pastors a measure of respect in this instance, just as we do from the simple members among the faithful. It does not demonstrate a very fine sense of spirituality to put one's hat or gloves on it; or make a sort of clothes rack of it, as is done during concerts, even "sacred" ones, given in some of our churches and cathedrals; or when we see it being made into a convenient counter where Sunday School teachers may put their classroom materials; or where the church wardens may spread the money from the offering plates to be counted, or where, finally, the ballot-boxes are thrown when the church council is elected. It is to be hoped that these inappropriate habits will soon be merely painful memories!

would take from it the right to signify the faith of the church. It is the memorial of a victory, the victory of the "faithful Witness" (Rev. 1:5 and 3:4), who died rather than give in to the pressures of the forces of evil and deny the Father. Therefore, he "made a public example of the powers of evil on the cross" (Col. 2:15). This "sign of the Son of Man" (Matt. 24:30) is in its rightful place in the churches; it is a sermon for the eyes, provided that it is fully understood through regular comment and clarification in the preaching of the word of the cross and by the liturgy. The naked cross ought to be preferred without hesitation to the crucifix. We do not feel we have the right to criticize or judge Christians of Roman persuasion, or Lutherans or Anglicans, who make a place for the crucifix in their churches. But we think that the simple cross is more in keeping with the second commandment: "You shall not make for yourself a graven image." It is a discreet recollection of the crucified Christ, whereas with the crucifix there is always the risk of its becoming a holy object. Finally, it expresses better the victory of the Risen One who is no longer and will not ever again be on a cross.[7]

If the nature of character of the room does not permit any other arrangement, the cross may be placed upon the holy table, but its dimensions should be proportionate with those of the table itself. It is preferable, however, if there be no window at the back of the choir, to fix the cross upon the wall; and in this case, a cross of larger dimensions, with its base on the floor, may be used. Or, one may place behind the table a credence upon which is set a cross of dimensions commensurate with the type put on the table. In both cases the practical advantage is to avoid having to remove the cross for the celebration of Holy Communion, as is inevitably the case when the cross is on the table. The credence also has the advantage of serving as a support for the open Bible and eliminates the objection made by Lutherans and Anglicans to our putting the

---

[7] See P. Romane Musculus, *op. cit.*, p. 70. The author expresses a point of view which appears to us to be judiciously slanted on the subject of images and paintings in a Reformed church: "One should not confuse worship of images with usage of images. The Reformed church is not iconoclastic; it does not discard all images except those validated in scripture... While recognizing that images may come to the aid of our spirits, the church will be very careful in using this power which images have to move and nourish our piety" (pp. 68-69).

book upon the table. Indeed, they declare that this is an in-dication of the characteristically Reformed domination of the word at the expense of the sacraments in which the book of the word lords it over the table itself, which is reserved for the sacrament, although it is rarely celebrated. However, if it is not possible to put the open Bible somewhere else than on the table, we could see in this a symbol of the complementary union of word and sacrament. In any case the open Bible de-clares to everyone who comes that the word of God is the source of our faith, the essence of all that makes the church, and the justification for the worship we render to God in his house. Moreover, it reminds the visitor who is poorly in-formed in things of the faith, that vague religiosity may not be of sufficient help to him and that only a knowledge and ac-ceptance of the biblical message can put us into a right rela-tionship with God.

By putting the cross and the Bible behind the holy table, we are in keeping with the practice of the early church which left the table free from everything except the eucharistic plates and cup at the hour of the celebration of the sacrament. It is desirable, however, that the holy table be decorated at all times with an *antependium*, a piece of fine linen decorated with an embroidered Christian emblem, for example, the chrism or the IHS. If the table is made of fine material the *antependium* should not exceed the proportions of a "table runner," so that as much as possible of the table may be seen. If this is not the case, then the *antependium* may cover the whole front of the table, but in such away that it falls without folds at each corner; otherwise it would have the appearance of a liv-ing room table. For the communion services care should be taken to avoid a white cloth that would fall too low and cover the whole *antependium*. Or if the cloth is of such dimensions that the *antependium* cannot help being entirely covered, then the latter should be placed during the celebration upon the credence where it will form a decoration at the back of and above the holy table.

Until now it was not a custom in Reformed churches to use the symbolism of light which is, however, beautiful and simple and easily caught by both eye and spirit. The Old

Testament knew the lamp of God in the tabernacle at Shilo (I Sam. 3:3), and the candlestick with the seven arms in the temple at Jerusalem (Exod. 25:31-39; 27:20-21). The seer of Patmos contemplated seven lamps burning in front of the divine throne (Rev. 4:5). He saw Christ glorified and standing in the midst of seven golden candlesticks representing the churches (Rev. 1:12-13, 20). During Jewish meals of some importance, especially meals associated with religious fraternities, it was customary to light a lamp while pronouncing a prayer of benediction, and it is almost certain this was the case at the last meal the night prior to Jesus' death. Even nowadays in every pious Jewish family the lamp of the Sabbath is lit regularly every Saturday. These Jewish customs have survived in the Christian *agapé*. Thus Luke notes that "there were many lamps in the upper room" of Troas where Paul preached the word and broke bread for the local community on the first day of the week, that is, Sunday (Acts 20:7-8). Out of these customs has come the daily practice of *lucernarium*, widespread in Eastern Christianity in the fourth century, which consisted of celebrating solemnly every evening the hour of the lighting of the lamps in the basilicas, while thanking God for the gift of light and for all the benedictions of the past day. For the *lucernarium* was composed the oldest known Christian hymn, the *Phôs hilaron*, still used today daily in the Eastern Orthodox church.[8] Conforming to the universal custom of people in antiquity, the use of torches and candles at funerals has been generally employed in the ante-Nicene church. With the Constantinian era, when the church was at liberty to develop its public worship, they began to light lamps or candles to make the reading of the gospel more significant. Little by little, for reasons practical as well as symbolic, the custom was adopted of lighting lamps above the altar and of surrounding the altar with big candles. It is only from the ninth century onward that the custom became general of putting candles on the altar.

We cannot really understand why the church would want to deprive itself of the symbolism of light. The flame of a lamp

[8] The English version is known as *Hail, gladdening Light of his pure glory pour'd*, in *Hymns Ancient and Modern*.

121

or candle is a sign of life, truth, and joy. The bright splendor of many candlesticks gives to any meal or ceremony a festive air. For Christians, it suggests the fire of the Holy Spirit (Acts 2:3). It symbolizes also love that radiates while consuming itself (*in serviendo consumor*). The Eastern church lights many candles during its services and the Roman church prescribes two candles as a minimum for a simple Mass and six or more for solemn Masses. The Lutherans and Anglicans have used light more discreetly, chiefly for eucharistic services. There is no scriptural reason for opposing the adoption of this custom again in the Reformed church, since it is fully understood that it is merely a matter of liturgical usage in the church at the hour of worship and not for the purpose of promoting private devotion as a meritorious act. The Reformed church does not fear any excessive use of small candles, once a year, on Christmas Eve. Now the Christmas tree is an innovation dating back only to the middle of the ninteenth century in French speaking countries, although it would be very easy to demonstrate pre-Christian naturalistic antecedents of it. Why should one be disturbed by discreet use of light during the whole year? It is not only on Christmas Eve that Christ is the Light of the world and that the Holy Spirit lights the church; every day the Christian has to be a child of light. Every service of worship, especially the eucharist, is a feast of the Lord in which light may play its part; Christmas has no monopoly in this regard! The Reformed church, with its emphasis upon moderation, can hardly use church-candles, properly called, that are excessively high; short white candles are sufficient. An exact regulation of the number of liturgical candles is unnecessary. Care must be taken merely to have an equal number symmetrically arranged on either side of the cross and Bible. There may be two or four simple candlesticks, or two candlesticks with two or three arms, or a miniature replica of the great candelabra of the old covenant with its seven arms. Care must be taken further to increase the light on feast and solemn days while retaining just enough through the moderate symbolism of two candlesticks on normal days. Whatever the number be, the candles symbolize Christ and his church (Rev. 1:12, 20) as the bearer of the flame and light of the Holy Spirit. On either side of the open Bible they testify "that Word and Spirit are inseparable in God's plan of salvation. The Word alone breeds dogmatism, the Spirit alone breeds sectarian enthusiasm; both together are sure and certain pledges of the proper upbuilding of the church."[9]

Associated with the symbolism of light is the question of the perpetual lamp in the sanctuary. If one has any symbolic intuition at all, he cannot deny the meaningful and clearly obvious value of this liturgical sign; the "eternal lamp." It was prescribed in the ceremonial ordinance of the old covenant (Exod. 25:37; 27:20-21; 30:7-8. II Chron. 13:11; I Sam. 3:3). This symbol was lighted only between the evening and morning. It is, therefore, truly biblical and its usage cannot drastically be abolished in the worship of the new covenant. In the Eastern church lamps are lighted in front of the icons during the worship; and in the Catholic church of the West, the lamp lighted day and night is an indication of the presence of the Holy Sacrament in the tabernacle on the altar, whether it be during worship or outside the hours of worship. From the Reformed point of view we can scarcely accept the fact of a symbolic lamp burning in front of a material element—icon or sacrament—which assumes then the value of an object of worship, and that this lamp goes out when the object is not there anymore. We can, however, conceive of and admit the symbolism of an inextinguishable lamp that may be the sign of the spiritual and eternal presence of God in his church. Still, this perpetual lamp in the sanctuary tends to reduce too greatly the necessary tension, which was a question earlier, between the universal divine presence and the particular presence of the Lord in the place where his people come together. We cannot recommend, therefore, any general adoption of it, but we believe that such an element of symbolism may, in certain cases, contribute to the realization of the presence of God in the church and to the worship of Protestants who have so little of it.

Floral decorations in the sanctuary depend essentially on a question of taste rather than on rigid prescriptions. It is a recent innovation. In the Roman church it first appeared in

[9] Max Thurian, *op. cit.*, p. 101.

the sixteenth century and in the Reformed church in the twentieth. When flowers are used solely for decorative purposes, they have no proper place in churches. Their use is justified only when they bring the worshiper to a remembrance of the splendor of God reflected in the great work of his creation. Therefore, flowers should be used in the church with moderation. Care must be exercised lest the House of God be made to resemble some kind of verandah or botannical garden. When used, flowers should be placed, wherever possible, around the holy table, or behind and above it on *ad hoc* supports or stands. They may be put on the table only when no other arrangement is possible. The Lord's table must not be made to look like a flower table in the living room. We must avoid any display that will confuse the worshiper about the relationship between the order of grace and the order of creation and nature.

The pulpit of the word of God should be placed at the side. Whether it is on the left of the holy table or on the right has no significance in itself architecturally, although the right side has been reserved traditionally for the reading of the gospel, God's word *par excellence*. The shape of the pulpit which harmonizes most adequately with the nature of worship is the old ambon, a side stage some steps higher than the holy table, from where one can have direct access to it. Standing sideways with the choir the ambon is directly adjacent to the table, and one catches sight of them in the same glance. Here is a visible expression of the balance that should be maintained between word and sacrament. Any other arrangement of the pulpit bears out this balance less clearly or betrays it entirely. If the pulpit is on top, at the crossing or axis of the edifice, and is big and ostentatious, with the table at its foot, the word dominates and overshadows the sacrament. If, moreover, the table occupies its normal place in the choir, and the pulpit is placed against a sidewall or a pillar of the nave, the word is again separated from the sacrament, or the sacrament is isolated from the word. In this last case, however, one can remedy this defective arrangement to a certain degree by means of a lectern placed on one side or the other of the table (preferably on the side opposite to the pulpit in order to balance the furnishings of the church). This lectern may be used for the reading of the scripture lessons, the liturgy of baptism, confirmation, marriages and funerals, while the pulpit is reserved for preaching at the main Sunday service. It should be made clear at this point that the lectern, and equally the pulpit or ambon, should not be used for the reading of the prayers. For the prayers the furniture should include a *prie-dieu*, placed sideways, near the lectern. The pulpit or ambon, as well as the lectern, may, and indeed, should be provided with paraments that harmonize with the antependium of the holy table, and bearing appropriately an embroidered Christian symbol.

On the opposite side of the pulpit or ambon the baptismal font or baptistry is normally placed as a permanent reminder of the sacrament of Christian initiation. Baptism should be administered, as a rule, before the congregation. The font, therefore, should occupy a position in full view of all. We are inclined to favor this location in preference to that in the Roman Catholic and Anglican churches where it stands at the entrance of the building as a sign of the fact that baptism is the introductory sacrament of the church. In these churches baptism is mostly a private ceremony embracing only the family of the baptized child. In such an event this location may be justified. It cannot be this way if we conceive, as we should, of the sacrament of baptism as the action of the whole gathered congregation, almost like the Holy Communion. Since baptism is the act of incorporation into the church, the moment of induction to the congregation of the children of God, it is right and proper that the congregation be present there and involved. Consequently the font should be placed in front and in sight of the congregation.

This, then, is how the house of God should be furnished for its children who live within its corporate body. Frescoes and stained glass windows may be included as the homage of human art inspired by faith in the glory of the God of truth, holiness, and beauty. But these elements do not add anything to what is essential: holy table, pulpit, font, Bible and cross, which are sufficient to certify that the Lord's presence is given and received in this place in its fullness. Wherever the

125

people of God set or erect these material symbols for the public worship of the Lord, they constitute in principle a "house of God," that is to say, a properly defined place which shows forth the marvelous event of the entrance of the Lord God into this world and of his habitation in the midst of his own.

12

The Proper Place
for the Liturgical Celebration

The place for liturgical celebration posed no problem at all in the Christian congregations of the ante-Nicene period. The church gathered privately in a certain house or secretly in some crypt of the catacombs. There was one table for the essential if not unique act of worship: the breaking of bread, or eucharist. Those who presided, that is, the bishop with his elders or the presbyter with his deacons, took their places around the table during the whole service. It was from very near the table necessarily and altogether naturally that the scriptures were read and the homily delivered. The Roman patrician villas, which frequently provided shelter for these congregations, were particularly well suited for Christian worship. The entrance hall (*atrium*) held the gathered congregation. At the back, the *tablinium*, one or two steps higher, was for the seats of the celebrant and his assistants. The *cartibulum*, at the entrance of the *tablinium*, became the Lord's Table, and the *impluvium*, a kind of pool in the center of the atrium, served as a baptistry. And the *triclinium*, adjacent to the *atrium*, was used for the *agapé* or love feast.

In the time of Constantine the church came out of hiding; now it could affirm and assert itself. And its worship, private and homely as it was, became public. Places of worship were constructed which reproduced on a larger scale the character of the Roman villas which were found to be so convenient. Behind the table the *cathedra* was raised, or the seat of the bishop, which was not a pulpit in the modern sense of the word, but rather a kind of presidential chair from which the bishop spoke while sitting. A bench for the presbyters formed a semi-circle around the table. For the scripture reading, a sort of podium on a higher level, called *ambon*, was placed at the side. Therefore, the worship was conducted entirely at the holy table or in the area immediately surrounding it. This is the normal consequence of the fact that the breaking of bread is at the center of Christian worship.

The heavenly worship in the book of Revelation is not held at the foot of a pulpit but in the presence of "the golden altar that is before the throne" (8:3) or that "is placed before God" (9:13). Other references are: Rev. 6:9; 11:1; 14:18; and 16:7. The Lamb that is "as though it had been slain" is "in the midst of the throne" (5:6 and 7:17). It is not upon the altar, for its sacrifice has been consummated "once for all" (Heb. 9:28) and is not repeatable; but the throne dominates the altar and on this altar are offered "the prayers of all the saints" (8:3). For the prayer is a "sacrifice of praise" (Heb. 13:15, in the context of 13:10 "we have an altar"); it is the offering of incense going up to the throne of God (Ps. 141:2). If it is believed that according to the scriptures God has to instruct us by means of the symbolism of heavenly worship, it is doubtless for the purpose of our deriving from it some useful teaching for the earthly worship of the church. Unless we want to feel more spiritualistic than the Holy Spirit who inspired the scriptures, then we may, and indeed we must, regulate to a certain measure the worship of the church militant according to what has been revealed to us typologically about the worship of the church triumphant. This worship is essentially adoration, praise, communion; and the altar is indicated there as the proper place for this spiritual offering. To ignore this fact is to be willing to deny that the material character of these places is a sign that assists the faithful in discovering the profound essence and significance of worship, and incidentally, is useful for the development of their piety. Prayers said from a pulpit, whether we like it or not, give the impression of a discourse, of a didactic exposition or harangue, of a "preachment" made to God, preceding or following the one delivered to the congregation. [1]

It was only during the Middle Ages, at the instigation of the preaching monks, that pulpits in the modern sense of the term were put in the churches, and these were fixed to a pillar in the nave. It was a matter of making popular evangelization easier in the big Gothic churches where the acoustics were so unfavorable. The only purpose of these pulpits was preaching; to use them for any other reason in worship would have appeared as nonsense and without any connection whatsoever with the worship of the early church. It is, therefore, a rather curious paradox that the pulpit of the medieval monks has become the proper place and the symbol of Protestant Reformed worship. Have some not gone so far in the Reformed church as to celebrate the liturgy of Holy Communion from the pulpit itself? It is somewhat as if one were to say grace as far as possible from the table served or set for the family meal. It is as if the Lord, while instituting the Holy Communion, had said grace from some remote corner of the upper room, from the level of some distant pulpit, rather than offering it at the table itself! The pulpit is not the place of of prayer or sacrament. The pulpit as such is only a speaker's rostrum, similar to those found in a large public room or university auditorium. Obviously it differs from it in that the words declared from it are religious and biblical, but it is not any less the appropriate place for discourse delivered to the public. The prayer, however, is not a discourse one pronounces from an elevated place to a crowd. When the officiant presents the prayer to God, he does so as a spokesman of the gathered congregation of which he, too, is a

---

[1] Of all the various church confessions and denominations, only the Reformed (Calvinistic-Zwinglian) has acquired the habit of celebrating the whole of the divine service from the height of the pulpit—in contradiction to Calvin's way of doing it. Most of the Reformed people (chiefly the ministers) have not taken the trouble to visit the worship of churches other than their own and have not been able, therefore, to experience the value and importance of the celebration of the liturgy near the holy table. Lacking such a point of comparison, they do not feel that there is anything theologically wrong in the tradition (very human and very narrowly confessional) of the worship being led entirely from the pulpit. As it has been said in good humor, the officiant is fixed there as rigidly as an egg in its holder.

member. Though ordained to a particular order or mission he has, for this action, to remain, in a certain sense, among the ranks, on the audience level of the church or of the congregation for whom he speaks.[2] Prayer offered from the pulpit separates, and indeed, isolates the officiant from the congregation; and, as he presents to God the prayer of them all, his place is down there at the level of the faithful near the table that witnesses to the presence of the Lord in the midst of his own and to the sacrifice in the name of which we may and dare to pray and offer also our sacrifice of praise and thanksgiving.[3] This location of the officiant illustrates the ascending movement of the dialogue of worship between men and God. When the officiant speaks in the name of the Lord while reading or preaching His word, his proper place is above the congregation. At that moment, he expresses himself as the proxy of Christ, as a minister vested with apostolic authority. He steps up to the pulpit to proclaim and teach. The pulpit symbolizes and gives place to the descending movement of the worship dialogue; from above the Lord addresses himself and speaks to his people below.[4]

The exclusive and utter domination by the pulpit in Reformed worship is a characteristic sign of the usurpation

[2] Cf. André Schlemmer, *op. cit.*, pp. 57-58.

[3] Cf. Robert Will, *op. cit.*, II: "The Protestant altar preserves its sacrificial significance. It is there that the community, through the office of the liturgist, presents to God the sacrifice of its praise and prayers. It is there it offers itself to God. The Protestant altar tends to call forth an atmosphere of refined spirituality" (p. 543). "The altar will be the focal point where the perfume of the prayers will rise to the Eternal. This symbolism, which is perfectly admissible, does not endow the altar with an intrinsic holiness, nor does it exclude prayer from the high level of the pulpit, if liturgical needs require it" (p. 336).

[4] Cf. the witness of a student who was present at an evangelical service of worship in Strasbourg in 1545: "The minister kneels before a table made of wood in the sense of an altar, which is not adorned except when one celebrates the Holy Communion of our Lord Jesus Christ, which is celebrated fortnightly... The said altar is placed nearly in the middle of the church where the minister is ... facing towards the people and offering the prayers for the people in the mother tongue, loud and clear, so that everyone hears it; when the prayer is finished, he goes up to the pulpit and gives the sermon." Quoted by G. van der Leeuw, *Liturgiek* (Gronigen: Callenbach, 1940), p. 237. In the beginning of the eighteenth century, Ostervald saw in Zurich the reading of the Bible done below, from the choir entrance, and not from the pulpit. J. J. von Allmen, *L'Eglise et ses fonctions d'après Jean-Frédéric Ostervald* (Neuchâtel-Paris: Delachaux et Niestlè, 1948), p. 87. In Neuchâtel, too, he would have wanted "different places for the preaching and for the celebration of worship"; in other words, that one would celebrate "the liturgies, as it is done throughout the whole of German Switzerland, in the place where the sacraments are administered, at the entrance of the choir." *Ibid.*, p. 38.

of the whole service by preaching. It is a striking mark of the *Predigtgottesdienst* in that the manner and style of the prayers, too, are often sermonic. The liturgy at the holy table and the preaching from the pulpit is, therefore, the proper principle of the "separation of the powers," so to speak, and which ought to govern the pattern of the worship. In Reformed churches built recently among us the elevated pulpit has been relinquished fortunately in favor of the *ambon* of the early church. It is from this *ambon* that the reading of the biblical pericopes must be done by different members of the congregation designated for this purpose and the preaching done by the minister.

What position ought the officiants take in relation to the holy table or altar of the Lord? During the first centuries the celebrant of the eucharist stood behind the table, facing the congregation; this is the normal position of the one who presides at a family meal. In the post-Nicene churches and basilicas the bishop, at the moment of offering the eucharistic prayer, rose from his *cathedra* placed at the back of the apse, and advanced several steps towards the table. From this comes the name or term *basilica position* given to this stance of facing the congregation which is the rule in the Reformed churches. But the early Christians continued under the influence of the Jewish custom of praying facing Jerusalem, even if they were reacting against Judaism. They, too, believed in a general way that the glorious Christ would come from the East (Matt. 24:27), and they turned almost instinctively in this direction while appealing for his return. Moreover, they lived within the orbit of Eastern religions which required their subjects to turn toward the rising sun for prayer. Out of these diversified factors combined was born the custom, already certified to in the second century by Pastor Hermas, Tertullian, Clement of Alexandria, and the apocryphal *Acta Pauli*, to pray towards the East.[5] When the church was able to build freely its places of worship, they were set towards the East, that is, the apse and the table

[5] On the question of praying towards the East, the classic monograph is by F. J. Dölger, *Sol Salutis, Gebet and Gesang im Christlichen Altertum, mit besonderes Rücksicht auf die Ostung im Gebet und Liturgie* (Münster: Aschendoffsche Verl., 1925), especially Chaps. 1, 4, and 9.

were put at the East side. In this way the congregation was turned towards the East for prayer. But the celebrant was the single exception; from behind the table his back was turned to the East. This seemed an anomaly, so the celebrant soon came to the front of the table in order to pray facing the East and therefore his back was turned to the people. This is how the *East position* took the place of the *basilica position*. It has found favor in the West in the development of private daily Masses without lay assistance; it is clear that a single officiant with one server would prefer to face the altar rather than an empty nave. The East position has become rooted in the Roman and Eastern churches. In the Reformation it has been retained in Lutheran churches. It was reintroduced in most Anglican churches in the nineteenth century through the Oxford Movement. This position does not conform to ancient usage and cannot be considered in a church founded essentially on the scripture and which wants to re-think liturgical questions in the light of the results of modern historical research. Moreover, it is significant that one of the objectives of the actual liturgical movement within the Roman church is the return to the basilica position, which is officially restored by the liturgical decrees of Vatican II. It is interesting that in Rome itself this old position has survived paradoxically unto our day in St. Peter's, St. John Lateran, and generally in the Roman basilicas for papal Masses. This position of the officiant behind the holy table means that the Lord is in the midst of his own and he is *surrounded* by the family as his guests; whereas the celebrant who turns his back to the congregation creates in a sense a screen between God and his people, between the congregation and the sacrament.

The East position, however, has in its favor the fine symbolism of the rising Sun which has come to visit us and to show us light in our misery. And above all it safeguards a certain element of truth none of us can afford to neglect: that the officiant is before the Lord in the same sense as the lowliest of the faithful. Officiant and congregation, appearing equally before one another, gaze together at the same divine Object which transcends both of them in common: the Lord and

Savior of all, both churchmen and laymen. The celebrant is truly the shepherd who walks ahead of his flock in order to lead them to the living God.[6] Consequently, when the matter of the eucharistic liturgy is put aside, the officiant must not pray facing the congregation, for by so doing he forms a screen between the congregation and its Lord. By his being turned in another direction from that of the congregation, he appears in a sense to be apart from them and to make a show of himself. His personality is put into bold relief and is therefore unduly conspicuous when it should be more reserved. In praying while facing the hearers the officiant gives the impression (which is often accentuated by the bad style of extempore prayers) that prayer is a sort of conversation with the public and not a request addressed to God. Facing the congregation, whether it be from the high pulpit or from before the holy table, the officiant makes himself the focus of every gaze and attention. And if, apart from the eucharistic celebration, he takes his place behind the table, he gives somewhat the impression of a storekeeper behind his counter, if one may say so.

There is one intermediate solution left which appears in the Anglican worship: the *side position*. The officiant stands aside from the table in profile towards the congregation, not turning his back, therefore, either to the table or congregation; he creates then no screen; he removes himself in a sense from before the Lord and the symbols of his presence: the altar, the Bible, and the cross. The accent is put, therefore, upon the objectivity of the divine presence, while safeguarding the legitimate aspect of the basilica position: the Lord's presence in the midst of the family of believers. The propriety or rightness of the side position is borne out clearly in the normal cases when the officiant offers on his knees, with the congregation, the prayers of humiliation and supplication; one can not conceive of an officiant kneeling upon a *prie-dieu* while facing the congregation; and the Reformed would not want it either, kneeling against the holy table, with the back turned towards the faithful. (This is recommended, however, by

---

[6] Cf. Robert Will, *op. cit.*, II, pp. 440-441; and Oscar J. Mehl, *Das liturgische Verhalten*, (Göttingen: Vanderhoek & Ruprecht, 1927), pp. 50-53, tries a justification, however debatable, of the East prayer which is used in most Lutheran churches.

Max Thurian, *op. cit.*, p. 95). It is necessary then that the kneeling chair be placed sideways to the table and the officiant appear there in profile. The same conclusion is true for prayer while standing. The prayer, while facing, has a place only in a limited, though not solemn, gathering, where they may be grouped as if in a family—in the mood of a prayer meeting.

In conclusion, the East position is to be discarded; the basilica position suggests itself for the celebration of the eucharist; and the side position for all other liturgical prayers. In a service without communion the rule to be observed is simple: for everything addressed to the congregation (Introit, words of grace and absolution, reading the Bible pericopes, benediction), the officiant faces the congregation; for everything addressed to God (prayer, hymns), he stands in profile in relation to the congregation. During the singing of the congregation, in which all normally join, the officiant and his helpers should stand in the side position, for the principal reason that the singing is really a prayer; and for the following practical reason: the officiant who is singing face to face with the congregation is tempted to look at them and to take this opportunity to check the members of the congregation present or absent from the worship, instead of really praying the words he is singing; and while singing, he may, by involuntary and unconscious mimicry which every singer has, become a subject of distraction or amusement for the faithful. Here, too, he must avoid creating a screen.

For the assistants of the principal celebrant: the readers, collectors, and so forth, *side* seats must be put in the choir of the church. In no case should the officiants be seated facing the congregation, for the faithful do not come to worship to be faced with a gallery of distracting faces, but to contemplate and listen to God.

13

Liturgical Vestments and Colors

Should the officiants in Christian worship wear special vestments in exercising their ministry or not? There is no single answer to this question which belongs really to the realm of *adiaphora*, i.e., those incidental things in which the matter of eternal salvation is not involved; it is merely a question of propriety or impropriety. Actually, while the priests of the old covenant wore liturgical dress described at length in Chapter 28 of the book of Exodus, the apostles and all of the bishops and presbyters of the first six centuries, on the other hand, officiated at the Lord's table without liturgical vestments at all. In the ante-Nicene church, Christian worship as a rule was private and conducted in homes without any ceremonial. When worship became public in the basilicas in the Constantinian era, at first religious clothing was used that bore no necessary distinction from civil or secular dress. The celebrants wore the usual vestments of their period and environment, whether Jewish or Greco-Roman.

In the third century, however, the bishop of Rome was already directing his presbyters not to wear for every day purposes the vestments reserved for the celebration of worship. It can be inferred then from this information that already the custom had been established of dressing for worship in particularly well-cared-for samples of traditional clothing. In the following century, Constantine gave the church in Jerusalem a sacred vestment (ἱερὰν στολήν), woven of gold which the bishop had to wear for the baptismal liturgy of the Easter vigil. At the end of the same century, there was the question in the *Apostolic Constitutions* of the splendid vestments (λαμπρὰ ἐσθής) which clothed the bishop for the eucharistic celebration. In neither case was the handsome vestment essentially different from the ordinary style of clothing of the period. But the time came when styles changed considerably under the influence of the new people who had broken through the boundaries of the Roman world, while the ecclesiastics continued the ancient modes. Eventually the difference was so great that the clothing of the officiants at worship no longer appeared as outmoded forms of secular clothing but as a distinctive and special mark of the clergy for liturgical acts, and one strove to justify it by more or less pertinent symbolic reasons.

From the second century the old Roman toga was replaced little by little by a long vestment of white cloth with narrow sleeves called an *alba*. Over the *alba* was passed another vestment with short sleeves which covered three-fourths of the height of the individual: this was the *tunica*. Finally, on certain great occasions there was worn over the *alba* and the *tunica* a large round piece of cloth with an opening in the middle for the head and which fell down on each side to the knees. It was called *paenula* or *casula* (meaning "little house"). With some modifications that occurred later, these secular vestments became the alb, tunic or dalmatic, and chasuble of church dress. A variant of the alb, influenced by the Nordic climate, resulted in the surplice. And the *pluviale*, a protective outer coat against bad weather became the cope. The only pieces of liturgical vestments which are an original creation of the church and serve as a distinctive sign for the celebrants of worship, are the *pallium*, a type of white cape marked with black crosses and covering the shoulders, and the *stola* (yoke), i.e., the stole, which is a narrow piece of silk hanging from the neck and falling in two parallel bands along the front of the body. The stole was worn by all the clergy, while the pallium was reserved for the more eminent members of the hierarchy.

At the Reformation three different attitudes or positions regarding liturgical vestments were discerned. There was the Puritan radicalism which demanded their suppression, purely and simply. This extremism, even in those cases where it could be imposed for a time, could not be maintained generally. There was the attitude of Luther which consisted of trying for pedagogical reasons to retain the liturgical vestments traditional in the church, while throwing out all legalism regarding their use: pure gospel and conscience were not involved in this question. Luther used great liberty when judging what vestments were useful but not indispensable. He approved of their continuation, but he made fun rather readily of those who attached any great importance to them. One day in October 1524, he preached in the morning in his monk's habit and in the afternoon in his academic doctoral robe. Also, a copper engraving of the period shows him officiating at the altar in a white liturgical vestment. In the third place, there was the attitude of Calvin and Zwingli who replaced the ancient vestments by the black academic robe; this is the "Geneva gown" which has prevailed in its use in the Reformed churches.[1]

Theoretically we could conceive in the church of today of an attitude analogous with that of the early church: the officiants could perform their liturgical acts in the ordinary clothing of our time. Nevertheless, anyone could ask himself if the style of men's clothing today is as much in harmony with religious fashions as those of ancient vestments. The various vestments that we can group under the generic term *robes* all reduce and eclipse in some sense the form of the body, which is the purpose of any vestment according to biblical teaching (Gen. 3:21). The trousers and jacket of today, on the other hand, emphasize and outline the human anatomy, and are thereby in the class or category of modern secularism which exalts physical attractiveness and favors *volens nolens* the breakdown of manners and morals. This phenomenon is somewhat parellel to

---

[1] P. Romane Musculus has stated regarding the history of the Geneva gown in the Reformed church that "at no time has the theological thinking of the church been exercised upon the liturgical vestments of its pastors," (*Verbum Caro*, No. 18, 1951, p. 95).

the use of secular melodies for the hymnody of the church; while certain songs about human love and various medieval hunting airs lent themselves with little difficulty to transformation into the singing of the sixteenth century church, yet it is obvious that such would not work to a similar extent with the large repertoire of music hall hits and jazz themes of our century. There are some deep and essential incompatibilities which belong to the nature of these elements whenever they are presented.

We must also take into account that clothing must correspond in some sense with the circumstances and function of the individual who wears it. Clothing varies according to sex, age, profession, and different circumstances of life, ordinary or unusual, happy or unhappy. It is natural, therefore, that the man who officiates in the worship of the church be clothed in a manner corresponding to the task assigned to him and expressing visibly what he does. Moreover, whoever leads in the act of worship does not perform as a private party but as a minister of the church; he is the representative of the community and the spokesman of the Lord. Hence, an especially prescribed vestment, a sort of ecclesiastical "uniform," is useful for reminding both the faithful and himself that in this act he is not Mr. So-and-So, but a minister of the church in the midst of a multitude of others. What was not any less indispensable in ancient times, when the sense of community and of the objectivity of cultic action prevailed, has become in our time a very useful aid, and indeed truly necessary, since individualism and subjectivity have become so deeply rooted in the piety of the Reformed churches. In addition, as Robert Will has said, "The vestment exercises a stimulating effect not only on those who see it worn but also on him who wears it. Clothes carry the man; they determine his attitudes and movements; religious dress discourages all extravagant movements. [2]

If anyone declines liturgical vestments on mere principle, consistency would require that one officiate in the customary business suit, and when weather permits, the light sport clothes which are so widely worn in our time. The black frock coat, the morning jacket, the wing collar and the white tie are

[2] *Op. cit.*, II, pp. 331-332.

a denial, in principle, of the usual clothing, and a survival of the nineteenth century just as much as a robe, a white surplice, or chasuble in the Middle Ages was a survival of antiquity. If, on the other hand, we grant the possibility of liturgical vestments, then it is necessary to ask the question afresh—what is the most adequate form for evangelical worship?—just as we have to inquire again in our time about all the theological, ecclesiological, and liturgical problems, as well as those of religious architecture. In such a widespread review, everything must be kept in perspective.

Is the use of black robes in the Reformed churches justified? In the sixteenth century it was the robe worn by doctors and professors, not only while lecturing, but when appearing in public as well. In our time, in many countries, it is still worn by professors, but also and particularly by judges and lawyers in the courts, and even by schoolboys and students during graduation ceremonies at schools and universities. The black robe is worn also by rabbis. It is not a garment or vestment used exclusively in Christian worship. In fact, its origin is associated more precisely with the all too didactic character of Reformed worship which the whole effort of a third of a century of liturgical movement has tried to rectify. If one adheres to the primacy of the moral law which has marked the Reformed confession from its origin, if one wants the essential element in worship to be didactic or the paranetic sermon patterned after that of the synagogue, and if one sees in the Sacrament of the Lord's Supper only an austere, and indeed, mournful commemoration of the death of Christ, then undoubtedly the black robe is still legitimate; it expresses visibly the essence of the worship. But if worship be an encounter with the God of love who receives us into the new covenant of grace; if the word he speaks to us is not entirely law and judgment, but the good news of free salvation in Christ; if instruction is subordinated to adoration; and if the celebration of the sacrament signifies thanksgiving, praise and joy in the presence of the victorious and risen Christ who is to come again, why is the black robe warranted? Have not the representatives of the new covenant, the witnesses to the good news, something better to put on as a more distinctive sign than the robe of judicial authorities, or of professors of secular learning, or of the representatives of the ancient people of God in mourning for their messianic hopes?[3] There is not a single reference to black robes in the Bible, whereas white robes and vestments are mentioned many times, either actually or symbolically.

Indeed, if there is one color that suggests itself as an adequate expression of the gospel and the evangelical divine service, certainly it is white. In the Bible white is the divine color *par excellence* because it symbolizes the holiness and perfection of God (Ps. 104:2; Dan. 7:9; Rev. 1:14; 19:11; 20:11). In the New Testament white plays a special role: the transfigured Christ appeared in a white vestment that was like snow or light, a glistening whiteness (Matt. 17:2; Mark 9:3; Luke 9:29). Herod, forcing Jesus to be clothed in a white tunic in derision (Luke 23:11), expressed unconsciously a great truth regarding the person of our Lord, even as Caiaphas prophesied that one man must die for all the people (John 11:51-52); or Pilate ordering his soldiers to cover Jesus with a scarlet cloak, the royal color (Matt. 27:28). Herod did not know that Jesus Christ is "Light of Light, very God of very God" (The Nicene Creed), but the white tunic said it for him. The angels who announced the victory of the resurrection and the Lord's appearance are described as being vested in white (Matt. 28:3; Mark 16:5; Acts 1:10). The ransomed who participate in the victory of Christ, in his divine Sonship and in his priesthood, appear clothed in white in the Apocalypse (Rev. 4:4; 7:9, 13, 14). Thus, the most beautiful robe given to the prodigal son upon his return (Luke 15:22) and the wedding garment signifying the right to enter the hall of festivity (Matt. 22:11-12) are along the same line of imagery as the white vestment of the Apocalypse, which is the sign of divine salvation, and of the heavenly purity and of the victory of Christ and his own (Rev. 3:4-5 and 18; 19:8).

In the ante-Nicene church it was already the custom to clothe the newly baptized in white at the Easter vigil. They kept this white vestment until the Sunday after Easter, called precisely *in albis*, but understood also as *deponendis* because on

---

[3] Regarding the use of "preaching tabs," the residue of the ancient collar, there is no justification for their liturgical use except as one may wish to recall the two tables of the Law which leads us back to the old covenant.

that day the white vestment was taken off. The practice has been continued in our Reformed churches until today of clothing the young children in white for the ceremony of baptism. For confirmation young girls now wear a white veil, having used formerly a black veil and dress which no one would tolerate any longer. (In French-speaking Switzerland, and in France, incidentally, they no more endure the black covering, similar to that used upon a coffin, which "decorates" the table or baptistry in German-speaking Switzerland). But we continue the use of the black pastoral robe. Worse yet, our missionaries have transmitted the practice to the native clergy of the African churches. The tropical climate and the natural taste of the Africans for color make the transplanting of such a usage absurd; and even among us, it does not escape criticism. Is not this robe the clothing worn in the city by the medieval schoolmaster?

The Lutheran churches in Germany had retained almost everywhere the ancient vestments until the *Aufklärung* of the eighteenth century. Then they were dropped gradually under the influence of the rationalistic movement, except in Würtemberg and in Saxony. The Scandinavian Lutheran churches have remained faithful to the liturgical vestments, and even today their pastors officiate at the altar in a white surplice or chasuble. The Anglican church, after a temporary eclipse in the eighteenth century, has also retained the ancient vestments; the Anglo-Catholics use the chasuble while the middle-of-the-road or average Anglican prefers the *cappa*; the "Evangelicals" use the white surplice. Among the more "Protestant" Anglicans, no one officiates any longer in black robes. In the United States the Lutherans who had customarily used the black robe are giving it up more and more in favor of the alb or white surplice, and many Reformed congregations are adopting the same view. Some American liturgists of the Reformed tradition sanction the abandonment of the "Geneva gown" and a return to the surplice or white dalmatic. In more than one American Reformed church even the parochial choir members wear a robe in which white predominates. This is a sign of liturgical unity in the same collective priesthood of the "clergy" and the "laity."

Our Reformed churches in Europe can no longer ignore the question of liturgical vestments. Undoubtedly the issue is not a fundamental one. It is not an *articulum stantis aut cadentis Ecclesiae*, and many religious problems are more essential and urgent. However, if worship is the place of assembling and of capturing the conscience of the church, nothing that contributes to the expression of its true nature can be treated with indifference. The Geneva gown, "this anti-liturgical, secular vestment, which appears in the color of the shades of darkness, this clothing which is comparable to the sack cloth and ashes of mourning in the old covenant, is the negation of the right of the church to rejoice and be consoled in the presence of the heavenly Bridegroom. Perhaps for the synagogue, in its tribulation, to wear such a vestment would be the normal thing. But in modern Protestantism it is a depressing sign that we are not more aware of the nuptial joy of the eucharist and that we do not believe in the victorious struggle Christ led against the world."[4]

We grant that the sobriety of the worship forms which are characteristic of the Reformed tradition would ill fit any recovery of the complicated and richly ornamented vestments of Catholic tradition, either Eastern or Western. It should be appropriate then to focus upon a simple robe in which white clearly predominates over the black, or to put over the black robe a white surplice which leaves visible only the collar and lower folds of the same robe.[5] An initial step, and an urgent one, would consist in abandoning without regret the insignificant rabat and replacing it with a white stole, symbolic of the easy yoke and light burden of Jesus Christ. Indeed, to be-

---

[4] Herbert Goltzen, *Die Stimme des Geopferten*, (Kassel: Stauda, 1949), p. 21.

[5] Cf. P. R. Musculus, "Le Vêtement liturgique dan l'Eglise réformée," (*Verbum Caro*, n. 20, 1951): "It is no longer admissible that one be treated as a Catholic sympathizer each time one speaks of adding a little white to all our black (p. 179) . . . Why, upon the black men that we are, should there not be thrown like a promise, a sign of our hope that is sure, the whiteness of fine linen?" (p. 181). The reference is to Rev. 19:8. In hospitals, medical and sanitary personnel are clothed in white, and no doubt the morale of the patients is affected positively by it. A book on this subject has been entitled *Les Hommes en Blanc*, by André Soubiran, (Paris: Didier, 1947). Why must we speak necessarily of *men in black*, when it involves those who preach the good news of salvation and offer to believers, at the holy table, the means to perfect joy in Christ? Must this nonsense go on forever in our churches? There is, moreover, a book entitled *Les Hommes en Noir*, by René Vigo, (Paris: Segep, 1953), but it deals with the world of judges and lawyers, i.e., the professional people of the law courts!

gin with, this restoration of white could be limited to the service of the Lord's Supper, in order to emphasize the element of eschatological joy so predominant in the beginning. As a book of liturgical orders of the German Reformation put it: "The holy angels were clothed in white to perform their duties. We also, in the future, will want to celebrate the joyous banquet of the Lord's Supper in white vestments, according to the custom."[6]

A question connected with that of liturgical vestments is that of liturgical colors.[7] It is well known and understood that the use of different colored ornaments prescribed according to the various seasons and festivals of the church year did not come early. Neither were organs, harmoniums, and other musical instruments of early usage in worship, which is not a justifiable reason for throwing them out. Liturgical colors are the creation of the Middle Ages, a period much disposed to symbolism in general, and particularly to colors. The Eastern church has not followed this development; even today it still has no official rule on this subject and the officiants choose according to their inclination and the circumstances between whatever diversely colored and ornate liturgical vestments are at their disposal. We can maintain that this differentiation of colors which has been imposed upon the Western church is a normal development from the very early adoption of white and that it is consistent with the general facts of biblical symbolism. In the Old Testament, colors had their significance in the clothing of the high priest and the furnishing of the holy place. Three colors are always closely associated by their shades with the tabernacle and the costume of the priest: azure blue, scarlet purple, and crimson. The dominant color of the sacerdotal vestments is blue; gold also plays its role in the accessory ornaments (Exod. 26:1, 4, 31, 36; 28:6, 8, 15, 28, 31, 33; 39:1-5, 8, 22-25, 29; Num. 4, *passim*).

Color is a teacher through sight, and it creates moods. We misunderstand human nature and the place of perception in our inner life when we downgrade this psychological factor in the worship life of the church. This is especially true in an age

[6] *Liegnitzer Kirchenordnung*, 1535.

[7] See Robert Will, *op. cit.*, II, pp. 489-490; Max Thurian, *op. cit.*, pp. 103-104.

when the masses are notoriously more sensitive to visual than to auditory impressions. We find evidence for such a conclusion in education, entertainment, advertising, and so forth. Why should the Reformed church alone deprive itself of these possibilities?[8] On Easter morning when the church appears at first sight to be decorated in white, in contrast to the violet of the preceding Sundays, each person will realize immediately that a new and joyful word is to be proclaimed and will feel carried away by the triumphant gladness of the resurrection.

The Roman church, after some tentative steps, codified the division of liturgical colors among the different seasons of the church year. It has used four basic colors—white, green, red, and violet: white for the joyous and glorious feasts of Christ, Mary, and the saints; green for the periods after Epiphany and after Pentecost; violet for Advent, Lent, and Passiontide; red for Pentecost and the anniversaries of the martyrs. Gold occasionally completes or replaces white. Black is used for funeral services. On the whole, this codification is understandable and acceptable. However, it does not seem entirely convincing; one can criticize certainly the use of violet for Advent, for this season is essentially not of the same character as the seasons of Lent and Passiontide. Its dominant note is hope and not repentance, and it is green–the color of springtime–that is recognized as signifying hope. Moreover, we are disturbed that azure blue, fundamental to the worship symbolism of the old covenant, has not been retained in the canon of liturgical colors in the West. The Eastern church permits it in its ecclesiastical ornaments, and it is not unusual to see an Orthodox priest celebrate in a blue chasuble on Ascension Day, because blue—the color of the natural sky—is best able to symbolize the spiritual sky, the invisible world. To assign to red the role of recalling the blood of the martyrs, appears to us to stem from a crude realism rather than from discerning symbolism. At that rate, however, it would be necessary to use it for Good

---

[8] Why be shocked by persons of very limited intelligence or the simple-minded who leave Reformed worship because it is too cerebral and abstract, and end up by living with practically no religion at all? It is not the same with Roman Catholicism and Eastern Orthodoxy, in which the most limited persons intellectually can find strength for his religious needs in a more concrete form of worship which is more adequate for us as beings of flesh and senses.

Friday when the blood of Christ, which alone has redemptive value, flowed for our salvation. Red has hardly any value other than richly decorative, and if it is necessary to give it symbolic value, we would prefer to limit it to recalling the fire of the Holy Spirit. Taking these observations into account we propose the following canon of liturgical colors:

The four Sundays of Advent: green

From Christmas Eve to Epiphany: white or gold

From the first Sunday after Epiphany to Lent: red

Lent, Passiontide, Holy Week: violet

From Easter Eve to Sunday after Ascension: white or gold

From Pentecost Eve to end of Church Year: red

Trinity Sunday: white

Here red is seen less as the color of Pentecost than as an ornamental color intended for "neutral" periods of the Church Year, that is, those which do not have a well-defined character. From this point of view, blue could be used eventually in the place of red. Blue would recall the kingdom of heaven, to which the church is moving, and red the remembrance of the fire of love that embraces the whole church. Both are fitting for the long series of Sundays after Pentecost, which is properly the "season of the church," the time of pilgrimage of the church on its way into the Kingdom of God. Let us remember also that violet comes from deep purple, which in past times was the royal or imperial color; Christ was clothed in it for derision by the Roman soldiers who hailed him as King of the Jews; thus by transposition, violet in Passiontide signifies the King of kings humiliated and sacrificed.

The *antependia* of the altar, the pulpit, and lectern in liturgical colors are like "signs of the Son of Man" and contribute with their decorative value to make of the house of God the "lovely dwelling place" (Ps. 84:1) in which we can "behold the beauty of the Lord" (Ps. 27:4). The value of the liturgical colors is above all pedagogical and mystical, in order to lift us by visible signs to invisible realities, and to help us relive by faith the successive stages of God's saving work in the world through his Son, Jesus Christ.

14

Singing and Music in Worship

From apostolic times there has been singing in worship. Not only was the singing of biblical psalms picked up from the synagogue, but the new hymns, original compositions and creations of the new covenant, have been used.[1] A whole hymnological literature was brought into being during the first four centuries. From this abundant collection there remain only a few bits of things, because the church was obliged to place a curb upon it in reaction to the fantasies and heresies which marked many of these compositions. The *Phos hilaron* of the Eastern church, the *Gloria in excelsis* and the *Te Deum*, and the few hymns called Ambrosian of the Roman Office, are the only surviving ones still used from these numerous materials.[2] The music of these hymns was in recitative form, resembling the cantilena of the old Greek tragedies, or the monodic chant that followed the natural inflections of the

---

[1] See Eph. 5:19; Col. 3:16; I Cor. 14:26; James 5:13. The New Testament contains examples of these primitive hymns: Rev. 5, 7, 12, 15, 19, and the three hymns of the protogospel of Luke (Chaps. 1 and 2). See Max Thurian, *op. cit.*, pp. 52-54. It is the "new hymn" of the last days (Rev. 5:9 and 14:3; 15:3).

[2] Several well chosen examples may be found in Adalbert Hamman, *Prière des premiers chrétiens* (Paris: Fayard, 1952), Part II, Chaps. 1, 3.

spoken text.[3] The musical notation of the *Hymn of Oxyrhynchus*, found in 1922 during some excavations done in Egypt, gives a characteristic example of it. It was this kind of music that Pope Gregory the Great altered and codified in the sixth century and that has become what is called the Gregorian or plain chant. By its very nature this chant, which is of real musical and religious value and significance, could never be popular and hence became the business of specialized singers. Thus the Christian congregation was reduced to passivity. During the whole of the Middle Ages Christian people incapable of using Latin were unable to express their faith through singing.

At the Reformation, Luther, who was very musical, had his heart set upon giving to the faithful the opportunity of singing their faith. Inspired by the themes of the plain chant, he made of it a grave and rhythmic chant of the church, namely the chorale, which because of its simple melodic lines and rhythm enabled the congregation to participate. The Luther "chorales," with their substantial text and their burden of sound evangelical doctrine, multiplied between the sixteenth and eighteenth centuries. This type of sacred choral music may demand, and rightly so, to be recognized as the chant *par excellence* of the church founded on the gospel.[4]

We cannot say as much about the "Reformed" chant, Calvin having rejected all other musical texts except the paraphrases in verse of the biblical psalms of the Old Testament.[5] In spite of their indisputable musical value,[6] the Huguenot psalms, several of which are derived from medieval Gregorian melo-

---

[3] In the early church the chant was considered as a prophetic pneumatic phenomenon or element. "The chant of the church contains some indication of this pneumatic-prophetic elevation, a mark of this prophetic ecstasy which cannot be separated from the essence itself of the Ecclesia without observing the eschatological character of the church," *Leiturgia*, I, p. 324.

[4] Cf. Robert Will, *op. cit.*, I, pp. 283-307. "The chorale is particularly apt to create the feeling of collectivity and to constitute the *Corpus Christi* (p. 285) . . . The chorale forms, better perhaps than the Credo, a *church conscience*. The church finds there the basis of a spiritual unity, solid and wide. One could almost say that it is the chorale that created the Protestant congregation" (p. 302).

[5] On the question of the chant and music in the Reformed church, one might consult profitably the chapter *Psaumes et cantiques*, by Pierre Scherding, in *L'Esprit du Culte Protestant*, pp. 45-73.

[6] On the text and music of the psalms, see Joseph Ver, *La cantilène huguenote du XVI siècle*, (Réalville; Tarne-et-Garonne, 1918), and Charles Schneider, *Un problème actuel: La restauration du Psautier huguenot* (Neuchâtel-Paris: Delachaux et Niestlé, 1932). Cf. as well the fine analysis by Robert Will, *op. cit.*, II, pp. 148-149.

dies, can not presume to be *the* chant or song of the church, because they reflect only the word of the Old Covenant, and the good news of Christ, therefore, has remained silent in the song of the Reformed churches until the eighteenth century.[7] In this period, the few hymns by Benedictus Pictet based on the tunes of the psalms have given finally to French Calvinistic congregations the means, as yet abridged, of singing of Christ and his work at Christmas, Easter, Ascension, and Pentecost. The one-sided biblicism of Calvin has been shown to be as untenable in practice as it was false in theory; once the breach was made, Reformed worship opened itself widely for hymns. Unfortunately this happy change in attitude coincided with the worst period in the singing of the church. In fact the nineteenth century is marked by a disastrous corruption in the quality of its sacred music: the sweet sentimentality of the Anglo-Saxon revival tunes invaded the sanctuaries. For the grave music without sadness and the solemn tunes without pomposity of the chorales and the psalms were substituted sweet melopoeia unworthy of the glory of God.[8] The Sunday Schools also have contributed much, unfortunately, to this end by instilling within the heart of three or four generations the same commonplace hymns and cradle songs, thus smothering any proper understanding of church music, as well as simple good musical taste.[9] In the past forty years there has been a definite recovery, but there is a considerable distance

[7] "Calvin has reduced our Reformed churches, which were illuminated by the light of the Gospel and liberated—at least in principle—from the dominion of the Levitic Law, to sing as hymns only a version of the psalms of these same Levites." It is in these severe terms—he also speaks of "rigorous biblicism, dogmatic narrowness"— that Henri Vuilleumier, *op. cit.*, p. 331-333, evaluates Calvin's attitude as compared with Luther's. Let us remember, however, to the credit of Calvin and the first Reformed congregations, the singing of the Lord's Prayer, of the Apostles' Creed, and of the Ten Commandments, which has been entirely lost since then and for the return of which we wait impatiently in a future edition of the French-Swiss hymn book.

[8] In all this it had been forgotten that Calvin wrote: "Care must be taken always that the singing be neither light nor flighty, but that it have weight and majesty, as Augustine said, and that there is a great difference, therefore, between music made to be enjoyed by people at the table at home and the psalms sung in church, in the presence of God and his angels" (Epistle to All Christians and Lovers of the Word of God, 1543).

[9] "The spontaneity, frankness, and robustness of the Huguenot tunes have made way for the accents, sometimes soft or neatly choregraphic, of so many modern hymns." Cf. Charles Schneider, *L'évolution musicale de l'Église réformée de 1900 à nos jours.* (Neuchâtel-Paris: Delachaux et Niestlé, 1952), p. 31. Numerous apposite reflections on music in worship are to be found in this interesting work, although its materials could have been set in a more methodical format.

to go before the Reformed congregations in the French language are reeducated. The new hymn books in France and in French-speaking Switzerland, have incorporated much inferior material and have permitted too great a compromise with mediocre substance, frequently and clearly of bad taste. Faced with the corruption of the musical tastes of too many of the faithful, the task of the church is not to lower itself to this inferior level, but to make an effort to raise its members to a higher level in the field of hymnology as well as in that of Christian faith and life, and to reform gradually their musical sensibilities and tastes. Too many spiritual leaders follow the flock in this regard instead of leading it, often because they have never received sufficient musical instruction themselves, but chiefly because the teaching of sacred hymnology has not yet found its rightful place in many theological faculties.

The musical deficiencies of our French hymn books are aggravated by their basic textual inadequacies. Where the Lutheran and Anglican books are rich with a well-rounded biblical theology and contain a great number of christocentric hymns, our Reformed psalters are, comparatively speaking, marked with a certain undeniable poverty; and the hymns in adoration of Christ as Lord and Savior can be quickly counted. Popular evangelical hymns, inappropriate during the Sunday worship of any congregation, occupy a place out of all due proportion in these books. Just as some of the bad prayers of earlier Reformed liturgies are more properly sermons than real prayers, so are the bad hymns harangues addressed to the people who are absent or laborious appeals to sentimentality, rather than praise or requests to God and Christ.[10] Furthermore, the liturgical responses are still insufficient in number and offer very little melodic variety.

Generally speaking our church singing consists basically of Lutheran chorales, of those Huguenot psalms where the melody was capable of being assimilated by modern ears, and of a certain number of examples from the Anglican hymnology. (The quality of much Anglican hymnology is very uneven. Be-

---

[10] "The hymns that preach, teach, or engage in polemics, that is, that look to man rather than God . . . may by their evangelistic accents stimulate the will of the Christian, and even, indirectly, move his religious conscience; it is not less true that these hymns aim at other goals and purposes than those appropriate to prayer." Robert Will, *op. cit.*, I, p. 288.

sides the numerous hymns that have no musical value, there is a certain number of quite remarkable ones of a really distinctive character as compared with Lutheran chorales, and which could lend another complementary note to our worship). It is desirable also that the psalmody be restored to our Reformed worship, or the modulated recitative of texts in prose for such hymns as those of Zechariah, Mary and Simeon, the Beatitudes, and the *Te Deum*. It should not be permitted that such honorable biblical texts be sung only in verse form, which mutilates somewhat the inspired original simply for the sake of rhyme. Regarding the psalms it is difficult to formulate a precise statement for the present. French Christian vocabulary, Catholic as well as Protestant, is generally feeling its way. The traditional versified text and its frequently imperfect adaptation to the music provide no satisfaction anymore. The Dominican fathers in their *Bible de Jérusalem* have attempted a translation into prose which retains all the power and sharpness of the Hebrew original. The French priest Gelineau has composed a rather successful musical accompaniment for them which could become popular. Presently, however, we must continue to hope that eventually we shall have a metrical version of the psalms worthy of the biblical original and set to the beautiful Huguenot tunes, and also a text in prose that conforms to the euphonic demands of the French language and conducive to being sung.[11]

Congregational singing ought to be in unison. This is to conform to the Reformers' idea and the original practice of the Lutheran as well as Reformed churches. Singing in four voices or parts is justified only it if is prepared well in advance. The sporadic projection of an alto, tenor, or bass, from discrete individuals scattered throughout the congregation can only disturb and throw the whole group off pitch.[12]

[11] Cf. André Schlemmer, *op. cit.*, Appendix III, pp. 68-70; also pp. 20-22.

[12] "In French Switzerland, one presumes that the people are capable of singing in four parts without previous practice. Let us suppose our musical acumen permits such boldness; it would be essential that the right proportion of voices be guaranteed, in order to secure the proper effect . . . The first reform to introduce into the singing of the faithful is singing in union. This may seem to be a retreat, but it would be progress," Gustave Doret, *Musique et Musiciens* (Paris: Fischbacker, 1919). Pierre Pidoux writes accordingly of ''exercises in sight reading which too many engage in Sunday after Sunday on the pretense of singing in four parts the praise of God,'' *Le Culte Protestant et La Musique*, in *Revue de Théologie et de Philosophie*, Lausanne, No. 130, 1944.

We have to leave to the organ the task of rendering the melody harmoniously or to the choir of the church to sing a piece of music in four parts which they have prepared carefully. The faithful individual who really wants to pray his chant can do so only while keeping the melody that is traditionally associated with the text; whereas any attempt, either well or badly or in an improvised manner, to sing in a voice part can only distract this amateur singer of the text, which is, however, the essential matter. For it is upon this that one has to focus steadily: the music in worship is only the servant of prayer. Musical art in the church is subordinated definitely to the word and glory of God. It does not figure in the divine service autonomously or as an end in itself.

This is a matter no one should forget regarding the organ, the instrument specifically for worship, but which is apt to occupy an overwhelming place and to foster the priority of aesthetical factors rather than those elements that are more properly spiritual. Let us remember that the Eastern church has never permitted instrumental music in its worship; its thought is that only the human voice, the expression of a conscious personality, may celebrate divine praise. Zwingli and Calvin adopted the same radical position regarding organs; it was only by the eighteenth century that the Reformed churches returned to a less inflexible attitude and that the organ was reintroduced into worship.[13] Certainly we would declare today that this instrument has a justifiable right to be in our churches, but on the condition that the organist remembers that its function in worship is not to give a concert or to display his own professional talent, but to sustain the singing of the congregation and to aid in silent prayer and meditation. Long preludes which force the officiant to remain at a standstill and make the beginning of the service late, or the endless interludes which interrupt the progress of the liturgy, must be avoided. Normally preludes ought to be a paraphrase of the proper chorale or psalm of that Sunday

[13] Earlier, that is in the beginning of the seventeenth century, trumpets began to be used to sustain the singing of the psalms. The first appeared in the Collégiale in Berne. Scripture, Old Testament (Num. 10:1; II Chron. 29:26-28; Ps. 98:6; 150:3) as well as New Testament (Rev. 8:2), justified this innovation. In certain ceremonies of solemn and triumphal character, it is quite proper and acceptable to use trumpets to produce a striking effect. Cf. Henri Vulleumier, *op. cit.*, II, pp. 342-343.

of the church year[14] and the interludes must be simple phrases at the conclusion of a reading or a prayer. Every prelude, as short as it may be, is to be avoided as introducing a response; the organ must confine itself to giving only the initial note, and then the congregation has to come in immediately. Organ playing *pianissimo* during the Lord's Prayer or the creed, very much a fashion at the beginning of the century, ought to be rejected in principle as an expression of an aestheticism that favors sentimentality. We may tolerate it on occasion or provisionally, but only as a temporary substitute for the collective recitation by the congregation and as a preparatory stage to it.

The church or parish choir does not displace the congregation and sing the liturgy in its stead. If it must assume such a role, it should be only temporarily; that is, until the congregation is sufficiently educated liturgically to sing the responses itself and until our hymnbooks are complete in this regard. The function of the choir is to lead and sustain the congregation and to perform the sacred masterpieces that are too difficult for the congregation: motets, cantatas, and so forth, which complete and comment upon the message of the word.[15]

The place of the parish choir, or *sacred chant*, is at the organ loft or gallery, therefore, above and behind the congregation, in order not to be visible to them.[16] For the choristers are not artists or amateurs coming to present themselves before the public or audience on the occasion of worship. Their task is not to "embellish" worship by some concert piece that figures as *hors d'oeuvre*. We ought to reject severely and without reservation the still too widespread custom in our churches of

---

[14] "At any rate this organ prelude speaks a clear word only to those who are acquainted with the chorale . . . But when the chorale is known, it is quickly recognized in the form of organ music. Then it can become the collective prayer of the congregation, a veritable act of worship," Pierre Pidoux, *op. cit.*

[15] "It is necessary that the artistic style of the choir does not surpass the level of the average among the assistants and that the singers are aware of the fact that they are not enrolled for the aesthetic enjoyment of the minority, but for reciprocal and collective upbuilding," Robert Will, *op. cit.*, I, p. 304.

[16] In Anglican worship, and in a general way in the Anglo-Saxon denominations, the singers are placed in the choir on either side of the altar, in side benches, in two equal groups that face each other and are seen in profile by the congregation. They sing the liturgy from their place, without direction, led only by the organ. They wear mostly a uniform liturgical dress, gown or robe. In principle there would be no opposition to adopting this practice in the continental Reformed churches.

choirs who, at the announcement of the officiant, leave their place in the nave and gather together at the foot of the pulpit or in front of the holy table, facing the congregation as if it were an audience and under the leadership of a director who is standing on a tripod and swinging a baton. When the piece is performed the singers go back to their seats with the inevitable hurly-burly, while the minister, from his high pulpit, offers thanks effusively. It is inconceivable that the ridiculous character of this moving around should escape the attention of the majority of the parishioners, even though they be blind to this deplorable confusion between worship and concert or social production. Let us insist upon the fact that the singers in the parish choir are among the leaders of the act of worship and subject as the other officiants to the rules of the whole liturgical function. In the place assigned to them in the choir loft they will sing spontaneously and without announcement or introduction the complete texts inserted in the order of worship.[17]

On the other hand we can only lament the divorce that exists in our churches between worship, properly called, and the art of sacred music. On one side, acts of worship are celebrated with great poverty of expression, in which the word and the words alone have the right of way, with several hymns rendered in a mediocre way (in both senses of the word) by the congregation. On the other side sacred concerts are organized, with occasionally paid admissions, in which Passion music, cantatas, and motets are sung as artistic productions in churches which have become for the occasion commercial concert halls; it is only just that applause for such performers has never become a fashion. Will there come a time when the idea will be general among responsible people that these masterpieces by Schutz, Bach, Handel, Haydn, and other great composers, written mostly for worship and sung at the time within the context of Lutheran worship, should be again what they were in other days? Without a doubt it is improper to trans-

---

[17] "This choir will not be heard as one listens to the performances of a music group which are strange to the worship life of the church; it will pray its chant and the congregation will pray it . . . The church choir is part of the congregation in worship and not an isolated society. It should be in its place by right every Sunday and officiate as leader, indeed as liturgist, for the singing congregation," Pierre Pidoux, *op. cit.*

form Sunday worship into a concert as had become sometimes an abusive practice in German Lutheranism of the eighteenth century. However good the preparation and performance may be sometimes, a monumental presentation is frequently the exception. They could take place, however, within the context of a liturgical evening service, under certain special circumstances. At least we might be able to retrieve the organic unity of the worship of the Lord and of sacred music composed to the glory of this same Lord.[18]

Let us conclude with Calvin: "Certainly if the singing is adapted to the solemnity that is appropriate in the presence of God and his angels, it is a beautiful means of giving grace and dignity to the praise of God and it is a good way to incite their hearts and enflame them with greater ardor to pray. But care must be taken always lest the ear pays more attention to the harmony of the singing than the spirit for the real meaning of the words." And Alexander Vinet has said, "Adoration is a state of soul that only singing can express."[19]

---

[18] This case put apart, it has to be avoided as much as possible that soloists permit themselves to be heard above others during worship. The personal factor and individual vanity should not occupy a disproportionate place.

[19] *Op. cit.*, p. 185.

Part Three

Ecclesiastical Order

The religious services of the Christian churches of all denominations ought to be classified into two categories of distinctly historical origin: the dominical *service* of word and sacrament; and the daily *office* of praise and prayer concentrated upon the psalms.[1]

The first is the normal service of the people of the church, the official parish worship, both under its integral form, as in all the churches of the "Catholic" type, and under its truncated form, reduced to the word only, as the case often is still in churches of the "Protestant" type. The other type of worship, the divine office, has not been and still is not practiced regularly and integrally among religious congregations. Church people are involved in it merely partially and occasionally. For instance, the more pious Roman Catholics attend Sunday Vespers or Compline in addition to the Mass. Frequently an important exception must be noted: in Anglicanism, up to the doctrinal and sacramental renewal of the Oxford Movement of the eighteenth century, the morning office (Morning Prayer or Matins) constituted the normal parish worship on Sunday morning. It is still thus, to a certain degree, in Anglican parishes, especially of the evangelical or *Low Church* persuasion, but it is fading away.

[1] Cf. Max Thurian, *op. cit.*, p. 140: "For clarity in liturgical vocabulary, we distinguish the various cultic acts according to two expressions—services and offices."

15

The Normal
Sunday Morning Service

The Lord's Day service of word and sacrament is the result of a fusion between the new act, specifically Christian, of the breaking of bread, and the service of expository reading of the Holy Scriptures which originated in the synagogue. When the disciples came together after the Master had left, their purpose was to continue and fulfill in his memory the action of the upper room called *the breaking of bread*. For the rest of the time they continued to attend the services of the synagogue and the temple.[1] The relentless hostility which resulted from the Jews and the complete rupture between the synagogue and the church motivated the Christians to constitute a service of reading and prayer peculiar to themselves which was called *synaxis*. So the ante-Nicene Church had two different types of service in the beginning: the breaking of bread, afterwards called the *eucharist*, which was a continuation of the last meal of Jesus with his disciples; and the *synaxis*, which was inspired by the worship of the synagogue and consisted of readings from the Holy Scriptures, a homily and prayers. Occasionally these two services were joined one to the other. Their fusion, which occurred more and more by the beginning of the second

[1] See Acts 2:46; 3:1; 9:20; 13:5; 14:1; 17:1-3; 18:4, 26.

century, became the general rule as late as the fifth century. The combined word and sacrament which resulted from this union has maintained, nevertheless, the distinction between its component parts.[2] In the pre-Constantinian period this differentiation was necessitated by the ecclesiastical discipline, by virtue of the fact that the non-Christians, the catechumens or candidates for baptism, and the penitents were excluded from all participation, even passive, in the sacramental act. Authorized to attend only the service of the word, they were dismissed as soon as the first part of the service was over. Only the baptized, the full members of the body of Christ and the church community, were allowed to participate in the eucharistic celebration. In the West this was called *missa fidelium*, mass of the faithful, whereas the first part of the service was named *missa catechumenorum*, mass of the catechumens. With the Roman Catholics of today we would say Mass and Fore-Mass whereas with the Anglicans we speak of Communion and Ante-Communion. But, whether these two sections were joined or not, it mattered not in the early Church because the eucharistic sacrament was celebrated every Sunday.[3]

Actually, in Reformed churches the Holy Communion is in most cases only the exceptional appendix to what is called "ordinary" worship; that is, the service of the word in which preaching has the central place. The error in this Reformed custom is not so much in splitting the service into two quasi-independent parts as it is the downgrading of the second section—the sacrament—to the rank of an occasional appendix to the first—the word—considered as normally complete and sufficient. This is a lamentable rejection of the apostolic custom of celebrating Holy Communion every Lord's Day, a practice which no church of the "Catholic" type has ever abandoned. How could this deviation have occurred with the Reformed? It is after all only the result of a very old Catholic fault: passive attendance at eucharistic worship without taking communion. This withdrawal from communion dates back very early from the post-Nicene period. It comes from a false

[2] For these historical questions, see Henri Chirat, *L'assemblée Chrétienne à l'Âge Apostolique* (Paris: Editions du Cerf, 1949), chaps. 2 and 4; Max Thurian, *op. cit.*, pp. 42-45.

[3] See André Schlemmer, *op. cit.*, pp. 33-38.

conception of the sacrament as a fearful thing that inspired holy terror. Also, it was the result of admission to the Mass of non-Christians in the church. After all, in the Middle Ages one received communion only once a year, at Easter. It is only reasonable then that the Reformers wanted to restore the authentic idea and integral practice of the sacrament. They devoted themselves to reintroducing the communion with the two elements available for all present in the act of worship. But it was not possible to uproot at once a habit of almost one thousand years. Indeed, for lack of communicants the weekly celebration of the Holy Communion could not be re-established. And since the Reformers refused to continue the erroneous system of the liturgical Mass-drama, at which the faithful were present as passive spectators without receiving communion, the result was an extreme dilution of the celebration of the sacrament.[4] In Geneva, Calvin had to renounce the weekly communion before the power of a secular atavism which found its expression in the opposition of these civil authorities. "It would be very desirable," the Reformer writes, "that the communion of the holy table should be at least the custom every Sunday . . . While waiting until the people who are still weak to become more mature, let the Holy Communion be customary once a month."[5] He could not obtain, however, even this monthly celebration and had to accept the practice of communion three times a year, at Christmas, Easter, and Pentecost. In Geneva and Neuchâtel they began rather early a fourth communion on the first Sunday in September. But Calvin always reproached himself for having capitulated to the obstinate incomprehension of his parishioners: "Certainly this custom which commands our taking communion once a year is certainly an invention of the devil . . . The communion of the Lord should be offered at least once a week to the congregation of Christians.[6]

[4] In *Ways of Worship*, the reformed theologian, Julius Schweizer of Basle, shows how a service of preaching, independent from the Mass, had been introduced during the fifteenth century in the principal cities of South Germany and the Helvetic Confederation. This service, much appreciated in humanistic and experimental circles, was the basis from which the partisans of the Reformation worked out the new worship when the Mass was abolished, pp. 130-131.

[5] *Calvini Opera*, X, 1, vii.

[6] *Ibid.*, IV, p. 1051. Cf. *Institutes de la Religion chrétienne*, IV, 18.

The Lutheran churches, German as well as Scandinavian, and the Anglican church which wanted in the sixteenth century to keep at any cost the principle of the eucharist on every Sunday, even by retaining sometimes the old name of Mass,[7] had been led little by little in the seventeenth century to give in: the sacrament was celebrated only once a month, sometimes even more rarely. The early word and sacrament service of the universal church gave way to a mutilated service, deprived of an essential element—the meal of the Lord.[8]

But the early church, and the Reformation in its original and pristine stage, understood Christian worship as an ellipse with two foci. The early church gave to the word its full importance: the reading of biblical pericopes was considered to be an important part of divine worship, particularly for the instruction of the catechumens and for preparing the faithful for communion. The homilies and sermons of men such as Athanasius, Augustine, and John Chrysostom are still witnesses to the important role of the word in worship in that era. But if the Reformation renewed gloriously this heritage, it has not been able to return like for like and preserve the original and legitimate place of the sacrament. With the Lutherans the *Predigtgottesdienst* has become the rule; in Reformed circles one went to "the sermon" or to the "preaching." Things had come even to this point that a century after the Reformation preaching had dethroned and almost eliminated from worship the reading of the Bible itself. The preacher did not read anything more than the verse on which his sermon was built. The Bible was read by a teacher or divinity student before the act of worship, during the last strokes of the church bell, and in place of the organ prelude we know today.[9] Osterwald com-

---

[7] The first eucharistic liturgical formula of Luther was called *Deutsche Messe*. Still today in the Church of Sweden Sunday worship without Holy Communion is called Hogdmass, that is, "High Mass."

[8] "What we know today as the church service both in Roman Catholicism *and* in Protestantism is a torso. The Roman Catholic church has a sacramental service without preaching . . . We have a service with a sermon but without sacraments. Both types of service are impossible . . . We do not any longer even realize that a service without sacraments is one which is outwardly incomplete. As a rule we hold such outwardly incomplete services as if it were perfectly natural to do so" Karl Barth: *Knowledge of God and the Service of God*, trans. J. L. M. Haire and I. Henderson. (London: Hodder & Stoughton, 1938), p. 211.

[9] Henri Vuilleumier, *op. cit.*, II, p. 339; III, pp. 593-594.

plained: "It is not enough to read the scripture in the churches only before the gathering is formed and the worship starts. Such a lection is not part of the divine worship; it is separated from it even by the time and the persons who read and by other circumstances, so that the people pay only scant attention and respect and even some of them are not yet present at all. All this proves that the reading of the Holy Scripture is regarded as being much less important than the preaching."[10]

It is time now for the evangelical church to find its way back to the fullness of the cultic mystery in the complementary interrelatedness of word and sacrament.[11] Sunday eucharist is a biblical demand. "We celebrate communion four times a year," writes Calvin, " . . . but please God, we might base more frequent celebration of it. For we see by Luke in the book of Acts that the early Church had it more often . . . By this we must confess it is our own fault in not following the example of the apostles."[12] The church does not have the right to abstain from offering every Sunday to the faithful the opportunity of partaking of the bread of life and the cup of salvation.

If and when things have been reestablished in their normal condition, a delicate problem is presented inevitably: Are those believers who are present at worship who do not intend to take communion required to remain until the end of the service, or can arrangements be made for their earlier dismissal between the two parts of the service?

In the early church this dismissal existed for the catechumens and penitents. It occurred after the sermon and before the "prayer of the faithful," that is, the prayer of intercession which is the gradual before the sacrament. This prayer, like the sacrament, being the privilege and prerogative of "the people of God" and the outward expression of the royal priest-

---

[10] *Préface de la liturgie neuchâteloise*, 1713.

[11] "It is perfectly in order that the question about the right form of service should never cease to engage the evangelical churches. It is not true that the right form of service was finally discovered and introduced in the sixteenth century. It is quite in order to ask, whether what is known to us today in the Reformed church as the service is really founded on obedience to the Lord of the church, or whether it ought not to have its form changed by the asking of the question as to this its primary ground," Karl Barth, *op. cit.*, p. 207.

[12] Letter from Calvin to the Senate of Berne, 1555. The reformer expressed his opinion in this subject in the official reports of the Council of Geneva: "curavi tamen referre in acta publica vitiosum esse morem nostrum, ut posteris facilior esset ac liberior correctio," *Calvini opera*, X, 1, 213.

hood of the redeemed, could be the act only of the baptized and not of the simple auditors. Historically a breach between the two halves of the service may, therefore, be justified. In our actual situation as "Christianized people" where only a minority is "faithful" and involved, the first part of the act of worship has to a degree the value of mission and evangelism to the auditors, while the communion concerns the active and involved members of the body of Christ. Therefore, the auditors and young catechumens should have the opportunity to withdraw.[13] If they are denied this and are obliged to be present at the celebration of the sacrament, a disruption is created in the eucharistic κοινωνία ; an injury is suffered by the fraternal community. Certainly we should grant that Christians can be present at a eucharistic service without taking communion, maybe refraining on account of a momentary lack of the necessary spiritual disposition, but in all probability with the intention of preparing themselves in this way to partake worthily on another occasion. But this practice cannot be either encouraged or generalized without the risk of following the wrong road of the Tractarian movement in Anglicanism: while wanting to rehabilitate the sacrament they finally made a "High Mass" out of the principal Sunday worship, a solemn eucharist, at which everybody attends, but in which only the celebrant takes communion. The act is then theologically justified by a unilateral stress upon the sacrificial element of the ceremony.

It seems on first thought that the difficulty could be solved by creating two separate services, such as in the early years of the church: a service of the word read and preached, and another service at another time in the morning (or in the evening as it was originally) when there would be only the sacrament. But in doing this we dissociate badly the word and sacrament.

---

[13] Max Thurian, *op. cit.*, pp. 141-143, proposes the following terminology: *Eucharist* would designate the principal complete service of the church with the reading and preaching of the Word, followed by the celebration of the sacrament of the bread and cup. *Worship* would mean the service of the Word only, the apostolic and missionary service for those outside and for the parishes which "had not yet reached the mature community stature and necessary spiritual understanding." *Holy Communion* or *Lord's Supper* would be reserved for those services where the sacrament alone is administered without the preaching of the Word, at a very early hour on Sunday, or during the week, or during a retreat. This judicious nomenclature, we believe, will not be easily adopted. In any case one should avoid at any price the frightful expression which is all too widespread: worship of Communion!

And if the followers of the service of the word do not seem to suffer greatly by being deprived of the sacrament, the communicants on the other hand would feel painfully the absence of the message of the word. If the early church came eventually to the fusion of the two services, it was only after some helpful experiences we would be foolish to neglect. It is necessary, therefore, to keep word and sacrament united in the principal service on Sunday and with the possibility of the non-communicants withdrawing before the communion liturgy. But this dismissal should be done in the most sober and discreet manner possible; they could leave, for example, during a brief organ interlude that prolongs the tune of a hymn of the congregation, and there would be no benediction given to those who withdraw. Thus the error will not be perpetuated by continuing a first service, complete in itself, followed by a second and optional service. It is necessary, moreover, that the liturgical text of the whole give the impression that the word read and preached is only half of the whole, the first part of an act of worship of which the culminating point is the breaking of bread.[14]

Originally, the first part of the service (the fore-mass) contained the reading of the scriptures, a homily, and a prayer of intercession called the *prayer of the faithful*, then the readings were preceded by a salutation and a short prayer. The second part of the worship (sacrament) included the offering of the elements brought in by the faithful, the thanksgiving or eucharistic prayer of consecration, the fraction, the communion and the dismissal. The non-Christians withdrew after the homily and before the "prayer of the faithful," which was actually part of the service of the word. This being the situation, must the prayer of intercession nowadays be inserted then within the framework of the word or of the sacrament?

Let us note, first of all, that those who withdraw "at the first leaving" are not the same as the pagan auditors or the non-baptized catechumens in the ante-Nicene period. They have, therefore, the right to participate in the act of worship called rightly the "prayer of the faithful," which is a general

---

[14] It is necessary, however, to allow and even to require occasionally the attendance of the young catechumens at the celebration of Holy Communion, prior to their first communion, so that they may become accustomed to it. See also *Leiturgia*, I, p. 334.

intercession for the various categories of persons—Christians or non-Christians. But the old eucharistic liturgy also contained a reference to the names of the communicants present who had brought their offering of bread and wine for the sacrament, as well as of the members absent from the local community and of those who had died. These items, however, would not be placed within the framework of the first part of the service, but would occur quite normally at the beginning of the second part where they belong more properly to the intimate and precise intercessions of the eucharistic community, the mutual commendation of the guests at the holy table. Historically this remembrance both of the living and of the dead has its place actually at the beginning of the eucharistic act. If its content is properly organized and limited, it should not appear as a second edition of the general intercession which concludes the service of the word.

Therefore, the divine service which the church of Christ celebrates every Sunday, the weekly recognition of its risen Lord, the day on which believers gather in the presence of this same Lord, must be like a prophetic sign and anticipation of the time when "the Son of Man will gather his elect from the four winds, from the ends of the earth to the ends of heaven" (Mark 13:27), and where the elect "will come from east and west, and from north and south, and sit at table in the kingdom of God" (Luke 13:29). The chief aim of the liturgical movement of our time must be the integral and universal restoration of this complete and balanced worship of word and sacrament. Wherever the word is veiled by a dead language and by careless or dull preaching, we must give back to the people of God the intelligible and living word. Wherever the sacrament of the body and blood of Christ has become like some fanciful matter reserved for great occasions, it is imperative that we set again the table of Christ every time Christian people gather in the name of their Lord on his day.[15]

---

[15] In rural parishes containing several churches or chapels and where the minister must conduct two or three services every Sunday, it is not necessary or possible to celebrate the eucharist in all these places. It will be sufficient to celebrate it once a Sunday alternatively in every place of worship in the parish.

16

The Service of the Word

We have said that essentially the service of the word contained in the beginning the reading of the scriptures, the homily and the prayer of intercession. The Constantinian era, which made possible a fuller and more complete unfolding of Christian worship, did not add much, however, to this early scheme. The chanting of a psalm in the West and of a church hymn in the East marked, at the beginning of the worship, the entrance of the officiants. To this new liturgical element was given the name *introitus* (entrance) in the Roman liturgy, whereas the Gallic named it *ingressus*. A biblical salutation introduced the readings. Very soon, however, between the introit and this salutation there was inserted a litany of intercession; some chants and responses also were put between the biblical pericopes.

The initial litany has been entirely maintained in the Eastern liturgies, with the numerous and varied requests punctuated by the responsive invocation *Kyrie eleison*, "Lord, have mercy," In the West, subsequently, the requests were abolished from the Roman rite in the interest of brevity, and everything was reduced to the single invocation *Kyrie eleison*, interrupted by the variant *Christe eleison*. The prayer of the faithful after the sermon was dropped as well. At the same time appeared the *Gloria in excelsis*, or "great doxology," a paraphrase in praise and supplication of the angels' song of Luke 2:14. This hymn, used first in the divine office and attested to from the fourth century, made its entrance into the Sunday liturgy where it took its place after the Kyrie. In the eight century in Gaul, and only in the eleventh century in Rome, the creed was inserted in the fore-mass after the reading of the gospel. One final addition was the *confiteor* or confession of sins right at the beginning of the service. Originally it was only an act of private devotion of the officiants in the sacristy, as it has remained in the case of the East. Then, at the end of the Middle Ages, it became an action done in public, spoken at the foot of the altar, either before or during the singing of the introit.

To conclude this very brief historical sketch we note that in the sixteenth century, on the eve of the Reformation, the Western book of order for the fore-mass had the following pattern: *confiteor* and absolution, introit, *Kyrie*, *Gloria in excelsis*, salutation, short prayer (called a *collect*), two Bible readings (epistle and gospel), and finally the creed. The *confiteor* has retained something of its individual and peculiar character, being composed in the first person singular, so that the introit was considered as indicating the true beginning of the act of public worship.

These then are the liturgical elements which the Reformation found already established in the church. Lutheranism retained them for its main service and in their traditional order, except for generally leaving aside the *confiteor* and absolution at the outset. In contrast with Luther, Calvin kept from among all these elements only the confession of sin, to which he gave a communal character by putting it in the first person plural. He introduced a chanted decalogue after the formula of absolution. Under the influence of Calvin, the Anglican liturgy of 1552 adopted the Decalogue and created an original combination by placing the old invocations of the *Kyrie eleison* between the commandments.[1] The Kyrie was, therefore, directed away from its early intention of supplicating intercession to serve as an expression of the humiliation of repentance.

[1] For the origins of the *Kyrie eleison*, consult Franz J. Dölger, *Sol salutis* (Münster: Aschendorff, 1925), Chap. 2; Josef A. Jungmann, *Missarum solemnia*, II, pp. 87-103. On the use the Lutheran Reformation made of it, see *Leiturgia*, II, pp. 17-22.

This is very probably what suggested to the French liturgical renovator, Eugène Bersier, the idea of building the *Kyrie* and *Gloria* of the old liturgy into the confession of sins and absolution. In this arrangement the *Kyrie* is the response of the congregation to the confession of sins pronounced in its name by the officiant, and the *Gloria in excelsis*, abbreviated and reduced to its sole biblical formulation, becomes the joyful response to the words of grace and absolution. A step in this direction already had been taken earlier by the Swedish Lutherans, for in the liturgy of the Church of Sweden, the *Kyrie* of the congregation follows the absolution, after which the officiant starts the *Gloria* which the congregation finishes.

Now, in the Reformed churches of the French language, the confession of sins is made an integral part of the worship. It is in fact preceded by the invocation, then by introductory biblical texts and a hymn by the congregation, elements which correspond to the ancient introit.[2] Bersier's scheme has generally prevailed: the *Kyrie* and *Gloria*, or other hymns considered equivalent, are inserted into the progression of the confession of sins and the words of grace. In some ways this rearrangement is regretted from both historical and theological points of view. For a thousand years the church universal had not known a confession of sins in the Sunday worship because Sunday was the joyful and glorious day of the risen Christ, and because the Christian congregation of these early times considered itself a holy and ransomed people, the community of kings and priests who had received mercy. Individuals were permitted and had to confess their weaknesses;[3] but the community as such, gathered to render service of praise and adoration to its Lord, was the holy and irreproachable Bride (Eph. 5:27).

Moreover, in certain services during the week and in Lent the element of abasement has found a place as well as in the practice of auricular confession and the sacrament of penance.

[2] See in Rene Blanc, *Etudes liturgiques sur le service divin*, (Paris-Strasbourg: Editions Lutheriennes, 1948), pp. 13-24, a very careful discussion of the place of the introit and confession of sin respectively. The author stands against the Reformed solution of this problem and pleads for the more traditional order as in |Lutheranism: confession of sin first, as a preparation for the service, then the introit which opens what is properly called the service. The same also in *Ways of Worship*, pp. 84-90.

[3] *Didaché*, 14:1, 2 and 15:3.

But circumstances have long since changed: the *Corpus Christianum* and its spiritual mediocrity has replaced the original "little flock." Christian people frequent practically no other worship than the one on Sunday. It appears to us now that the churches of the Reformation were acting rightly and realistically when they made the public confession of sin a constitutive element of the Sunday morning worship, and this more especially since they abolished or dropped into desuetude all private confession and sacramental absolution.

Let us come back now to the introit, which as its name implies, is the introduction to the worship. In order to understand this element of worship more fully, we have to refer to its historical origins. In Rome from the fifth century at least, it was customary for the singers who were grouped in two half-choirs to sing a psalm during the entering of the officiants. When these had taken their places near the holy table, they stopped the psalm and began the conclusion which was the *Gloria Patri* or Little Doxology (Glory be to the Father, and to the Son, and to the Holy Ghost). This was normal procedure during a time when no musical instrument was permitted in worship. Today, however, the entering of the officiants is done generally with organ accompaniment which is definitely no longer in the spirit of the early introit. In order to restore this spirit we should have to assign to the organ the simple role of providing a prelude to the singing which is done by congregation or choir while the officiants enter. This is the most common Anglican and Lutheran procedure. The Reformed could gain a great deal of inspiration from it also. However, the versified psalter in French does not contain all the psalms and the form in which they are presently written is often incredibly far from the biblical text. Our psalms, therefore, can not fulfill adequately the role of the antiphonal psalms of the introit of the early liturgy. Consequently, it appears more preferable to us to let the congregation or parish choir sing a hymn (or one of the appropriate psalms) related to the particular Sunday of the church year or expressive of the presence of God in his sanctuary. When this song is completed, then the principal officiant will pronounce the invocation, followed by a short biblical text designating clearly the distinctive character of the Sunday (*Eingangswort*). Then the appropriate psalm for that Sunday will be said antiphonally between the principal officiant and his assistants, or still better, if it is possible, between the officiants and the whole congregation. In this renewed form the introit becomes an even richer and more significant and harmonized whole than the introit of antiquity.

The introit is followed by the reading of the law which introduces and justifies the confession of sin. This is a pedagogical order. The theological order would request that the law be put preferably after the confession and absolution as Calvin had done. But we must not overlook the traditionally pedagogical character of the service of the word, hitherto in the early church, that permitted non-Christians and catechumens to attend. In our actually pluralistic situation it is better to give the law of God a role preparatory to the act of abasement and repentance than to make of it the program of a lifetime for the forgiven believer. As far as the text of the law is concerned we must avoid restricting ourselves exclusively to the Decalogue or the two great commandments which are the summary of it: the too frequently repeated use of these texts risks blunting its significance. In the churches where—like ours—they do not have private confession with the examination of conscience which such supposes, the law of God should be expressed in varied biblical texts that bring to focus precisely in every detail the requirements of the divine will in the moral field. The Bible is rich with texts of an ethical character appropriate for this liturgical usage.

The confession of sin benefits also from being stated or drawn up in a variable manner in order to avoid the routine, or prevent inattention or indifference. However, it would be preferable that a short and simple formula be chosen to be said periodically—for example, once a month. It should be suitable for catechism manuals and be memorized as the Lord's Prayer and the Apostles' Creed; indeed it might be said aloud by the whole congregation as is the case in the Anglican service every Sunday. The other formula, pronounced by the officiant alone, will be ratified by the *Amen* said by the congregation and by the singing of the *Kyrie*.

The *Kyrie* displaces in the worship the rather frequent biblical supplication to the Eternal or to Christ, with direct supplication without affectation and springing up from the depth of human distress. It is appropriate that this type of expression of it be preserved. To substitute for it a long versified strophe of a hymn is to falsify it. An exception may be tolerated, however, during Lent or Passiontide or a fast day in favor of the Anglican paraphrase of the Prayer Book of 1662: "Lord, have mercy upon us, and incline our hearts to keep Thy Law," or in favor of a short versified psalm strophe, like Psalm 61 or 130. In the old Roman liturgy, the invocation *Kyrie eleison* was repeated nine times, that is to say three times three times, in honor of the Trinity, and the second group was made explicit as *Christe eleison*. Luther, in his *Deutsche Messe* (1525) has simplified matters by reducing each of the three groups to one single invocation. So that the weekly singing then of the *Kyrie* does not create monotony, it is important that the church hymnbooks offer several different tunes for this invocation. On Sunday, when the confession of sin will be said by the whole congregation, the *Kyrie* may be omitted as superfluous.

Since the church is not any more under the law but under grace, it is necessary that the abasement of the confession of sin and the *Kyrie* be followed by the good news of the mercy of God in the form of appropriate biblical texts (words of pardon) and of a formula of absolution. The one used for private auricular confession has generally the deprecatory form which had universal use in the church until the eleventh century: "Trusting the word of the Savior: those to whom you have forgiven their sins, they will be forgiven, I dare to say; all that you have confessed . . . may God pardon it for you."[4] Since then in the Latin church a declaratory formula has replaced it for the sacramental absolution of the auricular confession. On the contrary, in the *confiteor* which prefaces the Mass, the Roman church has retained the deprecative formula: "That the Almighty God have mercy upon you, that he may forgive your sins and lead you to eternal life." This formula is said reciprocally by the representatives of the congregation to the

---

[4] In the Greek and Syrian churches. The Russian and Armenian churches use a declarative formula.

celebrant, and by the celebrant to the congregation. Then the celebrant pronounces the general absolution in which he includes himself: "May the almighty and merciful Savior grant *us* his pardon, the absolution and remission of *our* sins." It is worthwhile to note how in the Roman liturgy this feature is the opposite of clerical sacerdotalism.

The modifications Luther's reformation movement had determined gradually and in varied ways in the divine service during the sixteenth century often include the suppression of the *confiteor* and the absolution. But where the absolution has remained it has retained nearly everything of the Roman form. Calvin himself went still further than the Roman church in the matter of a declarative absolution: "That everyone among you recognize himself truly sinful, humiliating himself before God, and believe that the heavenly Father will be gracious to him in Jesus Christ. To all those who repent in this way and seek Jesus Christ for their salvation, I declare that absolution of sins has been given in the name of the Father, the Son and the Holy Spirit. Amen." We may reasonably say that "the Calvinistic formula is much stronger than those which figure in all the other Christian liturgies. It has indeed not just the form of a wish but of a proclamation."[5]

It appears that the Reformation in Strasbourg had really poured in a way the new wine into the old bottles. The *Deutsche Messe* of 1524 in Strasbourg introduced for the first time a biblical word of grace before the absolution: "The saying is sure and worthy of full acceptance that Christ Jesus came into the world to save sinners (I Tim. 1:15). I believe that: Lord, help my unbelief and save me. I believe that God forgives us and has mercy upon us all." This new way has been followed in certain respects by the Anglican liturgy; there the confession of sins and the absolution, foreseen in the heart of the communion liturgy itself, are concluded by the *comfortable words*, that is, three biblical texts: Matt. 11:28; John 3:16; and especially I Tim. 1:15. This is a good procedure for the church that wants to found itself upon the biblical word. It is necessary, therefore, that the confession of sins and the *Kyrie* be followed by adequate biblical texts, which may be varied, but

[5] André Schlemmer, *op. cit.*, p. 32.

which declare to the congregation from the lips of the Lord the divine grace that forgives. Then comes the formula of absolution, preferably deprecative or optative, but which may be declarative also, on the condition that the officiant in this act is only a minister and proxy of the Lord, and that forgiveness is really given only in response to the sincere repentance and personal faith of the believers. [6]

The words of grace and the absolution are answered by the song of praise of the congregation. The traditional *Gloria in excelsis* finds its place here normally in its simple biblical text from Luke 2:14. The amplification by the church in the Roman Mass, and which has remained in this way for some time in certain orders of Lutheran worship in the sixteenth century, is inconvenient for the pattern we follow. [7] Three of the invocations to Christ which it contains are an appeal from sinners for divine mercy and would be, therefore, a repetition of the confession of sins. The complete *Gloria*, this admirable specimen of the hymnology of the early church, would be proper only at the beginning of a service of praise when there would be no confession of sins, as in the divine office where it has a well-determined place. We can tolerate occasionally the simple *Gloria in excelsis* being replaced in our order of worship by the verse of a hymn of praise and thanksgiving, particularly by the first stanza of the paraphrase in verse Luther gave of the Gloria in the chorale *Allein sei Gott Ehr' in der Höh*.

In the old liturgical order, before the Reformation introduced the yoked confession-absolution, the *Gloria Patri* of the introit was followed by the biblical salutation, "The Lord be with you," or "Peace be with you," to which the congregation replied with the words, "And with thy spirit." Later, after the insertion of the linked *Kyrie-Gloria in excelsis*, the salutation came immediately after the latter. It prefaced originally the biblical readings. Afterwards a short prayer of petition was put between the salutation and the readings; it was

---

[6] An example taken from the liturgy of the Reformed church in France: "To all those who repent and seek their salvation in Jesus Christ, we declare in the name of the Father, and of the Son, and of the Holy Spirit, that *God forgives now their sins.*"

[7] On the origins of the *Gloria in excelsis*, see Josef A. Jungman, *op. cit.*, II, pp. 103-109; *Liturgy and Worship*, pp. 358-360; *Leiturgia*, II, pp. 23-29.

named a *Collect* because it "collected" or summarized the wishes and needs of the church.

Here the salutation is in an appropriate place for announcing the reading of the word of God. It may be expressed in forms different from what are given to it in the epistles. We do not feel that the response, "And with thy spirit," must be continued in the parish worship for it sounds a bit strange to our modern ears; it is really a semitism that says simply, "And with you."[8] Let us keep the apostolic greeting, which may be ratified eventually by an *Amen* spoken by the congregation. The collect has its full and complete significance here only if it asks, under different forms, for the grace necessary to understand the divine word that will be read. This is the character of the prayer prescribed at this moment in the service by many Eastern liturgies. In the Reformed worship it is permissible to use at this point the old collects of the Latin liturgy, while inflecting them slightly in the sense indicated. After the greeting and the collect come the scripture readings, followed then by commentary and explanation in the preaching or sermon. This is certainly the most reasonable order if the preaching is really an actualization of the inspired text. In principle nothing can justify the intrusion of any peculiar element between the scripture readings and the sermon, except short responses by the congregation or choir after each pericope. In the complete service of worship, that is, with the celebration of Holy Communion, there is no difficulty: the order is logical and complete.

But in that truncated form of worship in which the sacrament is absent, which is current usage still in the Reformed churches, the lack of a prayer of adoration or thanksgiving, which has its place in the eucharistic preface, is felt severely. Without such a prayer, the service of the word would contain only the prayer of humiliation and that of intercession; an essential point of the Christian prayer would, therefore, be missed there. Where should we put, then, this prayer of praise and thanksgiving? If it is acknowledged that nothing must separate the word that is read from the preaching that explains it, the result is that this prayer must be placed after the con-

[8] It is a biblical expression. See Gal. 6:18; Phil. 4:23; Tim. 4:22; and Phil. 1:25.

fession and absolution and before the reading of the word of God. We do not overlook or minimize the inconvenience of joining, almost without interruption, two acts of prayer. But it is also the only way to respect the principle: word at the pulpit, prayer at the altar, in the frequently occurring case of only one and the same officiant leading the whole service. For in this instance the one who was in the pulpit for the reading of the pericopes would have to come down again for the prayer of praise and then return for the preaching, if this prayer were not placed after the biblical pericopes. In the case, which is infinitely more acceptable, in which the celebrant is assisted by readers for the pericopes everything is simple: the readers climb the *ambon* or pulpit to fulfill their office, and during this time the officiant remains in his stall in the choir from where he stands up when he wishes, after the readings, to deliver the prayer of praise. But we repeat that it is better not to separate the word that is read from the word that is preached.

Another question arises now: what about the confession of faith? Does it have a necessary place in the Sunday worship? In the West the confession of faith, be it the Apostles' or the Nicene Creed, is framed in the first person singular. This implies that its usage was limited originally to baptism and to being declared by the candidate as a personal confession of faith. It was not until the fourth century in Antioch that the Nicene Creed was integrated into the Sunday eucharistic worship. Rome waited until the eleventh century to adopt this view. This indicates, therefore, that the use of the creed in public worship on Sunday is not old.[9] Its use may be justified, however, for some good reasons: if the congregation comes together to be nourished and built up in the faith, it is a normal thing to confess its faith in unison. When the church is under the cross, when it is fighting against the vexation and persecution of a totalitarian civil power, then the confession of faith said by the whole congregation has such force and impact that all theological or liturgical justification of this usage becomes superfluous.[10] The Orthodox church, in the Byzantine liturgy,

---

[9] André Schlemmer comments similarly and consequently raises doubts regarding the necessity of the creed in Sunday worship, *op. cit.*, p. 52.

[10] Cf. *Leiturgia*, I, pp. 262-263, regarding short responses or acclamations: "Their true character is brought out by contrast when the state requires it."

puts the main reason for the recitation of the creed into proper perspective by introducing it with these words: "Let us love each other so that with a unified feeling we may confess (the faith)." This transposes it to the first person plural: "We believe in one God . . ." The saying of the creed during Sunday worship fills a gap there where it is no longer recited during the baptismal ceremony. And by the same token the importance of this act is diminished by the fact that it is not the baptized, an unconscious candidate, who declares the confession of faith under our method of baptizing infants.

Let us note, however, that the confession of faith recited in a service with Holy Communion is actually redundant if the eucharistic prayer (or preface) is properly said, for the latter is a calling forth in lyrical form of the facts of salvation in Christ, just as is the creed; it is nothing less than the *kerygma* in euchological form. It is a strange paradox, therefore, that in modern churches, Catholic as well as Protestant, the confession of faith should be pronounced only on the occasion of the celebration of the sacrament, precisely where it is not indispensable, but even superfluous. Thus, in the Orthodox, Roman, Anglican, and Lutheran churches, the Nicene Creed is said or sung during the eucharistic services on Sunday. And a number of Reformed churches use the Apostles' Creed (the only one they have) only on the occasion of communion services. The Anglican church reserves the Apostles' Creed for the offices of *Morning Prayer* and *Evening Prayer*.

However, in churches where a part of the congregation is present only during the first portion of the service and retires when the main sacramental liturgy begins, we can maintain that the recitation of the creed is useful; it takes the place for the non-communicants of the eucharistic prayer. In services without Holy Communion, the prayer of praise and thanksgiving, discussed earlier in this book, may in its turn be considered as a substitute for the confession of faith, on the condition that it mention in their sequence the central facts of salvation as the principal motive for thanksgiving. Furthermore, in worship the confession of faith must be considered as a prayer. The church has always understood it in this way: the occasional custom of kneeling at the *incarnatus est*, in the Roman Catholic Mass, as at the *crucifixus est* in certain Anglican services, is concrete expression of it. In the Alsace, the Lutheran people say usually, "to pray the creed," *den Glauben beten*. We concur, therefore, with a remark by Vinet, "The liturgy ought certainly to express the faith of the church, but, if I may put it in this way, in the contemplative state." [11]

The weekly use of the creed may become boring and vain repetition. This is certain when it is said by the officiant alone. Therefore, some variety is commendable: one should turn on one occasion to the Apostles' Creed, on another to the Nicene, maybe spoken at one time and sung at another, or to a prayer of thanksgiving framed according to the divine plan of salvation, or to a biblical confession of faith said by the officiant alone and ratified by the *Amen* or *Alleluia* of the congregation. As to the proper place for the confession of faith in the order of worship, it may be placed before the preaching as a response of the congregation to the message read from the divine word, especially if it is a short confession of faith comparable to a simple response; it may be put after the last of the biblical pericopes (that is, after the gospel), and immediately before the preaching. It could also be placed after the sermon, as a response to the message of the preacher.

The reading from the Bible has always been an essential part of Christian worship. At the beginning of the second century, Justin speaks already of the "recollections of the apostles" (that is, the gospels) and of the writings of the prophets that are read in the Christian congregation. [12] In the fourth century the *Apostolic Constitutions* foresee even five readings: the Pentateuch, the prophets, the letters, the Acts and the gospel. Even to this day some Eastern liturgies prescribe four readings, but early throughout the whole church the rule limited the number to three pericopes: Old Testament, epistle, and gospel. The Byzantine church and the Roman have even reduced this number to two: epistle and gospel. Consequently, the Anglican and Lutheran churches follow the same rule. Some centuries of feeling around were necessary before fixed lists of pericopes were established based upon the cycles of the

---

[11] Alexander Vinet, *op. cit.*, p. 191.

[12] *Apology* 1, 67.

church year. The eventual stabilization of the canon of scriptures, the fear of heresies, and the unfortunate experience of the all-too-fanciful liberties of officiants have shaped this evolution and development.

The system of fixed pericopes has the great advantage of protecting the congregation from the arbitrariness of the officiant and an entirely subjective choice of readings. Without the system or principle of pericopes the congregation is dependent upon the personal tastes and even theological leanings of its leader. On the other hand, by means of these judiciously established lists the faithful, after a given time, hear the whole essence of the biblical message in all its aspects, and the preacher finds himself deflected from his all-too-exclusively personal preoccupations and led back to a certain discipline that calls him to preach the word of God in all its richness.[13] In certain Lutheran churches, it is required that the preacher follow one of the pericopes of the day or a special verse taken from it. It seems that this is an excessive disciplinary requirement and that it would be more fitting to safeguard the liberty of the Holy Spirit. If a preacher feels inclined to treat another subject or another text than that of the pericopes for the day, the prescribed pericopes are still to be read.

The Reformed churches have never known the system of pericopes, except by chance.[14] Originally, the *lectio continua* was practiced voluntarily, that is the continued reading of a book of the Bible and the preacher's comments on it.[15] This

---

[13] Cf. Henri Vuilleumier, *op. cit.*, I, p. 328.

[14] However, in the seventeenth century, in the Pays de Vaud, by order of the authorities of Bern, the Classis of ministers imposed upon the preachers parts of the Bible on which they had to preach. One had been called to account for the inconveniences of too much individual liberty in this area. "Thus, in order to be free from the yoke of the Catholic and Lutheran pericopes, the pastors of the seventeenth century were not free absolutely—as much as they may have wished—in their activities where the choice of texts for their sermons was concerned," Henri Vuilleumier, *op. cit.*, pp. 355-356.

[15] Zwingli rejected from the beginning the system of church pericopes in order to have the *lectio continua*, with the laudable intention of making the whole Bible known to his flock. He began to preach on January 2, 1519, on the Gospel according to St. Matthew, then the book of the Acts, the first letter to Timothy, the one to the Galatians, the pastoral letters, the two epistles of Peter, and Hebrews. He did this until August, 1522. But the result was that during this time the parish congregation of Zürich had not heard a word of all the Johannine writings, of the letters to the Ephesians, Philippians and Colossians, of those to the Romans and Corinthians, or the Apocalypse, without mentioning the Old Testament in its entirety. Cf. *Leiturgia*, I, p. 501.

177

confuses, it seems, public worship with Bible study, which discloses once again the overly doctrinaire and didactic deflection of Reformed worship. We come back, therefore, to the system of pericopes where certain advantages have been noted[16] and with the hope of restoring it to better use than the churches which have conserved this principle traditionally. First of all, instead of limiting oneself to the letters and the gospels, the older principle of three readings is re-established, making a place thereby for the Old Testament. Secondly, the cycle of readings, instead of being annual, becomes biennial, triennial or even quadriennial. For the inconvenience of the traditional annual cycle lies in the impossibility to cover in fifty-two Sundays and some feast days all the riches of the Holy Scripture, without mentioning the frequent and monotonous return to the same readings. The epistles and gospels which recur each year represent only a minimal part of the Bible, and are, moreover, not always chosen as judiciously as one might wish. It is from the Lutheran church in Sweden that the initiative came in 1920 of a rotation over three years, and since then this idea has found acceptance.[17] This system has the advantage of permitting whoever is present at worship every Sunday during three years to hear the reading of the essence of the Old Testament and the whole substance of the New Testament. The triennial system of readings is of high origin and may revindicate a venerable tradition, since it was in force in the liturgy of the synagogues for the Sabbath at the time of Christ.[18] To avoid incoherence it is necessary obviously that the ecclesiastical authority, through a mandate issued to the pastors on a date close to Advent, remind them of what the series of pericopes is that they must follow during the forthcoming liturgical year.

The order of the readings is traditionally: Old Testament, epistle, and gospel. This order is not chronological, but honorary. It is the pattern of a graduated movement: the law or

[16] See the *Liturgie* of Bersier, *The Book of Common Order* of the Church of Scotland (1929) and the new liturgies of the French-speaking Churches of Switzerland (1940-1955). The *lectio continua* finds its most adequate place in the divine office.

[17] Cf. Emanuel Linderholm, *Svensk Evangeliebok*, Stockholm, 1920. This liturgical work has been translated, with certain adaptations and additions, by Rudolf Otto under the title, *Das Jahr der Kirche in Lesungen und Gebeten*, Gotha, 1927.

[18] Cf. Gregory Dix, *The Shape of the Liturgy*, (London: Dacre, 1949), p. 360.

the prophets, then the apostles are only the servants and heralds who announce the Master. The word of Christ or his life, in the gospel, is the culminating point of the revelation and the climax of the divine message in worship.[19] Thus can be explained the ceremony the churches elaborated in ancient times in order to exalt this prime moment in the divine service: the book was carried in processionally, escorted with lights and incense, and then it was kissed with reverent piety. The pericope was sung in order to give splendor and sound, and the congregation listened to it while standing. These rites have been maintained in the Roman and Eastern churches. These remain incomprehensible to anyone who sees in worship only teaching and edifying discourse, but they become clear and significant when they are seen as the faith and real presence of Christ coming and speaking himself to his gathered people. It would be out of the question to attempt to reintroduce to the full such ceremonies into Reformed worship. We could make the congregation more accustomed, however, to listen to the reading of the gospel standing, if not every Sunday, at least on the great festivals of Christmas, Easter, Ascension and Pentecost, and eventually even throughout Eastertide. We ought also to arrange to have the responses sung: "Praise be to Thee, O Christ" or "Glory be to Thee, O Lord." These would be joyful acclamations to him whose word has declared to his people the good news of salvation. We might request also that the readers, whether they be in the pulpit, *ambon*, or at the lectern, avoid holding before them in their hands, almost at eye level, a small-sized Bible or pocket edition of the New Testament. This is undignified. If there is on the pulpit or lectern a large-sized Bible of dimensions proportionate to the building in which it is used, and opened respectfully before the congregation, this Bible will tend to make known the majesty of 'the word of God, for "the Lord is pleased to make his Law great and magnificent" (Isa. 42:21).

Preaching is necessary in the principal service of worship on Sunday morning. The liturgical renaissance, so urgent in the

[19] The traditional order epistle-gospel does not seem to us to be absolutely mandatory. Without agreeing entirely with Robert Will, *op. cit.*, I, p. 312, that this rests upon "an unacceptable fiction," we have to recognize, however, that sometimes it appears to be artificial and inadequate for both the content and the logical course of the two readings. There are some cases in which the inversion is clearly imposed.

Reformed churches, must not work in any case to the disadvantage of preaching; liturgy and preaching are joint activities and interdependent. The parishioners of the Reformed tradition, since they are not acclimated to the liturgical spirit, will come only if there is preaching, to which they attach great importance, and if it is well done and has striking impact and power. They will resist any liturgical renewal if they suspect that preaching will suffer from it. Other reasons, of course, account for some failures in liturgical renewal. Only preaching that is Christ- and congregation-centered, deeply meditative and oriented towards the great facts of the faith: Trinity, incarnation, redemption, resurrection, *parousia*, church, and sacraments, can reflect that initial inspiration characteristic of apostolic Christianity. Only this can sustain and justify any liturgical renewal, for liturgy consists in helping us experience anew the eternal truths present in the successive stages and multiple aspects of the mystery of Christ the Savior. Preaching, for a regular one hour service, should not exceed twenty-five minutes; it may be limited to ten minutes for an evening service or a short morning service during the week.[20]

The organ music that follows the sermon is meant to encourage the personal and silent meditation of the worshipers and not to drown the noise of the people stretching themselves in their seats or coughing and blowing their noses without any discretion and seemingly in protest against the silence and immobility which the sermon imposed upon them for a time. For this it is necessary for the preacher and the others who officiate eventually to set an example themselves. The preacher who, as soon as his sermon is finished, turns from the right to the left in the pulpit to look still another time at his audience, or in order to gather up his papers, or to blow his nose, or to make loud guttural noises to be heard as he clears his throat,

---

[20] On the question of preaching in relation to the whole service of worship, no better treatment is found than in Robert Will, *op. cit.*, I, pp. 315-320, *La prédication comme Elément Liturgique*, which may be summarized in these words, "Preaching, far from dominating the worship, must be only a support, a means to an end, namely, the adoration," p. 316. See also in *L'Esprit du Culte Protestant*, Chap. 5, pp. 133-163, what Jean D. Benoît says on the importance of preaching; also see André Schlemmer, *op. cit.*, pp. 9-15. During the past twenty years, under the influence of Karl Barth, everything has been said among Reformed theologians about the value of preaching considered as an "event" or as "miracle" and of its "sacramental" character. We agree with all this, but do not discuss it further, lest we say less effectively what has already been well said by others.

cannot expect from the congregation an attitude more meditative than his own. He should leave the pulpit promptly and go to the choir; there he will stand near the holy table, in motionless adoration and meditation until the organ playing ends. The congregation, following his example, is less likely to be noisy or disrespectful.

During the organ playing or the singing, the offering will be received. The officiant will say first a biblical text referring to the spiritual significance of the offering of our possessions to God (II Sam. 24:24; Rom. 12:8; II Cor. 9:7; Gal. 6:2, and so forth). Then the persons responsible for collecting the offerings approach the holy table in orderly fashion, in pairs, not single file. The officiant will take from the table the plate on which the collection bags have been previously placed; standing at the entrance of the choir, he will present the plate to the collectors, each of whom will take a bag. The offering ended, the collectors will come together at the back of the church and will come forward then two by two and put the bags upon the plate which the officiant will present to them from the same place as before. Then the officiant will return the plate to the holy table and pronounce a brief prayer of dedication, during which the collectors will remain standing at the entrance of the choir or in front of the holy table as the representatives of the congregation. This procedure, followed in mostly all Anglo-Saxon churches, emphasizes and sanctifies the spiritual character of the offering.

The dominating characteristic of the closing prayer of the service of the word is intercession. This prayer must be said slowly and with brief periods of silence between the several petitions, so that everyone may pray really inwardly, and be able mentally to place the names of acquaintances and dear ones in every category of humanity for which intercession is made in a general way. In principle and within the context of a parish congregation, we should be able to mention by name those who need to be borne by this prayer. In practice there are difficulties; for example, in an urban parish where people do not know each other and the mentioning of such names would make no sense. In a rural parish there is always the danger of an unintentional omission of the mention of some names and the result is hurt feelings. Only in particularly tragic or painful cases is it wise to run the risk of mentioning names. Moreover, it ought to be done more freely during services that are somewhat intimate and restricted.

The Lord's Prayer, which sums up and contains all Christian prayer, must be said in unison and at the conclusion of the prayer of intercession. It may be sung entirely by the congregation or said by the officiant alone up to the request, "deliver us from evil" and then the final doxology be sung by the congregation (this is the Lutheran custom). The three procedures may be used alternately so as to avoid that monotony and formalism which attend the Lord's Prayer particularly. If Holy Communion is celebrated, the Lord's Prayer is omitted at this point and placed in the communion liturgy.

The *benediction* is a liturgical act which originated with the ancient people of God (Num. 6:22-27). The Levites raised their hands over the people and this gesture was a sign testifying that the name of Jehovah, that is to say his personal presence, rested with the community as a protective power. The priestly hands signified the hand of Jehovah himself placed upon the faithful. (Cf. I Kings 18:46; II Kings 3:15; Ezek. 1:3; 8:1; 37:1; 40:1). In the gospels we see the Lord using this gesture to bless the little children or his disciples (Mark 10:16; Luke 24:50). The church has taken over naturally this liturgical act which certifies to the congregation that its Lord, present during the service, does not forsake his own people when the worship is over but remains with them and accompanies them with his omnipotence wherever they go. The early church did not take over the Levitical formula of Numbers 6, which was put into use again at the Reformation. Some other formulas have been used, not always literally biblical. The Levitical or Aaronic benediction and that of II Cor. 13:14 are now among the most frequently used formulas in the evangelical churches. Other apostolic formulas, of which the epistles are full, may be substituted for them occasionally in order to avoid monotony. For pronouncing the benediction the officiant stretches his two arms slightly higher than his shoulders, while taking care not to spread apart his fingers. Early in the history of the church the sign of the cross, drawn with the right hand, accompanied the gesture of the outstretched arms. In certain Lutheran churches the two gestures, raising the hands and the sign of the cross are combined.[21]

The benediction, given generally from before (and not from behind) the holy table, is responded to normally by the *Amen* sung by the congregation. This *Amen* ratifies the benediction and, in a general way, the entire service. It helps the congregation to be aware of all that has been done and prevents it from retiring hurriedly. It is preferable that a moment of silence follow the *Amen*, so that each one is impressed fully by the divine presence that accompanies him as he goes from the worship into daily life. "I will not let you go unless you bless me" (Gen. 32:26). "The Lord will keep your going out and your coming in from this time forth and for evermore" (Ps. 121:8). After this moment of silent meditation, during which the officiant remains standing in his place, the playing of the organ is heard accompanying the leaving of the faithful.

The congregation may be made to tarry in their places for some moments at the beginning of the organ postlude while the officiants retire with dignity and in good order to the sacristy. This allows the minister time to come to the exit door to greet the parishioners and to shake hands with them. Through this both brotherly contact and community spirit are developed and strengthened.

The various parts at the end of the service may be arranged in a different way. The preaching may be followed by organ music, then directly by the prayer of intercession. Then would follow the singing of a hymn, during which the offering is held in the pews. The short offertory prayer is joined by the Lord's Prayer said in unison. This is the order adopted by the liturgy of the church of Geneva.

---

[21] For the matter of the gesture of benediction in the scripture, see Joseph Coppens, *L'imposition des Mains et les Rites Connexes dans le Nouveau Testament et dans l'Église Ancienne* (Paris: Gabalda, 1925), Chaps. 1 and 2.

17

The Sacrament
of Holy Communion or Eucharist

There is a historical order of the liturgy of Holy Communion;
however, it has been either ignored or forgotten in the Reformed churches. It is fortunate that the advances in historical
research in the liturgical field, accompanied by theological
concern to conform to the norms of the apostolic church, and
finally, the ecumenical aspiration to get back to communion
with the universal church, have contributed recently to the
restoration of a traditional eucharistic liturgy in churches that
hitherto have ignored it. This liturgy has the advantage of
objectively known facts. It is true that all liturgy includes
from its origin the more or less marked imprint of a personality. For example, the liturgies of the Eastern churches have
the name of an apostle or a churchman who is supposed to
have elaborated them (St. Mark, St. Basil, St. John Chrysostom, and so forth). The liturgies of the Reformation all have
at their source a doctor of the sixteenth century (Luther,
Bucer, Cranmer, Calvin, Olaus Petri). But the role of these
men was restricted for the most part to adapting or readjusting
the church liturgy to a new situation or to new demands.[1] In

[1] Unfortunately this is not the case with Calvin. He did not consider the traditional
data, and while producing some new things, "he drew up in a hurry, as he tells us
himself, under pressure from a thousand other works, the *Forme des Prières* that he ed-
ited in Strasbourg, then in Geneva. It is, however, this sort of improvisation, reedited
many times during his life and after his death, that constitutes the worship tradition
of almost all the Reformed churches," André Schlemmer, *op. cit.*, p. 61; also pp. 46-47.

no case was it a question of a creation *ex nihilo;* such would have been purely arbitrary and would lack any right in itself to be imposed upon the churches.[2]

The traditional eucharistic liturgy originated in the words of institution of the communion mentioned in the gospels and reported to us by primitive tradition. This account is unquestionably a stereotyped form which emerged from catechetical usage and perhaps also from liturgical practice in the apostolic communities. It is not possible to know precisely if this account was originally a necessary and integral part of the celebration of the Lord's Supper, and if so, what role it played there, especially if it had "consecrating" value. It was not until St. Augustine, however, that the church became conscious of the essential function of the words of institution in the administration of the sacraments. In this connection, the parallelism with baptism ought to play an important role: just as the baptism is effected through the declaration alone of the formula of institution of Matthew 28:19, without the necessity of any prayer, so have we been led to think that the words used by the Lord at the Last Supper were sufficient to perform the "consecration" and to enact or accomplish the sacrament. Scholasticism, especially since the promulgation of the dogma of transubstantiation in 1215, has generalized and made this point of view official. Luther carried the matter to its extreme consequence by reducing the whole consecrating canon of the Mass to the words of the institution only. By so doing, the Reformation departed from the original liturgical order certified by Justin Martyr and on into the first third of the second century. From the ecumenical point of view this is regrettable because the common pattern has been broken with the non-Reformed churches that have kept the old liturgical scheme. But what is still more decisive for us as evangelicals is that we should be equally removed, through this, from the

---

[2] Calvin entitled his liturgy: "La forme des prières et chants ecclésiastiques, avec la manière d'administrer les sacrements et consacrer le mariage, *selon la coutume de l'Eglise ancienne.*" Henri Vuilleumier writes on this subject: "One should notice at the end of the title these words: according to the custom of the early church. Historically these words are in no way justified. The order of worship established by Calvin does not correspond with either the worship of the primitive church, as far as we can judge from the apostolic letters, or the worship of the first centuries when everything gravitated around the communion as the central act." *op. cit.*, I, pp. 313-314.

supper in the upper room and from the apostolic "breaking of the bread." Indeed in the narratives of the miracle of the loaves as well as in those of the institution of the communion, it is said that Jesus started with thanksgiving.[3] He uttered a prayer of thanksgiving over the loaves and fishes and over the bread and cup. This prayer makes these elements, inconsequential in and by themselves, into nourishment given by God and used to his glory. Without imputing to it the idea of an intrinsic transformation of the food, we have to acknowledge that the two texts, in the Synoptics at least, suggest that the food is "blessed" or consecrated by this prayer.[4]

The apostles remained faithful to this Jewish custom which Jesus took up and even emphasized. "He who eats, eats in honor of the Lord, since he gives thanks to God" (Rom. 14:6). "If I partake with thankfulness, why am I denounced because of that for which I give thanks?" (I Cor. 10:30). A quotation from the pastoral letters points up the value and role of this prayer: "God created foods to be received with thanksgiving by those who believe and know the truth. For everything created by God is good and nothing is to be rejected if it is received with thanksgiving; *for then it is consecrated by the word of God and prayer*" (I Timothy 4:3-5). This last sentence is most important for the liturgy of Holy Communion. This latter is a meal; but in apostolic times no meal was conceivable without thanksgiving that blessed God and consecrated the food to his glory and service. The *eulogy*, or prayer of praise, recalling all the benefits of God towards his people, was inseparable from every Jewish meal of any importance. From the beginning it has been a constitutive part also of the sacred meal of the disciples of Jesus of Nazareth.[5] The "Word of God," according to the narrative of the institution, is not sufficient then to constitute the sacrament; a eulogy is necessary or a eucharistic prayer. We are not sure that the words of the institution were considered at the beginning as indispensable for the ceremony; but it is entirely certain that the eulogy was

[3] Mark 6:41 and 8:6; Matt. 14:19 and 15:36; John 6:11.
[4] Mark 8:7 and Luke 9:16.
[5] Certain New Testament texts, as Eph. 1:3-12; Phil. 2:6-11; Col. 1:12-20; I Tim. 3:16; Rev. 4:11; 5:9; 11:17; 15:3-4; 19:6-7, may give some idea of the way in which the apostolic communities prayed in order to make the eucharist out of the bread and the cup. Cf. *Leiturgia*, I, p. 207.

a mandatory part of the action of the breaking of the bread and the passing of the cup. In order to be in keeping with Christ's saying grace at the table the night before his death, and with the apostolic churches making the eucharist from the bread and the cup, a liturgy of Holy Communion must not only include the narrative of the institution, but equally so a rather long prayer of thanksgiving and of commemoration. For it is "by the Word of God *and by prayer*" that the elements are "sanctified."

We cannot emphasize this too much: the narrative of the institution is not the liturgy of Holy Communion. It is the pattern of it or the "order of the day." It enumerates for us the different steps or movements. The Lord 'took bread and the cup. Then he made the *eulogy;* in other words he raised to God his Father the praise and thanksgiving. Then he broke the bread and finally distributed it, along with the cup. Then the singing of the psalms concluded the action (Matt. 26:30). This narrative pattern of the gospel must be fulfilled; this is the real purpose of the church liturgy. The liturgy is the real substance of this formal framework; and the essence, if not the whole of this liturgy, is the "eucharistic prayer." The importance of this prayer arises clearly out of I Corinthians 10:16 (KJV)—"The cup of blessing *which we bless*, is it not the communion of the blood of Christ?" It is nonsense to pronounce this formula, considered as consecratory, and omit entirely the prayer of eulogy or eucharistic prayer that it mentions and presupposes, and that alone "sanctifies" (I Tim. 4:5) or consecrates the elements. [6]

Ought this prayer to include an explicit demand for the sanctification and consecration of the elements? In other words, must it contain an invocation of the Holy Spirit so that the bread and wine become a "pneumatic" element, a sacramental food? This is the famous question of the *eucharistic epiclesis*, which has divided for centuries the Roman and Eastern Orthodox churches and is the focus of numerous discussions among liturgical specialists. [7] We are unable to

---

[6] For more information on this matter, see *Liturgies de Communion*, Eglise et Liturgie, Lausanne, 1952, pp. 7-10.

[7] The literature on the question of the epiclesis is too numerous to make a catalogue of it here. It may be found in the article *Epiclèse in the Dictionnaire d'Archéologie et de Liturgie Chrétienne*, Paris, 1907, under the authoritative editorship of Dom Cabrol.

187

deal with this question here without departing from the theme assigned. As for the rest, from the Reformed point of view, it is not of primary importance.

The origins of the epiclesis are not clear. Irenaeus was the first to use the term in connection with the eucharist: "The bread having received the *invocation* (ἐπίκλησις) of God is not any longer ordinary bread, but the eucharist, and is composed of two things: an earthly and heavenly thing."[8] Irenaeus understood possibly nothing else under the term "invocation" than the eucharistic prayer as a whole. The explicit invocation of the Holy Spirit appeared with the Roman formula of Hippolytus only at the beginning of the third century, but its purpose there appears to be less the sanctification of the elements than of the faithful who participate in the sacrament. Here is the purport of it: "We ask Thee to send down Thy Holy Spirit upon the offering of the holy church; grant, while gathering them, to all the saints who receive it to be filled with the Holy Spirit in order to strengthen their faith through the truth."[9] Later the formula of the epiclesis became explicit in an invocation upon the communicants *and* on the elements (the principal emphasis being upon the elements) in the sense of a transformation or conversion of the bread into the body and of the wine into the blood of Christ. The churches of the Reformation, which refuse to interpret the sacramental presence of Christ in terms of substance, are unable at any price to embrace this point of view. But, under the modest and simple form it seems to have had in the beginning, such as in the *Anaphora of Hippolytus*, the epiclesis has its normal and logical place in the eucharistic prayer. There it appears as a development of the biblical words in John 6:63, "It is the spirit that gives life, the flesh is of no avail." In the sacrament, the body and blood of the Lord are nothing in themselves, but only insofar as they are instruments of the divine *pneuma*. The epiclesis reminds us, therefore, that the consecration of the elements is not accomplished in some sort of mechanical way, but in response to the humble and

---

[8] *Op. cit.*, IV, 18, 5.

[9] Hippolytus of Rome, *La Tradition Apostolique* (Paris: Editions du Cerf, 1946), pp. 32-33.

supplicating faith of the church. Finally, the eucharistic prayer, being a great "anamnesis" in chronological order of the divine plan of our redemption in Christ (as in the confession of faith), it is natural that it be concluded with recalling the work of the Holy Spirit who must penetrate and transform the heart of the elect, and who will one day change their bodies too in the last resurrection for the new heaven and the new earth. The bread and wine, "transfigured" by the Holy Spirit into the body and blood of the glorified Lord, are the indication and guarantee of this eschatological moment of the eucharist. The old *Maranatha* (I Cor. 16:22), this fervent appeal expressing the eschatological hope of the church, is linked then quite naturally with the epiclesis of the Holy Spirit in the conclusion of the entire eucharistic prayer.

Let us proceed now to a short description of the traditional order of the sacramental celebration. Whenever possible, it is fitting to have at least two officiants: the principal celebrant, who takes the place of the apostle, of the "prophet," or of the bishop of the early communities, and who delivers the consecrating prayer of thanksgiving; then an assistant, churchman or layman if necessary, who serves as a deacon. The task of the deacon is to read the gospel, to offer the prayer of intercession or the *memento* before the eucharistic prayer properly called, and to assist the celebrant in the distribution of the elements; that is, chiefly in the presenting or passing of the cup. During the service of the word and the beginning of the sacramental service, or until the end of the *memento*, the celebrant and deacon will be—one at each end of the holy table—facing each other.[10] It is only at the time of the eucharistic prayer proper that the celebrant comes behind and to the middle of the table, facing the congregation, while the deacon remains where he was until the moment of distribution, and then he resumes this same place again until the end of the service.

Originally the service began with the kiss of peace, the sign of brotherhood in Christ and of the mutual love of all the faithful.[11] It was accompanied by a wish of peace formulated

---

[10] The famous Anglican bishop and theologian Lancelot Andrewes (1555-1626) compares them with the two cherubim at either end of the mercy-seat (Exod. 25:18; 37: 7, 9). Cf. *Liturgy and Worship*, p. 190.

[11] Cf. Justin, *First Apology*, 65, 2. Also Rom. 16:16; I Cor. 16:20; II Cor. 13:12; I Thess' 5:26.

by the officiant and repeated by the communicants, one to the other. It was the greeting of the risen Lord to his disciples: "Peace be with you." Through the gradual evolution of custom the kiss of peace has fallen into disuse, and it would be foolish to attempt to revive it. Recently some have wanted to replace it with a handshake, but we have to admit that this is not such a good idea either. It is better to refrain from any gesture of this kind at this point in the ceremony and to restrict ourselves to the wish of peace declared by the celebrant, and followed, as is the case in many Eastern liturgies, by a biblical text expressing the commandment of brotherly love. Indeed we could consider as an equivalent to the kiss of peace the fact of being grouped around the holy table for the communion and of passing the cup to each other. This position and this specifically religious gesture have even more significance and expressive value than the very or all-too-"natural" gesture of the kiss.

The wish of peace is developed logically in a prayer for the assembled brethren and for those whom circumstances have kept from joining the congregation that day. This prayer will be given by the deacon. Originally in this prayer the names of those people were enumerated who, on that day, had brought their gifts in kind to provide the bread and wine of the holy table and to help the needy. It has not been this way for a long time, but names may be mentioned in this *memento of the living* when there are those who are seriously ill, brothers or sisters, grieviously afflicted, or in serious danger. Then, by way of inclusion, the prayer mentions the members of the congregation who have finished their earthly journey and have passed "beyond the veil;" this is the *memento of the dead*, which is not necessarily a prayer for the dead, but a recalling of their belonging to the κοινωνία of Christ. Finally this recollection expands to the great witnesses of the faith in the old and new covenant: patriarchs, prophets, apostles, doctors, martyrs, whom the old liturgies mentioned by name. This is the *memento of the saints*, or the *memento of the church triumphant*. This threefold memento makes concrete in the eucharist the "communion of the saints," that is affirmed in the creed. In this way the faithful "come to Mount Zion and to the city of the living God, the heavenly Jerusalem, and to innumerable angels in festal gathering, and to the assembly of the first-born who are enrolled in heaven" (Heb. 12:22). This first prayer of the liturgy of the Holy Communion gathers thus mystically the whole church, the body of the elect on earth and in heaven, around the communion table.

Then the eucharist, properly called, may begin; i.e., the prayer of thanksgiving over the bread and the cup which the officiant has just uncovered. The celebrant opens with the *Sursum corda*, in dialogue between the people and himself, one of the oldest liturgical forms. "Lift up your hearts: We lift them towards the Lord; Let us thank the Lord our God: This is worthy and right." This dialogue of Jewish origin was received probably in Christian worship from those early occasions when in the first century the eucharist followed the *agapé* (see Lam. 3:41, Col. 3:1, and I Tim. 2:8). When the *agapé*, that homely and quasi-casual meal, came to an end, the president of the gathering had to invite the guests to change their preoccupations and to lift their thoughts to higher things in view of the sacramental act about to begin. This initial dialogue, which introduces immediately the great eucharistic prayer, prepares the faithful to grasp and to live the fullness and grandeur of this prayer which is truly and specifically the eucharist.[12] At the very beginning of this solemn act, they are given the means of associating themselves explicitly with it, just as the final *Amen* permits them to conclude it themselves and ratify it. The restoration of this dialogue between the officiant and the congregation is one of the important tasks actually of the liturgical movement.[13]

Originally the eucharistic prayer was improvised by the officiant, but on a set theme—the successive stages of the intervention of God in our world to save sinful men. Creation, fall, the great dates of the Old Covenant and the redemptive work of Christ constituted the unchangeable model of this

---

[12] "The Communion was first called 'eucharist,' and as such, as thanksgiving, it characterizes the whole worship," Karl Barth, *op. cit.*, p. 181. This term has continued in use intermittently in the Reformed church until the eighteenth century. It is regrettable that it has fallen into disuse and it ought to be put back into circulation now. A letter of the ministers of the classis of Lausanne, dating from 1605, speaks even of "the sacrosanct eucharist!" Henri Vuilleumier, *op. cit.*, II, p. 423.

[13] Ostervald asked it already in his *Préface* in 1713.

long thanksgiving. At different times one or the other of these elements was more developed and better emphasized, according to the inspiration of the officiant or to local worship traditions. In later times the texts were crystallized and the officiants adhered strictly to the received and prescribed text. This text varies in different ways according to locale, churches, times, and feasts. But its fundamental unity is clear, and everywhere the narration of the institution has become invariably the center of it like a pivot.

This prayer is interrupted in almost all the liturgies by the chant of the seraphim of Isaiah, called the *sanctus* (Isa. 6:3). The location of the *sanctus* in this position is not old; but if it breaks the beautiful sequence of the prayer, it gives to the praise and thanksgiving an expanded resonance that compensates greatly for the seeming inconvenience. In a less solemn celebration of a more restrained and intimate character, it is suggested that the *sanctus* be omitted and that the older pattern (the ante-Nicene) of the eucharistic prayer be restored. The insertion of the *sanctus* has the effect of dividing this prayer into two distinct parts; in the West the name *preface* was given to this first part that precedes and leads to the *sanctus*,[14] and this *preface* has become variable according to the times and feasts of the church year; whereas the second part, called *canon* (rule), centered upon the words of institution, remained unique and invariable. In the East, on the other hand, the part of the prayer preceding the *sanctus* is generally a short praise of the divine Name, whereas the whole christological and soteriological development, that is the body itself of the prayer, comes after the *sanctus*. And the whole, called *anaphora*, is invariable.

The words of institution come at their logical and chronological place in the progression of the events of salvation, except in the special prefaces for Easter, Ascension, and Pentecost, where, through the necessity of things, the order of succession is not respected entirely. But after the accents of triumph of the *sanctus*, it is normal to "have silence before the

---

[14] In secular Latin, *praefatio* meant "invitation" or "pressing order." We are not surprised then that Cyprian meant by this word "initial dialogue." By extension, the term has been applied to the prayer that is linked to it, and which is an *invitation* to join the choir of angels in the singing of the sanctus.

Lord who comes." It is known that the *canon* of the Mass (that is, the unchangeable prayer prescribed for the consecration and offering of the sacrifice) which starts here has been said by the Roman priest in a low voice, practically in silence for centuries.[15] It is the same for the *anaphora* of the Eastern liturgy, with the exception of the words of institution which are said in a loud voice. This way of doing it is untenable from the evangelical point of view; furthermore, the promoters of liturgical renewal in the Orthodox as well as the Roman church, have begun to raise objections against this later deviation. There is, however, one positive element in safeguarding it, and the moment of silence preceding the words of institution provides us with the possibility for it. It improves these and gives to the consecrating prayer that follows a unique resonance.[16]

Luther wanted occasionally the words of institution to be sung by the officiant on the splendid theme of the traditional recitative of the preface. Robert Will describes rather casually the case of a congregation singing these words[17] and thereby giving maximum expression to the reality of the collective priesthood of all the faithful. When it is the celebrant who pronounces them, as is always the case now, he will do it with earnestness, with a certain deliberation, and with a reasonably lower voice than for the preceding preface. A short silence should be provided after the words concerning the bread, and in the same way after the words said over the cup.

The "Do this in remembrance of me" that concludes the institution calls very naturally for what is called the *anamnesis*, or shortened memorial and presentation before God, with the bread and wine, of the whole work of Christ the Savior. The epiclesis, which evokes the work of the Holy Spirit and invokes his presence and power in the sacramental act, ends the eucharistic prayer. The congregation concludes the whole with a solemn *Amen*, which Justin had specified already in the second century as an essential element of the

---

[15] It is gradually changing now, according to the liturgical decrees of Vatican II.

[16] Cf, Odo Casel, *Die Liturgie als Mysterienfeier* (Freiburg-im-Brisgau: Herder, 1923), pp. 149-151.

[17] *Op. cit.*, I, p. 251.

eucharist.[18] It is indeed indispensable to the expression of the community character of the action and the manifestation of the collective character of the people of God.

It is at this point, when the eulogy or eucharist is finished, that the *Maranatha* may, and indeed should, be introduced; this was familiar to the apostolic church but fell into disuse and oblivion at a very early date. Then the singing of the benedictus (Matt. 21:9, 15), for which there is evidence already at an analogous place in the *Didaché* (second century) and the Clementine liturgy (fourth century), takes on its real significance: "Come, Lord! Blessed is he who comes in the name of the Lord God. Hosanna in the highest heaven!" The coming of Christ in the incarnation, in the eucharistic sacrament, and soon in the *parousia*: this unique coming, though under three different modalities, is indicated and celebrated admirably by this acclamation of the crowd on Palm Sunday.[19]

The integral structure, therefore, of the eucharist is at the same time evangelical, apostolic, and "catholic" or ecumenical. Calvin had crossed it out with one stroke; Luther truncated it awkwardly in a massive and biased reaction against the sacrificial elements that had become predominant in the Roman Mass. The modern liturgical movement, within the context of ecumenism, has succeeded today in giving it back to the church and has restored, therefore, its spiritual riches. The dominant note in it is joy.[20]

The *Lord's Prayer* has its appointed place between the great eucharistic prayer and the act of communion; it is the prayer of the children of God gathered around the table of the Father

---

[18] *First Apology*, 65:3, 4; 67:4.

[19] The *benedictus* is obviously better placed here at the conclusion of the entire eucharistic prayer than when it is joined with the *sanctus*, as was the case before the actual liturgical renewal. Cf. *Liturgies de Communion*, Eglise et Liturgie, (Lausanne, 1952), pp. 111-112.

[20] The Reformed Communion has for a long time assumed "a strict and almost lugubrious character." Robert Will, *op. cit.*, I, p. 194. The "in remembrance of me" has been interpreted as meaning "in remembrance of my death." But the Greek word 'ανάμνησις has an entirely different significance and value than our word *remembrance:* it calls anew the person or event evoked and *makes them present. In remembrance of me* means in my living presence, and not in remembrance of my death. Furthermore, even in this last inexact interpretation, let us not forget that the cross of Christ is not defeat, but victory. It is the Crucified who is *Christus Victor*. Cf. Maurice Sweeting, in *La Sainte-Cène*, Etudes Luthériennes, No. 3, p. 28, and Julius Schweizer, in *Ways of Worship*, pp. 132-133.

of the family. The request, "Give us this day our daily bread," acquires here its full meaning.[21] Then the bread is broken for distribution; this is the *breaking of the bread*, in the more narrow sense of the expression.[22] And the cup is lifted in order to be presented to the communicants. Whether these two manual actions be emphasized or not by the text of I Cor. 10:16, they are in no way consecrating acts. It is important that we remove all confusion about this subject; it is the entire eucharistic prayer, culminating in the narration of the institution and the epiclesis, that consecrates the bread and the cup.[23]

There follows then a brief prayer of humiliation, called a *bowing prayer* in the old liturgies, and *prayer of humble access* in the Anglican liturgy. It may be omitted if the service of the word begins with a confession of sin already. Then, when the officiants have taken communion, the words of invitation or of "free access" call the communicants to the holy table.[24]

When the communion is ended, the elements that are left over will be covered again respectfully and the final prayer of thanksgiving and praise will follow. This must be short, so as not to repeat in essence the eucharistic prayer and to extend unduly a service that is already long. The service is concluded with a final hymn and the benediction in the same way we indicated for the service without the celebration of the Holy Communion.[25]

---

[21] Especially when we reckon with the interpretation of J. Jeremias of the Greek word ἐπιούσιος: the bread of the world to come. The Vulgate points to a similar meaning in translating: *supersubstantialis*, that is, the bread which is above all other substance.

[22] Let us point out that in the beginning the broken bread was not placed in any relationship to the broken body of the Lord. Furthermore, the fourth Gospel specifies that the body of the crucified Jesus had not been broken (John 19:32-36). The gesture of breaking the bread, other than its essentially practical importance in view of the communion, recalls the unity of the members of the Body of Christ, in the sense indicated in I Cor. 10:17.

[23] Consequently it is entirely erroneous for the officiant at that moment to place his hands on the bread and cup in a gesture of consecration.

[24] In *Ways of Worship*, the Anglican theologian A. H. Couratin gives a particularly thoughtful and complete synthesis of the eucharistic act. (pp. 191-194).

[25] We have not said anything here about the *Agnus Dei* that the Roman Mass provides at the point of the fraction and which has been retained in this place generally by the Lutheran liturgies. It was introduced into the eucharistic liturgy in Rome only at the end of the seventh century in connection with the growing emphasis upon the sacrificial motive in the conception of the sacrament.

A certain number of questions arise, however, regarding the manner of celebrating the sacrament.

What kind of bread should be used? No one can answer this question with absolute certainty because of our not knowing whether the Lord used unraised (or unleavened) or raised (leavened) bread in the upper room. In fact, the use of leavened bread has prevailed in the East while the unleavened in the West. This was, as is well known, one of the points of disagreement between Rome and Byzantium, and one of the reasons for the schism of the eleventh century. There is no well-reasoned doctrinal case for the preference for one usage or the other. In the churches issuing from the Reformation the usage of unleavened bread, inherited from the Roman church, has been maintained partially in the Anglican and Lutheran churches. It has the advantage of permitting the reservation of the sacrament for the communion of the sick. Now the Reformed churches have given up unleavened bread and have adopted the raised or leavened bread as in the Orthodox churches of the East.[26] Leavened bread indicates more clearly the symbolic parallelism between daily bread as the product of our work and food for our body and the Bread of Life coming from above, which feeds our souls and entire being for life eternal. But should it be unraised or unleavened bread, called *host* or *wafer*, leaves much to be desired concerning the symbolism of the breaking of the bread. The wafers are flat disks made beforehand, and of all that are distributed, the officiant breaks only one, the one he is to eat himself. The raised or leavened bread is usually present on the holy table in the shape of long strips of soft roll or crumb cut beforehand, a piece of which the officiant breaks off for every communicant. Nothing remains of the whole bread, the symbol at the time of the physical body of Christ and of his mystical body, the church, broken and shared among all the communicants in order to indicate and bring about their union and unity in their

---

[26] Some Zwinglian parishes, however, of the canton of Zürich still use wafers in our day. Berne had required this custom in 1538 in the Church of the Pays de Vaud, against the advice of Farel and Viret. But the idea evolved and a sovereign edict of 1605 replaced the thin wafers with common bread, made "with the purest and finest meal one could get." This change met resistance in the Pays de Vaud, and the new practice came into force only at certain communions in 1606. Henri Vuilleumier, *op. cit.*, II, pp. 422-425.

common participation in Christ. A practical and appropriate way should be found for breaking first a whole loaf, whether it be leavened or unleavened, and then this gesture should be repeated in some way for every communicant.[27] This would be the proper way of giving to this rite its distinctive significance, as was defined by St. Paul: "Because there is one loaf, we who are many are one body, for we all partake of the one loaf" (I Cor. 10:17). Some experiments must be tried in this area, if we wish to restore to the sacrament of Holy Communion its whole meaning for church people.

Should the eucharistic wine be white or red? Red wine seems more appropriate and more symbolic of the blood of the Lord. However, this argument should not be pushed too far, since in the beginning the cup seems to have had an especially eschatological meaning as the announcement and guarantee of the great feast of the Kingdom of God and of the eternal joy of the elect.[28] Yet the symbolism of the blood is more obvious for the average believer, both in those places where it is produced and its use is required, or where no wine is produced and they have to import it. However, white wine should be used in regions that produce it. Thus a very fine institution of the early church regarding the matter of the eucharistic sacrament takes better shape (of which Irenaeus was the principal interpreter): men bring to God the bread and wine, fruit of their work, and first fruits of the present harvest, as a sign of the offering of their life and powers to God in communion with Christ who offered himself as a sacrifice to his Father as the first fruit of the new eschatological creation.[29]

One bread calls for one cup. The uniqueness of the cup, as in the case of the bread, is as a clear and manifest sign of the unity of believers in the body of Christ. The Pauline text, "Because there is one bread, we are only one body," finds its extra-

---

[27] In this way it was understood by the ministers of the first generation in Vaud: while accepting the principle of unleavened bread imposed by Berne in 1538, they had some reservation and were able to celebrate effectively by replacing the small individual wafers with a kind of broad thin cake or waffle "of such dimensions that they could be broken into several pieces and therefore the principle of the breaking of the bread was kept at least." Henri Vuilleumier, *op. cit.*, II, p. 422.

[28] This point is very well stated by Jean F. Leenhardt, *Le sacrement de la Sainte Cène*, (Neuchâtel and Paris: Delachaux et Niestlé, 1948).

[29] Irenaeus, IV, 17:4. Cf. *Liturgies de communion*, Eglise et Liturgie, 1952, p. 13f.

canonical complement in this text from Ignatius of Antioch, sixty years later: "There is one cup only to unite us with the blood of Christ."[30] The plurality of cups on the same sacred table is nonsense, and it is made more so by the use of the Pauline text: "*The cup* of blessing which we bless, is it not the participation in the blood of Christ?" (I Cor. 10:16). For the strongest reasons the so-called individual cups should be forbidden, particularly as being the negation of an essential element of the sacrament of Holy Communion, which is the sacrament of unity, meaningful and constitutive for the church, the one body of the one Christ.[29] If there are questions of hygiene, for example, in the time of an epidemic, the custom of *intinction* may be adopted which is used in the Lutheran churches in the Baltic countries. A part of the piece of bread is dipped into the cup at the moment of giving it to the communicant; thus the two elements, bread and wine, are received at the same time, and no one has touched the cup with his lips. It is necessary then to have absorbent bread to prevent the wine from running. Intinction is an improved form of the Eastern Orthodox custom of giving the communicants bread and wine mixed, by means of a spoon.[31]

For the gesture of elevating the cup which follows immediately the one of breaking the bread, the officiant will perform this seriously by holding the foot of the cup with both hands and right in front of him. He will refrain from taking communion alone before his helpers and assistants. He will take care to have these by his side, so to speak, at the moment of the fraction and during the elevation of the cup. He will commune with all of them with the bread and then the cup. This indicates before the congregation the "corporate" unity of the different officiants and the principal celebrant.

The bodily posture of the communicants differs according to various churches. In the beginning communion was taken while standing. The Eastern church has retained this custom, whereas in the West kneeling prevailed in the Middle Ages as

---

[30] André Schlemmer, *op. cit.*, pp. 38-42, develops carefully all the practical problems the communion with the cup poses.

[31] This custom is practiced regularly in the church of St. John, in Lausanne, ever since the influenza epidemic in 1918.

a function associated with the development of the dogma of transubstantiation. Most Lutherans and the Anglican church have retained this usage as it has been inherited from the medieval church. But the Anglican Prayer Book of 1552 contains a special article on this subject called "the black rubric," reproduced with a slight modification in the 1662 version, and remaining in this form until this day. Here is the text of it: "It is prescribed in this office of the administration of the Lord's Supper that the communicants receive it kneeling. The purpose of this prescription is to emphasize that we humbly and gratefully recognize the benefits Christ offers in this sacrament to all those who receive it worthily. Another reason is to avoid any profanation and disorder which might result in another way of doing it. However, in order that this kneeling not be wrongly interpreted and altered by whomsoever it may be, through ignorance or weakness, or by malice and obstinancy, we declare here that this posture does not imply any adoration of the sacramental bread or wine, consumed physically in the communion, nor of any corporeal presence of the natural body and blood of Christ. For the sacramental bread and wine keep their natural substances and consequently may not be adored; this would be idolatry, a matter every true Christian abhors. The natural body and blood of Christ our Savior are in heaven, and not down here, and it is contrary to the reality of the natural body of Christ to be in several places at the same time."

The Reformed churches take communion standing or seated in the pews or around large tables as in certain Dutch congregations. This latter method seems to proceed from confusion between the Holy Communion and the early *agapé*. The former one recalls the crowd seated in rows for the miracle of the loaves, but abolishes unfortunately the role of the holy table, the place of the gathering of the communicants. Granted that the communicants must come near the table of the Lord, there are two ways then of doing it: either the communicants come to the table one by one or possibly two by two or they form a group in a semi-circle around it. The first method, called ambulatory, does not bring sufficiently into focus the communal character of the sacrament: each believer is alone in his turn at the table and takes communion in a way on his own account. On the other hand, by coming near in successive groups, that take their places around the table, the communicants are more fully aware of not being alone in an encounter with their Lord, but of being a family of brothers, a fraternity in Christ, reunited around the table of the heavenly Father. What might be called horizontal communion is put in relief as much as the vertical aspect of it. The effect of the successive groups is determined then by the space available near the table.[32]

Should some word be said to every communicant at the moment he receives the sacrament? No, because the liturgy, said beforehand, makes sufficiently explicit the meaning of the action performed without the necessity of adding anything further to it. In any case, the saying of a biblical verse without reference to the sacrament should be avoided lest it divert the attention of the communicant. The Reformed church has exalted the word enough already at the expense of the sacrament so that it need not overshadow it further with words that have little connection with it. If any one feels he is unable to distribute the sacrament in silence—which is defensible, however, and even advocated—he will use at least specifically eucharistic texts, especially those from the Gospel of John, Chapter 6.[33] By so doing we are in keeping with two of the most ancient liturgies known: the one of Hippolytus in the West, in which the officiant says to every communicant, "The bread of heaven in Christ Jesus," or the one of the Nestorians in the East, where it is said, "Receive the body of Christ and drink from his cup, in faith in his Kingdom," or better, "The body of our Lord, for the forgiveness of our sins, the blood of

---

[32] An extremely pertinent remark by André Schlemmer may be quoted here: "It is essential, in many churches where the communion is given at only one table, to abolish the waiting. It is a nuisance to meditation. It is impossible to continue in the attitude of inner prayer when one is confronted with the need during the whole duration of the ceremony to await his turn standing, either in the galleries or even around the table where too great a number of participants makes the distribution of the elements unusually long." *Op. cit.*, p. 43. We can cite such a parish where communion by groups has been reconsidered and abandoned because groups of too many communicants were created, with the endless waiting and standing that it involved. It is better to have more groups of smaller numbers. Max Thurian, *op. cit.*, p. 97, reflects a different opinion.

[33] In our churches, in the early years of the Reformation, the minister addressed to every communicant this same word: "May you remember that Jesus Christ died for you." Henri Vuilleumier, *op. cit.*, p. 344.

our Lord, for the forgiveness of our offenses, and for the spiritual banquet of life eternal." Let us note that in the Roman church the priest says as he gives the host or wafer to the believer, "That the body of our Lord Jesus Christ keep your soul unto life eternal." In the Eastern Orthodox church the priest says, "The servant of God receives the holy and precious body and blood of our Lord, God and Savior Jesus Christ, for the remission of his sins and for life everlasting." The Anglican liturgy prescribes these words: "The body (the blood) of our Lord Jesus Christ which was given (shed) for you keep your body and soul unto life everlasting. Take and eat this in the remembrance that Christ died for you and feed on him in your heart by faith with thanksgiving. (Drink this in remembrance that Christ's blood was shed for you and be thankful)." In the Lutheran church in Sweden the formula is more modest and could be used easily in the Reformed church, "The body of Christ given for you—the blood of Christ shed for you."

When the number of communicants reaches a certain size, it is quite appropriate for the congregation to sing some communion hymns, that is, during the lining up or while successive groups go to the holy table. This singing, performed by the faithful still in the pews awaiting their turn or having returned from the table, should be spontaneous; the organ and a singer, or the choir of the church, could sound the note and thereby engage the congregation.

It would be well to teach the communicants to answer *Amen* to the word that is said eventually to them when they receive the sacrament, and not to say "Thank you" as some among them do awkwardly. This is what the liturgy of Hippolytus already prescribed and it was current usage in the early church. In this way the consent or response of the faithful is expressed to the boundlessness of the divine mercy of which the sacrament is the sign and bearer.

In some Reformed churches the practice has been maintained of kneeling in the pew for a short period of individual prayer on returning from the holy table. This pious custom, a rule in some other churches, deserves to be revived everywhere.[34]

[34] This is, or at least it was up until some years ago, the case in parishes in the monutains of Neuchâtel. See also André Schlemmer, *op. cit.*, p. 45.

Communion at home for the sick dates back to the early origins of the church. Justin had mentioned already that "when he who presides has completed the eucharist and when all the people have responded, those whom we call deacons will distribute among all the assistants the bread with the eucharistic (consecrated) wine and water, and *they will bring them to the absent people*."[35] This custom is not widespread in the Reformed churches because the congregation of the faithful does not have such a keen sense of the necessity of the sacrament. Much remains to be done before the faithful, detained in their homes through sickness, infirmity, or old age, and those who are at the gates of death, desire to receive the bread and wine of the communion as a supreme grace. When the pastor is called to the home for a case of this kind on a day when communion has been celebrated in the church, normally he will use the elements consecrated at the holy table, while drawing the attention of the sick to the fact that this is a sign of the participation of the isolated in the community of brothers. These elements, therefore, will not be reconsecrated. If the pastor has just taken communion in the church during the Holy Communion of the parish, he will communicate again with the sick only if he considers it necessary because the person is alone, and to show to him that fraternal communion of which the sacrament is the sign and the means. He will be excused from this in a case where there are one or more persons surrounding the sick who communicate with him. He will then administer the sacrament only to the people present. On the other hand, if there has been no public celebration of the Holy Communion that day, the pastor will make it his duty and joy to communicate with the sick and his associates or friends. If it is not possible to use the consecrated elements from the parish communion, the pastor will proceed to consecrate the bread and wine near the sick on a table properly arranged for this purpose, and he will use in this case an abbreviated liturgy.

The left-over consecrated elements will be disposed of in a decent manner. Without attaching any superstitious importance to this matter, it must be admitted that there is in the

[35] *First Apology*, 65:5 & 67:5.

Reformed tradition at this point much "laissez-aller" and sloppiness that betrays a somewhat deficient evaluation of the sacrament. The completely profane manner in which the left-over consecrated elements are treated is sometimes shocking. The bread may be eaten respectfully by the officiant in the sacristy or by the minister and his family in the manse.[36] Still better, it could be burned, analogous with the prescription of Moses on the subject of the remainder of the Paschal Lamb: "And you shall let none of it remain until the morning; anything that remains until morning you shall burn" (Exod. 12:10). What is left over of the consecrated wine, if it cannot be drunk entirely by the officiant at the end of the ceremony or in the sacristy, should be spilled on the ground outside the church as a product of the earth being returned to the earth. The other non-consecrated elements may be distributed among the poor.[37]

Order of The Divine Service

I. The Word

Introduction

Entrance of the officiants, during organ playing and a hymn of the congregation or the choir

Invocation and introductory text (*de tempore*)

Hymn of the congregation: Lord, be among us

Introit psalm antiphonally

Singing of the *Gloria Patri*

Humiliation

Reading of the Law

Confession of sins

Singing of the *Kyrie*

Biblical word of grace and *Absolution*

Singing of the *Gloria in excelsis* or the *Alleluia* or a verse of a hymn of praise or thanksgiving

[36] Luther wished that the officiants eat it together at the end of the ceremony.

[37] See Justin, *op. cit.*, 67:6.

Instruction

    Apostolic greeting

    Reading of the Word of God: (a) Old Testament
                           (b) Epistle
                           (c) Gospel

    After each reading, the response of the congregation
    (Thanks be given to God; Praise to Thee, O Christ) or
       singing by the choir

    (Confession of faith or equivalent chant)

    Preaching

Offering and Intercession

    (Confession of faith)

    Singing of the congregation and collection of gifts

    Short offering prayer

    Prayer of intercession

    Leaving of the non-communicants or (in case that the
       sacrament is not celebrated):

    Organ

    Prayer of intercession

    Singing of the congregation and collection of gifts

    Short prayer of offering and Lord's Prayer

    Benediction

II. The Sacrament

Introduction

    Wish of peace

    Memento of the members of the congregation, alive and
       dead, and affirmation of the communion of the saints

Great Eucharistic Prayer

    Initial dialogue (*Sursum corda*)

    Preface

    Singing of the *Sanctus*

    Silence of adoration

    Words of institution of the communion

    Anamnesis or memorial of the Lord and presentation of
       the elements

    Epiclesis or invocation of the Holy Spirit and *Amen* of
       the congregation

    Maranatha and singing of the *Benedictus qui venit* . . .

    Lord's Prayer

Breaking of the Bread and Communion
    Words of the fraction of the bread and elevation of the cup
    (Prayer of humble access)
    Communion of the officiants
    Invitation
    Communion of the faithful

Conclusion
    Short final prayer
    Singing of the congregation (*Doxology*)
    Benediction
    Singing of the *Amen* by the congregation or choir

18

The Divine Office

The term "office", from the Latin *officium* (duty), means the service of praise and thanksgiving due daily by sinful man to his God, Creator and Savior. Whoever says the office says it with moral obligation and regularity, as an accomplished duty, not necessarily with compulsion, but freely and with gratitude. But freedom is not a synonym for irregularity and capricious whims or imagination. It implies every day, and not intermittently, and it is at certain moments of the day, suggested by the very nature of things: it is morning, afternoon, and evening that human praise must rise to the throne of the Lord. Already under the old covenant there were fixed hours for prayer as well as for acts of private piety in the program of the temple. The book of Acts shows us how the apostles continued to include themselves in the daily rhythm of Jewish prayer and indicated in this way that the duty of regular praise to God existed fully in the new covenant also. The twelve, gathered for prayer on Pentecost, received, therefore, the Holy Spirit on the third hour (Acts 2:1, 15). At the sixth hour, or at noon, Peter withdrew in order to pray (Acts 10:9). With John, "he was going up to the Temple in order to pray at the ninth hour" (Acts 3:1). In that same ninth hour, that is, at three in the afternoon, Cornelius, who feared God and whose life conformed to the prescriptions of the Jewish religion, had a vision which decided for him his future (Acts 10:3). Some decades later, the *Didaché* prescribed that the Lord's Prayer be said three times a day.[1] Tertullian, Cyprian, Origen, and others make references to the duty of praying on the third, sixth, and ninth hour. The *Apostolic Tradition* of Hippolytus, at the beginning of the third century, prescribes prayer upon arising; then at the three daily hours already mentioned, suggested by the remembrance of the events of Good Friday; then in the midst of the night, with reference to Matt. 25:6, 13; and finally at sunrise, when the cock crows.[2] In all these there remains also private devotion or in a restricted group such as the family. In the ante-Nicene period it could scarcely be otherwise, because the church was not free to carry on its program in public. It had to restrain itself to a bare minimum and be content with the synaxis and the Sunday eucharist. From the second century onwards, however, the week was marked by fasting on Wednesday and Friday, to which already the *Didaché* refers;[3] these two days soon became *stated* days, that is, days for assembling for worship. Moreover, according to the Jewish and Roman way of dividing time, the dividing line between two days was drawn at six o'clock in the evening and not at midnight. Consequently Sunday began already the day before in the evening and people got into the habit of celebrating a service called the *vigil* in between Saturday and Sunday. The idea that the Lord's return would occur in the midst of the night and that one had to be watching and praying for this event played a particular role in fixing this vigil. Tertullian wrote: "Prayer is the wall of faith: her arms and missiles against the foe watch over us on all sides. And, so never walk we unarmed. By day, be we mindful of Station; by night, of vigil."[4]

These divine services during the week in the ante-Nicene period were in a sense a prehistory of the divine office. With

[1] *The Didaché*, 8:3.
[2] Hippolytus, *op. cit.*, 35.
[3] *Ibid.*, 8:1.
[4] Tertullian, "On Prayer," *Ante-Nicene Fathers*, III, ed. A. Roberts and J. Donaldson (New York: Chas. Scribner's Sons, 1903), 29.

the coming of the Constantinian era and the freedom it provided, the church gave a public and communal complexion to the traditional hours of private prayer. In the fourth century the *Apostolic Constitutions* spoke of two main daily public services, one in the morning and the other in the evening, without mentioning the secondary hours—the third, sixth, and ninth hours—which were later called the "small hours." The movement which in that period tempted many Christians to withdraw from the world in order to practice asceticism and contemplation had influenced no doubt the elaboration of a daily cycle of hours of public praise and prayer. But this influence has not been conclusive. The divine office is explained essentially by the habits of "lay" piety in the first three centuries. It is not, therefore, a monastic peculiarity; it is, in the broadest sense, the act or affair of Christian people and of the entire church. This is how Luther understood it, and Cranmer after him. In an article dated 1523 the German reformer asserts immediately that the worship of the church of Christ consists in the Mass, matins, and vespers. "The divine office which is now everywhere is a thing as Christian and as beautiful as the preaching service."[5] The same year, in Wittenberg, the low Masses during the week were cancelled and replaced by a divine office of morning and evening in the manner of the old canonic hours. These, as we know, reached in time to eight in number: matins, lauds, primes, thirds, sixths, ninths, vespers, and complines. Luther reduced them to two, for as he said, "One does not have to overburden souls to the point of wearying and disgusting them, as they have up until now in the monasteries, where they have imposed upon themselves a donkey's burden."[6] Matins and vespers are focalized again upon the word of God, while conserving their traditional format. These are celebrated by pastors, students in the schools and candidates for the ministry. The people are not forced to assist, but they may join in and participate without the impediment of a dead language or the complications of ritual. In fact, at the beginning of the Lutheran reformation

[5] "Von Ordnung Gottesdienstes in der Gemeine," 1523, quoted in Leonhard Fendt, *Der lutherische Gottesdienst des 16. Jahrhunderts* (München: Reinhardt, 1923), p. 106.
[6] *Ibid.*, p. 111.

there was always a nucleus of believers present at prayers both morning and evening.

In England Cranmer, after some wavering, followed the same course. The first Prayer Book of 1549 provides for two daily offices: *Matins* and *Evensong*, called *Morning Prayer* and *Evening Prayer* in the revised version of 1552. The reading of scriptures and the singing of biblical hymns (the Songs of Mary, of Zacharias and Simeon) occupied considerable space. Cranmer's purpose, clearly explained in the preface of the edition of 1549, was to resume the order of public prayer of the era of "the early Fathers," established by the latter "for the greater advancement of piety" and in order that the scriptures be read entirely during the course of one year. Cranmer, however, had not seen that in reality the ancient divine office was based more upon psalmody, that is, upon the prayer and praise expressed in the psalms, than upon the reading of the scriptures. We could say that the spirit which animates and gives life to the Lutheran and Anglican office finds expression in the words: "Thy word is a lamp to my feet and a light to my path" (Ps. 119:105), whereas the inspiration of the early office is declared rather in this other saying: "Seven times a day I praise thee for thy righteous ordinances" (Ps. 119:164). The Anglican and Lutheran offices, moreover, might be considered as the remarkable success of the new wine of the Reformation poured into the old bottles of the ancient office. If the Lutheran church has not always known how to conserve this treasure, if it has allowed the office to fall generally into disuse under the disastrous influence of the Enlightenment, the Church of England in return has held faithfully to it; nevertheless, today the average Anglican goes to church on Sunday morning for *Morning Prayer*, or if he is not able to make it, he will go in the evening to join in *Evensong*.

The structure of the divine office may vary in details as it follows the "hours" or confessional traditions. But always it allows itself to be reduced to three fundamental elements: the praise of the psalms or psalmody, the reading of the Holy Scripture, and prayer in the form of collects or litanies. The biblical songs and church songs or hymns come second in order. Antiphonal psalms are the prayers *par excellence* of the

Christian community united with its divine Head, Christ.[7] "Christ sings first, says Calvin, and in the way he says it he gives us the tune that we may sing psalms after him."[8] We know that Christ, the Son of God, used the psalms freely during his life on earth; he read, quoted, prayed, and even sang them (Matt. 26:30). For the psalms are inspired prayer given to God's people of the old covenant, of which David—the royal psalmist—was the principal interpreter. Jesus Christ, Son of David; Jesus Christ, Head of the new people of God, has made the prayer of the psalms his own, either in taking for granted his own strictly personal role in those psalms properly called Messianic (Pss. 2, 72, 89, 110, 118, etc.) or in assuming it in his capacity as Head of the body, or representative of humanity, or the second Adam who supports us all in himself, who bears the sins of men, and who utters their repentance and their appeal for God's mercy.[9] With reference to Psalm 42 Augustine speaks of "the accents of Christ the Savior, singing and sighing, exulting in the Spirit or sighing before the dull reality." The psalter is Christological, not in the sense that every psalm contains some typological allusion to the person of Jesus-Messiah which artificial allegorical exegesis would demonstrate, but the psalter is the prayer of Christ, Son of God made man, identifying himself with the humanity he came to ransom. The psalms, prayed communally in the office, express the union of Christ, the second Adam, with the new humanity, the church, the gathering of those who are in Christ. They demonstrate also the mutual communion of the members of the body, where the needs of some become the needs of others and where everyone carries the burden of others before God in prayer. They declare the presence of Christ praying in his own community which adds

---

[7] On the fundamentally liturgical character of most psalms and their usage in the worship of the old covenant, see the remarkable introduction of Number 14 of *Das alte Testament deutsch, Die Psalmen I*, übersetzt und erklärt von Artur Weiser, (Göttingen: Vandenhoeck & Ruprecht, 1950). See also Robert Will, *op. cit.*, II, pp. 366-369, and Pierre Pidoux, *Du portique à l'autel*, (Neuchâtel, 1959).

[8] Quoted in "La vie liturgique," by M. Sweeting, *Le Semeur*, (*Paris*, June-July, 1946), p. 673.

[9] In order to put on the Psalms of David the seal of the new covenant, the early church adopted the custom of concluding them with the Trinitarian doxology of the *Gloria Patri*.

its unanimous voice to him who is the supreme and true "prayer." Therefore, in the office the psalms could not be, as a general rule, a reading, but a prayer; and the antiphonal method as well as the chanted version is the only sensible transposition, the incarnation of the "corporate" character of the prayer of Christ, of the Christ who has made himself one with his church.[10]

A certain number of psalms are not, properly speaking, prayers; such as, psalms 37, 45, 49, 50, 52, 55, 78, 81, 82, 87, 105, and 106. These should be removed from the cycle of the psalmody if the complexion of praise and prayer of the divine office is to be maintained. These psalms, because of their didactic character, could be used as readings.

We have spoken already of the important place of the reading of the Holy Scriptures in the Lutheran and Anglican, that is, the evangelical, versions of the office. The medieval office left only a very limited place to Bible reading; only the matins contained some fragments of it; the other hours were restricted to one or two verses, called "capitules." However, the daily office is the proper place for the *lectio continua*, which Calvin practised in Geneva by preaching every working day. Today no one would support a daily sermon, but the divine office provides for the reading of Holy Scripture followed and meditated upon in silence.

The prayers, collect or litany, are prescribed in such a way as to reflect the feelings and needs of the community in conjunction with the hour of the day or the season of the church year.

The Reformed church has dropped the divine office purely and simply, instead of revising or revitalizing it, as did the other churches that were born out of the Reformation movement. This is one manifestation of that massive and one-sided

[10] Through the prayer of the psalms, one is made everything to everyone: one rejoices with those who rejoice, one weeps with those who weep (Rom. 12:15). A legitimate allegorical transposition of certain realities is performed. Israel is the church; the enemies, which are evil, are sin, Satan, the demons and the world; the Babylonian captivity is the state of *simul peccator et justus*, of man sinful and justified at the same time; it is the captivity of the church which without being of the world is in the world; the king is Jesus Christ descending from David. Certain verses, however, can not be prayed by the church, because they belong to an inferior spiritual state of Israel; these are the cries of anger; of hatred and vengeance. These will be eliminated from the office." Max Thurian, *op. cit.*, pp. 169-170. Cf. also A.G. Hebert, *Liturgy and Society*, pp. 215-216.

radicalism of this branch of evangelical Christianity and of the incomprehensibility of Puritan circles regarding the traditional *ordo* of the church prayer. The history of the discussions which took place in England regarding the development of the Prayer Book, between Cranmer and his group on the one hand and the extremist or Puritan reformists on the other, is very significant. These latter, for example, did not want to know anything of the Magnificat, of the songs of Zacharias and Simeon, though biblical, for they had formed an integral part of the old office! They rejected the litany, the requests and responses of which were, according to them, "fragments and rests, more wishes than prayers." They preferred long prayers in sermonic style.[11] Doubtless the principle of religious offices on workdays was accepted and maintained until the eighteenth century in several Reformed churches. In ours they were characteristically called *prayers*, in contrast to the *sermon* or *action* of Sunday morning. Prayer was celebrated in the afternoon, in certain parishes every day, and once a week in the country in turn in each of the annexed localities which formed the parish.[12] But these offices had almost nothing in common with the old divine office.

The Reformed church needs very much to recover now the practice of the daily office, as in other churches, especially if it is to re-enter the ecumenical communion from which it isolated itself by rejecting experience and tradition. Has not Karl Barth, the great Reformed theologian of our century, restored the accent upon the sovereign transcendence of God, which removes him from the limitations of our emotions and personal "experiences"? At once we are made conscious of the duty of adoration, of thanksgiving, of supplication and of praise, which is incumbent upon sinful men respecting the Very High and Very Holy. Interior prayer is not merely a privilege we make use of or profit from when we please, according to the state of our souls or the disposition of the moment. It is a necessary service and a duty from which nothing can exempt us. Exterior prayer is the visible expression of it, conditioned by our organic placement in time and space. It must be

[11] *Liturgy and Worship*, p. 269.

[12] See Henri Vuilleumier, *op. cit.*, I, p. 319, and II, pp. 332-335.

performed regularly and under discipline, and with all of the faith and love which have been given us. There is nothing magical in this, but prayer thus conceived is the indispensable recalling of our state of dependence upon the Lord of life; it is the sign of our humble condition as servants under orders from our Master. Pure inwardness and personal fantasy do not have a biblical basis. A Reformed Christian, submissive to the word of God, does not feel anything in common with Hegel who, in responding to his wife's order to join her in church, said, "I honor God more while thinking than while praying."

The religious communities that have risen from the soil of the Reformed churches in the course of these later years have felt the need immediately of regulated common prayer. The perpetual improvisations and individual spontaneity of pietism soon run out of inspiration and tire rapidly. It is necessary, therefore, to come back to the divine office of the church universal after it has been revised and readjusted according to the complexion or character of the Reformed spirit and the needs of Christianity today. In this respect, the Reformed church has something new and specific to infuse into the old office. It may integrate with it whatever is true and valuable in pietistic individualism. In other words, besides the inviolable rights of the "institution," there are also those of the "event;" besides the directed prayer, there is a place also for spontaneous prayer. In the divine office of the strictly established churches, where the dogma of the incarnation develops its ecclesiastical consequences in a rigid and unilateral manner, everything is stereotyped, and free inspiration is not permitted to express or manifest itself. This is the case with the canonical hours and the Roman breviary, with the Eastern Orthodox Horologion, and also, in a certain measure, with the Anglican and Lutheran offices. With the Reformed church rests the duty of safeguarding the balance between the institution and the event, between the church and the Spirit, between history made and history yet to come. Its divine office must arrange, therefore, the right place, after the fixed and prescribed prayers, for those requests the Spirit dictates, *hic et nunc*, for the officiants and even for all of the brethren present. These free prayers, it must be understood, ought to be brief, concise, communal, and limited in number. It is necessary, moreover, that those who say them will have learned the art of praying in and with the community and that they know the difference between a prayer with and for the brethren and a prayer offered individually in the privacy and secrecy of their room. The tendency to lay bare one's soul and to display extravagantly one's personal feelings is not possible without falsifying entirely the sense of the office or unbalancing the structure of it.

The divine office, as we have indicated, is not limited to certain monastic communities. It may, and indeed must, become the daily morning and evening prayer of the urban parishes. If the rural parishes can not do so for practical reasons, they can at least celebrate the office once or twice a week during the times of the year which permit it. As in the time of the Reformation, there will never be the attendance on workdays that we have the right to expect at Sunday worship. But if the "little flock" is present, the nucleus of the active and responsible members of the parish faithful to their duty of praise and intercession, the church of Christ is there, which wakes and prays while waiting for its Lord. Religious and liturgical education of the faithful is necessary so that the divine office is fully experienced and the church truly edified among contemporary people. The Reformed, through their forefathers, have lost to such a degree the habit of this common prayer that the task of education is not without present difficulties. But what is at stake is worth the trouble. The church ceases then to be merely a theoretical entity, but takes concrete shape in the "prayer of the centuries," in the stream of which the divine office keeps the believers open to this truth: there is no reference to God our Father without reference to our brothers; we can not know Christ according to the Spirit if we are not a member among the members of his body; none of us can pray alone on his own account, but we truly pray only as "the communion of the saints."

214

CONCLUSION

Worship, or more precisely the liturgy, which is the organized and social form of the cult, should not be, and indeed never is, an arbitrary creation of a single individual or ecclesiastical authority. It is *given*, coincident with the initial religious fact, and receives its form organically from it. Christian worship reflects and re-echoes the unique event which was the appearance on earth of Jesus, the Christ. It represents and continues *hic et nunc* the divine transcendent reality perceived in him through faith. Those familiar with and experienced in the gospel, gathering for prayer, "call upon the name of the Lord." At the heart of the worshiping assembly the image of Christ, the Lord and Savior, rose in the spirit of the faithful and they lived "in the Spirit" the things that had happened in the past "during all the time that the Lord Jesus went in and out among us" (Acts 1:21). They invoked his presence; they still heard his voice in the oral tradition of his gospel; they ate and drank with him, the unseen resurrected One, just as they had done before the "cloud" of the ascension took him from their sight; and they called his return or manifestation, 'ἐπιφάνεια (Titus 2:13), of which the worship, particularly the eucharist, was an anticipation: *Maranatha, Lord, come!*

Thus, Christian worship re-presents and relives the Christian fact; although some say "the Christian myth," and deny this conception of worship. The main question is to know where the boundary line is to be drawn between myth and fact. The real question is whether the incarnation of the Son of God is a historical fact or if it is only a mythological veneer upon the commonplace life of Jesus of Nazareth. If the Holy Scripture has some authority for us, and if the faith and worship practices of the apostolic community have any normative significance for us, then the worship of the church today cannot be very different from what has been described and justified in this book.

The great lacuna in Reformed worship, as it has been understood and celebrated until recent times, is to forget that spirituality can only be for us men—and more especially for Christian men—an *incarnate spirituality*. Reformed worship has never been able to be honestly liturgical nor honestly charismatic; it has been neither communal nor prophetic, whatever pretensions it had to be so in its confrontation with traditionally ritualistic and clerical cults. The traditional worship of the church of Christ, such as we have tired to outline in its form, is without doubt much more in line with biblical anthropology, christology, and ecclesiology, as interpreted in recent years by the immense work of the present generation of theologians of all denominations, who join on the higher levels of ecumenism.

We are not pure spirit, nor are we separated spirits or juxtaposed units, but personalities immerged in the corporeity, interdepending personalities, conjointly in space and time, and communicating among them through the corporeity. Our religion, therefore, can not be individual; it is not *Privatsache*; it is personal and communal. We are not "free," in the individualistic sense of the word; we are mutually linked, gathered from our birth into the *Corpus Christianum*, initiated through baptism into the people of God, the church, which is the body of Christ. Our praying is necessarily affected by it: it may not be any longer our individual performance; it is sustained, amplified, and corroborated by those of our brothers of different Christian centuries and diverse places. We pray the words of praise and supplication with our brothers in faith, with those in the past in the idiom of their generation, and with those of today in theirs. Our brotherhood in Christ is not merely an idea or an inner feeling; it is confirmed and witnessed to in concretion of the corporeity; it is incarnate in the prayer formulated for the common denominator of all, and in the words that are spoken in common.

Incarnated spirituality: it is the word of the hour in the liturgical movement which actually excites all the denominations and all the Christian churches. Let us take care lest in this formula the adjective swallow the noun or the noun absorb the adjective. The balance and health of the worship life of the church depend upon it.

Index

221